Border Crossings

Scripture is taken from the New Revised Standard Version of the Bible, copyright 1989 by the Division of Christian Education of the National Council of the Churches of Christ in the USA. Used by permission.

Library of Congress Cataloging-in-Publication Data
Clapp, Rodney
    Border crossings : Christian trespasses on popular culture and public affairs / Rodney Clapp.
        p.   cm.
    Includes bibliographical regerences (p.).
    ISBN 1-58743-003-7
    1. Christianity and culture—United States. 2. United States—Religion—1960–
I. Title.

BR115.C8 C52 2000
261'.0973—dc21   00-040352

For current information about all releases from Brazos Press, visit our web site:
http://www.brazospress.com

Border Crossings

Christian Trespasses on Popular Culture
and Public Affairs

R O D N E Y   C L A P P

Brazos Press
A Division of Baker Book House Co
Grand Rapids, Michigan 49516

Dedication

To lifelong sustainers:

    my mother, Barbara;
    my brother, Kerry;
    and my sister, Kim.

Contents

Nonlinear Reading Guide to this Book

If you *are* a body and do not just *have* a body, go directly to chapter 6.

If you want to know the biggest single challenge facing the church in the incipient twenty-first century, go directly to chapter 10.

If you find Winnie-the-Pooh amusing, but sometimes vaguely disturbing, go directly to chapter 16.

If, brilliant and most excellent person you are, you regard John Coltrane as the be-all and end-all of twentieth-century music, go directly to chapter 17.

If you know whether it's Hank or Tennessee Williams most likely to be toting a guitar, go directly to chapter 2 or chapter 19.

If Christmas is *not* your favorite holiday, go directly to chapter 8.

If Thanksgiving is *not* your favorite holiday, go directly to chapter 7.

If you find the word *epistemology* intimidating (or worse), but know agent Scully's phone number and pray nightly for protection from the Cigarette Smoking Man, go directly to chapter 3.

If you find the word *epistemology* positively exciting, and keep Descartes on your nightstand, go directly to chapter 1.

If you wonder what earthly good theologians might be, go directly to chapter 5.

If you are trying to figure out how Bill Clinton can, policy-wise, be so much like Ronald Reagan and George Bush, go directly to chapter 4.

If you think the devil has all the good music, go directly to chapter 18.

If the Religious Right frustrates (scares, irritates, bores) the living daylights out of you, but you still don't want to give up on Pat Robertson and Jerry Falwell as brothers in Jesus, go directly to chapter 11.

If you always suspected there was something wrong with family values, but could never quite put your finger on it, go directly to chapter 12.

If you were raised Catholic or fundamentalist, or are a practicing psychologist, or currently have a psychologist practicing on you, go directly to chapter 9.

If, like the author, you can somehow imagine heroes more inspiring than Lee Iacocca, Rupert Murdoch, Alan Greenspan, or Donald Trump, go directly to chapters 13, 14, and 15.

Linear Reading Guide to this Book

or, The (Somewhat) Conventional Introduction

1. There is no such thing as common sense.

I grew up on a farm, with tractors and combines and pickup trucks. Common sense is a much prized commodity on farms. Although my father never took me aside and showed me, step by step, "This is how you take apart a carburetor," I was supposed to know these things. One day, while I was in high school, Dad came by the field and caught me driving the tractor and plow in the wrong direction. He was upset (and no doubt embarrassed, wondering how many neighbors had witnessed his eldest plowing ignorantly), but I was shocked and confused. How could there be a wrong way? Did the weeds care whether or not you ran over them clockwise or counterclockwise? I had no aptitude for these things, and instead knew how to get around in books and libraries, and so I was often accused of lacking common sense. As if it were a genetic deficiency.

Of course I could have been more observant. But exactly there was and is the point, for matters at hand in this book. Even had I had the farming aptitude, and been more a naturally astute plowboy, I would still have learned by watching and working alongside people who earlier watched

Key

and worked alongside other people (my dad following my granddad, for example) and so coming to be proficient farmers. Farming knowledge was not genetic at all. It was not inborn to all normal human beings, common to and shared by all people. People learn how to farm, just as they learn how to read or build jet airplanes, from watching and listening and being apprenticed to masters who were themselves earlier apprentices.

So in this regard there is a certain kind of common sense. But it is not the universal, innate-to-all-normally-endowed-human-beings common sense I, as an inept farmer, was suspected of lacking. It is instead a sense common to (or shared by) members of a specific culture or way of life. It is not common to all of humanity. Those who have never been a part of the culture of accounting or warmaking or newspapering will not instinctually know how to construct spreadsheets or launch ground-to-air missiles or write a news story. There is no universal common sense. The right question to ask anytime we are presented with common sense as a reason for doing or not doing something is, "Whose common sense is this?"

2. Eight anti-commonsensical exercises.

1. Get out your phone book and see how many places of worship there are in your community. Count them to see how many different religions are represented. How many Christian denominations?
2. Ask "what is truth?" on a World Wide Web search engine and explore the variety of sites dredged up in answer to that query.
3. Channel surf. Pause at least five minutes on different stations. Ask yourself, what is important to these people? What gets them up in the morning? What kind of things do they want to buy or own, and why? What do they consider worth killing for? Dying for?
4. Leave the preset stations on your car radio. Find an African-American or Spanish or some other station outside your typical world. Listen to what they report as news, and how they report it, and what excites them.
5. Seek childrearing advice from a great-grandmother, a contemporary working-out-of-home mother, a bachelor uncle, and two popular self-help parenting books. Compare and contrast.
6. Visit a library or newsstand and read some magazines and newspapers besides such establishment giants as *Time* or *Newsweek* or *The New York Times.* See how different the world looks for gays and les-

bians, Jews, Buddhists, self-identified secular humanists, ham radio operators, poetry buffs, mercenary soldiers.

Subscription advice: For an incisive view of the world coming from an organ not already owned by a corporate giant, subscribe to *The Progressive Populist*, P.O. Box 487, Storm Lake, IA 50588.

7. Recall what breakfast foods were regarded as eminently healthy when you were a child. If you are not over your twenties, ask your parents what was a good, foursquare breakfast when they were little.

A brief and pertinent autobiographical note: I'm 42. When I was a kid a certifiably, no-doubt-about-it, live-long-and-prosper breakfast was two eggs, bacon, buttered toast, and a glass or two of whole milk. Of course, that was long before awareness of the evils of cholesterol.

8. The nineteenth-century German philosopher Arthur Schopenhauer, who was wrong on all sorts of things, said this: "All truth passes through three stages. First, it is ridiculed, second, it is violently opposed, and third, it is accepted as self-evident." Can you think of a single scientific, religious, cultural, technological, economic, or political innovation that disproves this Schopenhauerian axiom?

Hint: It wasn't Copernican heliocentrism, or the law of gravity, or the alphabet, or the typewriter, or the Sermon on the Mount, or even, shocking as this seems in light of contemporary economic theology, the free market.

3. A reading recommendation.

If you still don't believe there's no such thing as common sense, and seek a careful, rigorous, Christian argument of this point, read Philip Kenneson, *Beyond Sectarianism* (Trinity Press International, 1999).

4. Another reading recommendation.

If you still don't believe there's no such thing as common sense and want a lively argument from an agnostic who models his writing style on C. S. Lewis, read Stanley Fish, *The Trouble with Principle* (Harvard University Press, 1999).

5. Christians should not care that there is no such thing as common sense.

Christianity, like the Judaism that is its parent or older sibling, has never believed in universal common sense. The Jews knew that Yahweh, a particular God, was not known simply by virtue of the knower being human, or observing the stars, or watching how animals treat one another. Instead, Yahweh was known through the telling of the story of how God led the Israelites out of Egypt (see Exod. 10:1–2) and a worship which remembered and reenacted that story (see Exod. 12:14–20). Christians, to learn who God is and what God's ways are, look to the same story, but through the later story of Jesus of Nazareth.

At a given point in history, certain Europeans invented universal common sense. They said that all normal, rationally endowed human beings, no matter their time or place, could arrive at foundational Truths, and from these foundational Truths judge the rightness or wrongness of all particular truths. (For more on this, see chapter 1, following.) Eventually, through philosophies but also through economic and military and political institutions, much of the western world came to believe in universal common sense. (It is at the root of classical liberalism, embraced down to this day by the likes of both Ronald Reagan and Bill Clinton—about which more, see chapter 4, following.) The church, under tremendous pressure, worked at buying into universal common sense. But that attempt has always been, at best, awkward. It is, after all, the abiding conviction of confessional Christianity that it is through Jesus Christ that Gentiles come to know God. According to the first chapter of the Gospel of John, there is nothing more basic (or foundational) that Christians can say than, "In the beginning was the Word, and the Word was with God, and the Word was God," and the Word was Jesus the Messiah, who "became flesh and lived among us."

Guess what? Time has passed and quite a variety of people (such as feminists and postmodernists and Islamic fundamentalists) have insisted that universal common sense is not universal, but is indeed the invention of particular peoples and places. Christians still have plenty of things to be embarrassed about (not least our own and ongoing behaviors), but "the scandal of particularity," as it has been called, is not one of them. It turns out (as the Bible had it in the first place) that all Truth, as it is known and spoken of by human beings, has particular provenance. All Truth suffers (if that is the word for it) from the scandal of particularity. So Christians need not get all red-faced and blushy when they say, in accord with long-standing Christian tradition, that God is known through learning and rehearsing the story of Israel and Jesus Christ. There is no better or deeper way to know God, because this is how God chose to be known.

6. Yet another reading recommendation.

There are many good books on this matter of God and history, and the God of Israel's penchant for getting tangled up in the history of God's creatures. I could rummage through my library and provide a careful list, with running and developed commentary. But (a) it's Saturday afternoon and there are other things I want to do, like take my daughter and the dog to the marsh; (b) book introductions are best kept short and simple; and (c) I just last month finished one of the best and most accessible books I have read on the subject. So here I will only point you to Gerhard Lohfink, *Does God Need the Church?* (Michael Glazier, 1999).

7. It all begins with baptism.

The Letter to the Ephesians says it all.

People are always about coming up with categories. That's how we make sense of the world. For the world of the first readers of the Letter to the Ephesians, the most important categories of all were Jew and Gentile. Nothing was more basic or determinative. And for those who think the biblical story is true, even into the twenty-first century, nothing else should be more basic or determinative. Race is not more decisive. Sexual gender or orientation is not more decisive. Being an American or a Canadian or a Mexican is not more decisive. God knows, registering Republican or Democrat is not more decisive. This is the most important binary for distinguishing human beings: Jew and Gentile.

God chose and will never forget the Jews. We Gentiles were utterly lost without the God of Israel. We were cosmic vagrants, the addled and wandering bag ladies of the solar system. We were strangers to the covenants and promises through which the God and King of the Universe would save and reconcile the creation. We had no genuine citizenship, but were "aliens from the commonwealth of Israel" (Eph. 2:12).

Then, Jesus.

He was the messiah of Israel, and the gateway of us Gentiles into citizenship in Israel: "In Christ Jesus you who were once far off have been brought near . . . So then you are no longer strangers and aliens, but you are citizens with the saints and also members of the household of God" (Eph. 2:13, 19).

That is why, for Christians, baptism is the most important mark and determinant of our identity. Indeed, "As many of you as were baptized into Christ have clothed yourselves with Christ. There is no longer Jew or Greek, there is no longer slave or free, there is no longer male and female; for all of you are one in Christ Jesus" (Gal. 3:27–28). Baptism makes us honorary Israelites.

Once upon a time, Christians believed this and tried to practice it. But it has been harder, especially after that point in the sixteenth and seventeenth centuries when European Christians decided they could kill one another in the name of their differing national allegiances and then tried to unite one another not through baptism, but by universal common sense. Several things followed. The body was separated from the soul, so that Christians might kill one another's bodies and remain ostensibly united in the soul. Faith was made a private rather than a communal matter, so that Christians might divide their allegiances. The church, henceforth, was to restrict itself to "personal" and "spiritual" matters, leaving economic and political concerns to the market and the government.

Christianity without physical bodies and corporate bodies. Christianity without a politics and economics. Baptism made less than what it is: a physical (as well as spiritual) rite of citizenship, an induction into a way of life.

All the essays in this book are about taking baptism seriously. And dreaming, taking a few tentative steps toward imagining how different the world might be if Christians once again had bodies, were bodies—socially and physically.

8. Bodies are public, and can cross borders.

I mean it when I talk about dreaming and taking a few tentative steps. For several centuries now, we have disembodied the faith and dismembered (that is, individualized) the church. All kinds of things will have to change, and if they change can only change slowly and fitfully, if we are to take baptism seriously. It is all right for it to take time. That is how history works, and Christians have learned from the Jews that stubborn notion that God is involved in and with history.

But we have a long, long road to travel, with all manner of obstacles, in making Christianity public again. In fact, categories are so mixed up that many will denounce taking baptism seriously (as induction into a culture, or way of life) for being "sectarian." They worry that people like me, who think the language of the church should be the most basic language Christians speak, are withdrawing Christianity from "public" concerns and responsibilities. From my vantage point, they are still captive to one or another derivative of the illusion of universal common sense. The publics to which they call Christians, supposedly more broad and nearly universal than the church, are publics such as the global economy or America the beneficent hegemony. But these "publics" are themselves particular. And though Christians may move about and work in them, to one degree or another, they are not the Christians' primary public and central polity. We already have the church.

The essays that follow work from that common base. They do not at all (as some detractors of the ecclesiocentric perspective would have it) deny Christian interest in and engagement of popular culture or economics or public affairs. They simply presume that Christians should engage these matters first and foremost as Christians. Thus they cross borders supposedly closed to the explicitly Christian. Philosophy, television shows, the Louvin Brothers and Charlie Parker, global capitalism, pop psychology, family values—all these and more are taken up. Christians can inhabit the whole world—public and private, body and soul—exactly as Christians. These essays are attempts at showing, rather than merely telling, that that can be so.

Since the essays that follow were written for different occasions and a variety of settings, they really do not have to be read in a set order, though reading parts one and two first will make a certain sort of logical sense. You are welcome to hop around and about (and of course could do so with or without the author's blessings, but I give them freely). A book with a title such as *Border Crossings,* and a subtitle boasting of trespasses, cannot rightly claim control of how the reader navigates its contents. A few favorite biblical texts and telling quotations or statistics are used in more than one chapter. I have left these as they are so that each essay can stand—and be read—best on its own.

9. Nine activities that will enhance your reading of this book.

1. Daily read from the Gospels, the Psalms, an Old Testament book, and a New Testament letter.
2. Daily recite the Lord's Prayer and the Apostle's Creed. Remember that you did not make them up.
3. Worship corporately, preferably in a building that looks more like a church than an office complex, at least once a week.
4. Make yourself responsible to and for a child. (If you don't have children, don't forget nephews and nieces, or a godchild.) Pledge yourself to love that child for the rest of his or her life, and to let him or her know that he or she is loved no matter what. Keep the pledge.
5. Comfort the afflicted and afflict the comfortable.

6. Enrich your music collection with at least two albums from among the following, and use them as the soundtracks of your life as (if not exactly while) you read this book:

George Jones, *Cold Hard Truth* (Asylum 62368-2)
Billie Holiday, *Greatest Hits* (Decca GRD-653)
Bob Wills, *Encore* (Liberty CDP-7242-8-30276)
Hank Williams, *24 Greatest Hits* (Mercury 923 293-2)
Duke Ellington, *The Blanton-Webster Band* (Bluebird 5659-2-RB)
John Coltrane, *Live at Birdland* (Impulse! IMPD-198)
Emmylou Harris, *Profile* (Warner Bros. 3258-2)
Elvis Presley, *The Memphis Record* (RCA 6221-2-R)
Charles Mingus, *The Black Saint and the Sinner Lady* (Impulse! IMPD-174)
The Mingus Big Band, *Blues & Politics* (Dreyfus FDM 36603-2)
Miles Davis, *Kind of Blue* (Columbia CK 64935)

7. Celebrate with food, drink, and friendship. Often. Very.
8. Practice resurrection. Look, wherever you look, for signs of the kingdom of God.
9. Pray, "Lord, I believe. Help me in my unbelief."

PART 1
The Inevitability of Borders

o n e

How Firm a Foundation

Can Evangelicals Be Nonfoundationalists?

Once when I was in college, an evangelistic group visited our dormitory. A pair of incognito evangelists appeared at my door, bearing clipboards and announcing that they were doing a survey. No poll takers ever showed up in the country town of my origins, so it seemed to be an opportunity for validation as a real citizen of the modern world—one who has not merely voted, but has responded to a scientific survey. I flung the door open and gratefully awaited my anointing. But then the first question was, "If you died tonight, how certain are you, in percentage points, that you would go to heaven?" As I soon found out, the only answer acceptable was "one hundred percent." Zero to ninety-nine percent made no difference—anything other than absolute, unqualified, mathematically certifiable certainty betrayed a soul adrift. My "eighty-five percent" response, calculated to combine confidence with becoming humility, elicited not a declaration of fellowship but a full-scale evangelistic presentation.

How could I have known? I was just a little Methodist boy, saved enough to refuse beer drinking my entire freshman year in college, but who grew up in a rural part of Oklahoma once known as "No Man's Land" and strained to pass basic algebra. Years later, settled in the evangelical subculture in Wheaton, Illinois, I learned that this particular evangelistic strategy and its opening question came from D. James Kennedy and his Evangelism Explosion. I learned yet later to put a name to the epistemology framing that question and its ideal reply: foundationalism.

And today, nearly two decades after that encounter in my dormitory room, I want to suggest that evangelicals are better off disavowing foundationalism, and argue that one of the better reasons for abandoning it is that the abandonment will enable us to be more devout Christians and less devout liberals.

Foundationalism by the Numbers

By "foundationalism" I mean what has been called "the pervasive Western philosophical doctrine that in a rational noetic structure every non-basic belief must ultimately be accepted on the basis of acultural and universally compelling beliefs or realities, themselves in need of no support."[1] Foundationalism is that theory of knowledge usually chased back to Descartes.

René Descartes was a man living in chaotic times. The Reformation, which occurred nearly a century before his prime, was putting to bloom not only the flowers of truth but also the toxic weeds of dissension. Luther had insisted on the power of all Christians to discern right and wrong on matters of faith. Calvin had looked to the absolute certainty of inner persuasion. There came to pass in consequence a crisis of authority—or should we say of authori*ties*? There were in fact now more authorities than before, and potentially innumerably more authorities, since each individual conscience theoretically constituted its own separate pope. The result, as Jeffrey Stout writes, was that "for over a hundred years, beginning roughly at the end of the last session of the Council of Trent and continuing throughout most of the seventeenth century, Europe found itself embroiled in religious wars."[2] This was the playing field of history onto which Descartes stepped.

Descartes was not alone in his anxiety about the violent disagreement surrounding him. Nor, I should add, was the worry solely over religious chaos. As the historian Lorraine Daston observes:

Seventeenth-century science was a battlefield where rivals and factions stopped at nothing to scientifically discredit and personally abuse (the two were seldom distinguished) one another. [To name only stars of the first magnitude,] Galileo relished blistering polemics and was a master of the *ad hominem* pamphlet title, and Newton crushed his adversaries by fair means and foul. . . . Newton nearly drove Robert Hooke out of the Royal Society over a priority dispute concerning the inverse square law of attraction; he not only stacked the Royal Society committee to which Leibniz had appealed for an impartial settlement of the priority dispute over the invention of calculus—he wrote its report, thus embittering relationships between British and Continental mathematicians for nearly a century. It comes as no surprise that the 1699 regulations of the Paris Academy of Sciences had to explicitly forbid its members to use "terms of contempt or bitterness against one another, both in their speech and writings."[3]

Thus situated, it is not hard to imagine how Descartes and others yearned for less partisanship and a more widely shared method for arriving at certainty. The problems at hand seemed clear: time changes everything, including beliefs. And ideas or identities based in localities—whether cities, cantons, or states—are a veritable recipe for interminable fighting. But no longer were philosophers, scientists, and politicians answerable to the church. Furthermore, the church was no longer a unified, consolidated authority, the generally accepted conduit of truth eternal, truth from beyond time and place, for all times and places. Thus Descartes sought a secular, or nonecclesial, foundation of knowledge that rested on grounds beyond time and place. This turned out to be his famous *cogito ergo sum*. This knowledge was at once indubitable and universally self-evident, unbeholden to any concrete and disputatious set of religious convictions. From this sure foundation one might reliably deduce the truth on any number of otherwise controvertible matters, across the range of human endeavor. Without recourse to the now-discredited church, a singular and compelling authority was thereby regained. The wars—scientific and religious, figurative and literal—could cease.

With such aims, it's hardly a wonder that Descartes modeled his epistemology on mathematics. Stephen Toulmin has pointed out that the comprehensive term *logic* is confusing because it can be modeled on the rationalities of several different fields: his own preference of jurisprudence, as well as psychology, sociology, technology, or mathematics. Descartes, tapping into a deep, age-old well, chose the latter. As Toulmin puts it, the "history of philosophy [is] bound up with the history of mathematics." Plato directed a school of geometers and saw geometrical proof as the ideal of all sciences. In a similar frame of mind, Descartes invented a branch of mathematics known as "Cartesian Geometry" and was attracted, Toulmin says, "by the idea of establishing in a quasi-geometrical manner all the fundamental truths of natural science and theology." Surely Descartes, Leibniz, and others gravitated toward mathematical logic in large part because pure mathematics is "possibly the only intellectual activity whose problems and solutions are 'above time'" and heedless of place.[4]

Thus "foundationalism" as I am now using the term is characterized by mathematical certainty, individualism, and acontextualism:[5] its truths aim to be indubitable and precise, along the lines of the geometric or scientific proof, and they are supposedly available to rationally able, well-intended individuals quite apart from any particular tradition or social context.

As my college encounter with the evangelists indicates, foundationalism as such has long been attractive to North American evangelicals. George Marsden's *Fundamentalism and American Culture* abounds with examples of how evangelical intellectuals assumed foundationalism as they popularized the Common Sense Realism of Thomas Reid. On this account the Princeton theologians Hodge, Alexander, and Warfield taught that "any sane and unbiased person of common sense could and must perceive the same things" and that "basic truths are much the same for all persons in all times and places."[6]

Protestant liberal foundationalism was based on experience, beginning with Schleiermacher's putatively universal feeling of absolute dependence. But the evangelicals, of course, turned to Scripture as the universally and individually accessible foundation, which implies that it stands as such apart from the church. So Charles Hodge could declare, "The Bible is a plain book. It is intelligible by the people. And they have the right and are bound to read and interpret it for themselves; so that their faith may rest on the testimony of the Scriptures, and not that of the Church."[7] In true and crowning foundationalist fashion, Hodge saw theology as concerned with the "facts and the principles" of this perspicuous Bible in just the way natural science is concerned with the "facts and laws of nature."[8]

However, foundationalism was in dire philosophical straits well before Hodge's time. In our time even those who hold to it do so with qualifications that, I would argue, effectively put them in a different world from that of the Princetonians, let alone Descartes.[9] Historically, foundationalism eroded because that singular, universal, supposedly nonparticular foundation could never for long or everywhere be agreed on. Soon enough Descartes's *cogito* crumbled. Hume championed the affections, Kant exalted innate reason, and these were only the first in what have now become myriad trains of positions (including evangelical biblical inerrancy) that are not all gauged to run on the same tracks. The problem, as Toulmin describes it, involves the eventual recognition that

the exercise of rational judgement is itself an activity carried out in a particular context and essentially dependent on it: the arguments we encounter are set out at a given time and in a given situation, and when we come to assess them they have to be judged against this background. So the practical critic of arguments, as of morals, is in no position to adopt the mathematician's Olympian posture.[10]

Because foundationalism followed the mathematical model of rationality, Toulmin argues, it failed to see logical categories as contextual or "field-dependent." It sought instead "field-invariant standards of validity, necessity and possibility."[11] By doing so, it hoped to make foundationalist logical necessity a necessity stronger than any religious, historical, social, or even physical necessity. All these other "necessities," after all, were particular and local on one scale or another, and as such clearly open to contention. But one large difficulty soon became apparent. Foundationalism's abstracted, idealized, and impractically rigorous epistemological standards invalidated the undeniably field-dependent work and conclusions not just of theologians and scientific quacks but also of astronomers, archaeologists, historians, ethicists, and psychologists—not to mention car mechanics, bricklayers, plumbers, farmers, and others whose skill and knowledge undergird the conduct of our daily lives.

Evangelicals and the Foundationalist Habit

Foundationalism, in short, demands a kind and degree of certainty and decontextualization that is simply not available to most, if any, substantial human endeavors. Even mathematics, if it is to be material and applicable, cannot escape context. For example, it is not true that in all times and places seven plus nine equals sixteen. Computer programmers can correctly tell us that seven plus nine equals ten—in a base sixteen system.[12] The importance of taking context into account is being recognized more and more broadly. Accordingly, I am not sure which, if any, contemporary evangelical thinker would, if pressed, hold to the virginal, innocent foundationalism of the seventeenth century, or even to the initiated (but married and chaste) foundationalism of late nineteenth-century Princeton. But many evangelicals still hold to the mood and rhetoric of foundationalism.

Consider the work of Ronald Nash. Professor Nash admits that "the degree of influence or control that a particular belief has within any given noetic structure will be person-relative." He has read his Plantinga and argues that noetic structures contain a number of significant beliefs presupposed "without support from other beliefs or arguments or evidence." He affirms that different presuppositions will lead to different conclusions, that "one's axioms determine one's theorems." He can on occasion use W. V. O. Quine's web metaphor, employed by the holist Quine in explicit opposition to foundationalism. He even speaks about conversion from one worldview to another in terms that would warm the cockles of the holist's heart, insisting that conversion occurs gradually, over time, in response to several cumulative causes. Then somehow a gestalt clicks, and, "quite unexpectedly, these [converts] 'saw' things they had overlooked before; or they suddenly 'saw' things fit together in a pattern so that there was meaning where none had been discernible before."[13]

But as Nash develops his epistemology, he seems the philosophical equivalent of someone trying to quit smoking.[14] He appears convinced that the foundationalist habit will lead to no good, but he must sneak a drag here and there. Then, before the chapter ends, the nicotine kicks in and, forget it, Nash will remain a foundationalist, if only in moderation. Pretty soon he's reenlisted Descartes's "innate ideas" and is dropping confident allusions to the "dispositions" Thomas Reid says were endowed to all by the Creator.[15] By now we are past the point of a smoke after dinner and back on the way to a pack a day. Human beings are assumed to be *sometimes* capable of "approaching sense-information in an impersonal and detached way." And sense-information is itself somehow separable from interpretation of it.[16]

At last Nash withdraws to the parlor with the confirmed foundationalist (and smoker) C. S. Lewis. He quotes Lewis to the effect that there is for all persons in all times and places a singular and innate sense of fairness. So, says Lewis, when two people quarrel, one seldom says,

> To hell with your standard. Nearly always he tries to make out that what he has been doing does not really go against the standard, or that there is some special excuse. . . . It looks, in fact, very much as if both parties had in mind some kind of Law or Rule of fair play or decent behavior or morality or whatever you call it, about which they really agreed.[17]

This, I allow, may have freighted cogency in Lewis's forties and fifties England. But today our society is sufficiently pluralistic and candid that it is exactly different standards that seem to be at work. Thus the pro-choicer's "decent behavior" is the pro-lifer's "murder"; the Muslim fundamentalist's "fair play" is Salman Rushdie's unconscionable censorship; and the homosexual's "morality" is Jimmy Swaggart's "sodomy."[18]

Professor Nash does not mention such objections, which seem glaring to me. But by now he has regained his smoker's cough and is reevaluating the habit. He concludes by resorting to mostly holist strategies for judging between worldviews: "Honest inquirers say to themselves, *Here is what I know about the inner and outer worlds. Now which touchstone proposition, which world-view, does the best job of making sense out of all this?*"[19]

He allows, "Once one leaves the arena of purely formal reasoning for the world of blood, sweat, and tears, one is required to abandon logical certainty for probability." A nonfoundationalist could nuance and live with either of these statements. But Nash remains enough of a foundationalist that he still wants certainty, even if it can now only be "moral" or "psychological" certainty.[20]

Similarly, the evangelical statesman Kenneth Kantzer commends evangelicalism as the truth because "it fosters a sense of life on a higher plane of human existence than is provided by other alternatives" and offers a "more coherent, fully elaborated world and life view by contrast with any presented by its contemporary rivals."[21] Unless I grossly misread George Lindbeck, William Placher, Stanley Hauerwas, John Howard Yoder, James McClendon, Nancey Murphy, and other nonfoundationalist theologians, this is quite similar to the sort of argument they want to make for Christianity. Dr. Kantzer says Christianity "fosters" a higher "sense of life," and I take it that such fostering acknowledges the importance of specifically Christian practices for Christian formation, as do all the nonfoundationalist theologians just cited. James McClendon and Nancey Murphy, like Dr. Kantzer, also explicitly appeal to coherence.[22] And if Dr. Kantzer sees Christianity opening the way to life on "a higher plane of human existence," Stanley Hauerwas, in his unbuttoned theological style, can declare that God has entrusted the church with "the best damn story in the world."[23]

Of course, there are important differences between Kenneth Kantzer's apologetic and the "unapologetic" theology of the nonfoundationalists.[24] It is crucial that Dr. Kantzer couch his apologetic in abstracted, highly conceptualized rhetoric that conceals any point of view. The nonfoundationalist theologians also confess Christianity as uniquely and finally true, but they are profoundly aware that this truth, like any truth, must be confessed or professed. That is, it can be lived, believed, and put forth only from a specific perspective or point of view. As George Lindbeck writes,

> The issue is not whether there are universal norms of reasonableness, but whether these can be formulated in some neutral, framework-independent language. Increasing awareness of how standards of rationality vary from field to field and age to age makes the discovery of such a language more and more unlikely and the possibility of foundational disciplines doubtful.[25]

Thus Lindbeck and other nonfoundationalists recognize the assertion of Christianity's unique and final truth as an argument far from settled. It is necessarily an assertion open to profound, honest, multifaceted, and ongoing agreement. But, perhaps misled by his own quasi-foundationalist language, Dr. Kantzer retreats to the fortress of certainty built by the likes of

Gordon Clark and Cornelius Van Til. Therefore, he sympathetically summarizes Clark's presuppositionalism accordingly:

> The regenerate believer can show a higher degree of internal consistency or coherence of the data on the basis of his Christian theistic supposition than is possible with all alternatives which are necessarily inconsistent at their foundation. In this way Clark presents the unbeliever with a challenge either to speak rationally and in a Christian-like manner or to be silent in irrational unbelief.[26]

How Foundationalists Really Argue

Again, Clark, Nash, Kantzer, and other conservative evangelicals seem to work with many nonfoundationalist tools.[27] They admit, for instance, that their base beliefs are presuppositions, not universally shared predispositions. But they persist in presenting their conclusions in foundationalist rhetoric, with the foundationalist attitudes of aperspectivalism and absolute certainty. In fact, I suspect that all the real work in their thinking and writing is done with nonfoundationalist tools.

What happens when they encounter actual, serious disagreement? Of course it takes no one anywhere to simply declare to the Muslim interlocutor, "Your way of life is inconsistent and irrational at its foundation. Get objective and start talking like a Christian or shut up." Instead, Professor Nash or Kantzer would respectfully initiate the painstaking process of examining and comparing Islamic and Christian presuppositions. They might argue from history, philosophy, theology, psychology—or even the experiences of missionary friends. They might attempt to locate the nub of their Muslim interlocutor's objection to Christianity and respond to it. They might try to learn what it is about Islam that fascinates and compels the Muslim, then seek to show that Christianity is more fascinating and compelling on analogous grounds. In the give-and-take, they would no doubt allow their Muslim friend some points, and admit some difficulties with the Christian case. And since Drs. Nash and Kantzer certainly are admirable and compassionate men, concerned to win others to the truth, they would welcome the opportunity to continue the conversation, not insisting that the Muslim either convert on the spot or fall silent.

Let me try to drive home this point by locating the disagreement closer to home, within evangelicalism itself. What happens when two evangelical, confessedly foundationalist parties disagree? Take the issue of gender egalitarianism. You will have no trouble locating evangelical feminists and evangelical antifeminists, each convinced that they are objectively, foundationally right and that the others are objectively, foundationally wrong. Since they are all (at least in their own eyes) evangelical, they spend a great deal of time arguing about what the Bible "really says" about the role of women. Thus the argument comes down to who is reading the Bible correctly. How is this to be decided? Again, in actual practice it is not going to be substantially decided in any foundationalist, objectivist sense. That is, one side is not suddenly going to fall down and say, "Silly us. We had our prejudices, our pet ideas, our traditions, and our personal histories. Now we've decided to set those aside and be objective. We know that all along you've been beyond traditions and prejudices. And we congratulate you on being right."

What actually happens is exemplified by the description of their own hermeneutics provided by the evangelical antifeminists John Piper and Wayne Grudem. Like Nash and Kantzer, Piper and Grudem cannot let go of foundationalist rhetoric, but even in this language their recommendations of hermeneutical practice betray a fundamentally holistic, perspectival method. So they pose for themselves the objectivistically couched question "How do you know that your interpretation of Scripture is not more influenced by your background and culture than by what the authors of Scripture actually intended?" But initially they respond not by insisting on their absolute and incontrovertible objectivity, based on a foundationalist certainty from beyond time and place. Instead, they admit their own fallibility and susceptibility to "the forces of culture, tradition, and personal inclination, as well as the deceitful darts of the devil." They suggest that they probably do not have the final or perfect interpretation of Scripture on women's roles, and they pledge openness to correction. Then they admit that it will take no one anywhere to simply impugn the other side's motives and lack of objectivity. "It is clear from the literature that we all have our suspicions."

Finally they list five "facts" that undergird their confidence in their convictions:

> 1) We regularly search our motives and seek to empty ourselves of all that would tarnish true perceptions of reality. 2) We pray that God would give us humility, teachability, wisdom, insight, fairness, and honesty. 3) We make every effort to submit our minds to the unbending and unchanging grammatical and historical reality of the Biblical texts in Greek and Hebrew, using the best methods of study available to get as close as possible to the intentions of the Biblical writers. 4) We test our conclusions by the history of exegesis to reveal any chronological snobbery or cultural myopia. 5) We test our conclusions in the real world of contemporary ministry and look for resonance from mature and godly people. In humble confidence that we are handling the Scriptures with care, we lay our vision before the public for all to see and debate in the public forum.[28]

It seems clear on many counts that what these very conservative evangelicals appeal to runs against the substance of foundationalism. Rather than being an individualistic epistemology, their epistemology develops its conclusions within the tradition of biblical exegesis and submits its conclusions to the public for all to see and debate. It cannot pretend to be beyond history and in fact hopes to be checked and corrected by history. It does not disallow ongoing, difficult, contestable judgment; in fact, it implicitly demands such. There is, for instance, regular prayer and searching of motives. There is also the imperative of testing conclusions in light of the discernment of "mature and godly people." Yet not only may "mature and godly people" differ among themselves, it is an ongoing event of judgment to determine who are and what makes "mature and godly people," to say nothing of the "best method" of biblical study.

The False Dichotomy: "Objectivism" Versus "Relativism"

What then? Are we all practically, if not rhetorically, rank relativists? It is only the lingering power of the foundationalist schema that makes us believe we must choose between the polar opposites of timeless and placeless objectivity and sheer, arbitrary, and solipsistic relativism. As Alasdair MacIntyre has painstakingly shown, and as Piper and Grudem's hermeneutical method demonstrates, traditional inquiry is constrained by many powerful checks and must always answer to the world around it, however exactly that world is perceived. Foundationalism, modeling its logic on mathematics and striving for an analogous kind of precision and certainty, led philosophers, theologians, and others to regard anything less as bogus knowledge. But the goal was set too high, or, to say it better, was of the wrong sort. Allow for different logics and you immediately achieve possibilities other than absolute objectivism and rank relativism.[29]

To put the matter metaphorically, it is as if foundationalists are on the playground of knowledge and insisting that everyone frolic only on the slippery slide. They believe that only there can knowledge be safely found. Foundationalists fear that, freed from the slide alone, some relativistic children may tire of any restrictions and wander into the street. But I think foundationalists need to admit that there is no such thing as safely and absolutely secured knowledge. Knowledge is particular and perspectival, and as such is always contestable. And it is after all not entirely safe living atop the slide, which is why those who do so are obsessed with slippery slopes. Dismounting it, we are at least freed to accurately assess danger in all its varieties. And we are freed to admit that danger is inescapable in a finite (and fallen) world.

In short, if evangelicals can be coaxed down from the slippery slide, they can admit to themselves that they, like other practicing holists, rationally examine any worldview in regard to consistency, coherence, and the adequacy of beliefs to experience.[30] But of course those still half-on the foundationalist slide, sneaking a few more puffs of the objectivist weed, will now protest: "How do I choose between competing worldviews?" The question itself betrays residual foundationalist hopes of achieving some Archimedean point beyond time and space from which the pristine individual can detachedly lord over all "reality" and exercise imperial choice—but I will not dwell on that. I instead refer again to Alasdair MacIntyre's work.[31]

MacIntyre insists that all inquiry is tradition-constituted and tradition-dependent. Translation of concepts from one tradition to another is always difficult and sometimes impossible. But we can, and in fact often do, learn the language of another tradition as a "second first language." Then we can sometimes show that a rival tradition has key problems it cannot answer. Our tradition may not have these key problems and is in that regard a stronger tradition. Better yet, it may have resources to solve the other tradition's key problems, and thereby show itself to be the superior tradition.

Of course, the opposite may also happen. In the real world the Christian does not always win—and perhaps most often no one "wins," at least not in the full-scale sense of converting another to one's own faith. But in any event nothing is gained by resorting to the foundationalist mood and rhetoric. In fact, foundationalist rhetoric actually makes conversation and conversion more difficult, since it inclines us toward believing that those who disagree are necessarily benighted or ill-intentioned. And who of us tries to listen harder to someone who regards us as stupid or immoral?

Lest we forget, the Christian confession is that we all see through a glass darkly and it is only on the last day that every knee shall bow and every tongue confess Jesus as Lord. We do better, I think, to come down from the foundationalist slide, recover an eschatologically informed epistemology, and place that epistemology firmly in the bed of ecclesiology. It is the community called "church" that teaches people the language and culture that enables them to know Jesus as Lord. And it is the church in the fullness of its life—not primarily its arguments—that draws others to consider the Christian faith.

It is not foundationalism, but in fact the commonly occupied ground of testimony and witness, that allows us to commend and defend the faith to others. So when asked by the non-Christian to provide reasons for the hope within us, we appeal to the (quite contextual) considerations that produced our own judgments. As vividly and persuasively as possible, we show the relevance of our analyses to our interlocutor's experience. And finally we try to point out the desirability of the change we propose (ultimately confession of Jesus Christ as Lord and baptism into his body) in relation to our interlocutor's own (quite contextual) interests and projects. By drawing others into Christian friendship, telling Christian stories, and sharing Christian worship, we may alter the way others interpret their experience and introduce a new set of desires into their desires.[32]

Foundationalism and Liberalism

Such, at least, are Christian evangelism, mission, and apologetics as I understand them.[33] It is of course altogether possible, according to the terms of my own argument, that with all this and more I will fail to coax any conservative evangelicals down from the slippery slide of foundationalism. But I have one more appeal.

I have learned, primarily from my postliberal brothers and sisters, that foundationalism and liberalism are of a single species. Now I do not mean liberalism in the unfortunately shallow political sense in which it is used in the United States. "Indeed," as George Parkin Grant writes, "what is meant in the U.S. by 'conservative' is generally a species of modern 'liberal.' 'Conservatives' want to hold onto consequences of the earlier tradition of our liberalism which more modern 'liberals' are willing to scrap in the interest of the new and the progressive."[34]

That earlier and deeper liberalism, a liberalism that too easily engulfs us all, is the liberalism of Kant, Locke, Rousseau, Mill, and other beacons of the Enlightenment. This is the liberalism that told us we must escape the particularities of history and tradition, substitute state neutrality for the pursuit of any substantive common good, and allow individuals in "public" to choose autonomously, answering only to the principles of a supposedly universal and innate reason.[35] As MacIntyre writes, "it is of the first importance to remember that the project of founding a form of social order in which individuals could emancipate themselves from the contingency and particularity of tradition . . . was and is not only, *and not principally*, a project of philosophers. It was and is the project of modern liberal, individualist society."[36]

In short, it is primarily the liberal project that has privatized faith, obsessed us with the nation-state and led us to neglect the church, and made us defer speaking about the God of Israel and Jesus Christ as our firm foundation until we have first proven ourselves in the supposedly more basic terms of foundationalist, universal reason. I have argued that in the pluralized, postmodern world in which we now live, few if any careful thinkers actually rely on foundationalist reasoning. I am now arguing that it is also time to leave foundationalist rhetoric because it is, in the beginning and the end, liberal rhetoric.[37]

If we quit foundationalist rhetoric we can claim the specifics of the Christian tradition and forthrightly speak the name of Christ in any public forum. We can admit that our argument is contestable, as are the arguments of Marxists, Hindus, free-market capitalists, and every other party, then speak unapologetically as Christians.

If we quit foundationalist rhetoric we can more easily perceive and draw attention to liberalism itself as a tradition. Otherwise liberalism is free to hegemonically normalize all it encounters while pretending it has no norms. If I may be so bold as to paraphrase Stanley Fish, foundationalist liberals create a situation in which they can say, "We're for fairness and you're for biased judgment; we're for merit and you're for special interests; we're for objectivity and you're playing politics; we want religion everyone can affirm and you want the Jewish tribal faith of Christianity."[38] Admitting foundationalism for what it is—part and parcel of a particular tradition—we are free to challenge head-on "objectivity" and other liberal prejudices.

Finally, and most important, if we quit foundationalist rhetoric we can leave off the inevitably violent ways of liberalism and live true to Christ's nonviolent, nonhegemonic persuasion.[39] The God revealed in Jesus Christ is the God who created a free world, and when that free world wrecked itself, God entered into the suffering, confusion, and ambiguity of that world to woo it back. True to the character and ways of such a God, Jesus "has always admitted that if we entrust our life to him and his cause, we will never be proven right until beyond the end of this story and cannot count on being positively reinforced along all of the way."[40] We are not liberals who have come to tell people what they always already really knew. We are evangelicals. We confess that Israel and the church are not characters in a greater story called "the world," but instead that the world is a character in God's story, a character that does not even know its true name apart from Israel and the church. We are not liberals come to make the gospel intelligible to the world, but are evangelicals come to help the world see why it cannot be intelligible without the gospel.[41]

Nonfoundationalist *Because* Evangelical

In short, I am saying that we should be nonfoundationalists exactly because we are evangelicals. And, as John Howard Yoder writes,

> For a practice to qualify as "evangelical" . . . means first of all that it communicates *news*. It says something particular that would not be known and could not be believed were it not said. Second, it must mean functionally that this "news" is attested as *good; as shalom*. It must be public, not esoteric, but the way for it to be public is not an a priori logical move that subtracts the

particular. It is an a posteriori political practice that tells the world something it did not know and could not believe before. It tells the world what is the world's own calling and destiny, not by announcing either a utopian or a realistic goal to be imposed on the whole society, but by pioneering a paradigmatic demonstration of both the power and the practices that define the shape of restored humanity. The confessing people of God is the new world on its way. . . . [And] the credibility of that which is both "good" and "news" consists precisely in its vulnerability, its refusability.[42]

Just so, I think. And so might evangelicals move from decontextualized propositions to traditioned, storied truths; from absolute certainty to humble confidence; from mathematical purity to the rich, if less predictable, world of relational trust; from detached objectivist epistemology to engaged participative epistemology; from control of the data to respect of the other in all its created variety; from individualist knowing to communal knowing; and from once-for-all rational justification to the ongoing pilgrimage of testimony.[43]

two

Tom T. Hall and the Necessity of Narrative

In a society of advanced capitalism, theologians probably cannot avoid becoming consumer consultants on religious options. Every aspect of our lives, from automobile selection to child care, is presided over by experts who present our vast array of choices and advise us in choosing what is best for us. So it may not be fair to get impatient with theologians who present us with whole catalogs of theologies and hermeneutics and ethics, and even update the catalogs annually. They are only doing what we expect of contemporary experts.

Still, laypeople get tired. Somehow, theologies are not as easy to change in and out of as last fall's wardrobe. So suspicion arises about fads, fashions, and trends emanating from the seminaries and graduate schools. And those lay people who have heard about one of the recent developments, namely narrative theology, may wonder if it is worth the time and trouble of their investigation.

I want to say that narrative is not just a fad. Instead, it is necessary for Christians to describe our faith, to talk about the way we understand the world and our place in it, to see persons in all their complexity. I don't suppose many people outside seminaries and graduate schools will be convinced of the case by abstruse academic arguments. So here I gratefully note the theologians and philosophers and literary critics who have forcefully and eruditely demonstrated, to me and many others, the necessity of narrative—Lindbeck, H. R. Niebuhr, Hauerwas, McClendon, MacIntyre, Crites, Alter, Burrell, Frei, Goldberg, Stroup, Tilley—and that is it so far as arcane references go. The rest of the way the scholars will offer cues from backstage and I will draw on an eminent authority of a different sort, the country singer and songwriter Tom T. Hall.

As an Oklahoman, I am no more disposed to apologize for esteeming a country-music artist than would an Austrian be for admiring Mozart. Suffice to say that Hall is no fool: as novelist Kurt Vonnegut put it upon his first meeting with him, "Right away, Tom T. wanted to talk about the Harvard philosopher Alfred North Whitehead, about whom I still know next to zip, and about whom I guess he knows just about everything. After he realized how ignorant I was, we got along just fine, and remain good friends today."

But more seriously, the necessity of narrative will be underscored if we talk about it in everyday, ordinary language. If we don't need technical jargon to make the case for the centrality of story, we may feel all the more certain it is not merely faddish, one in a series of complicated games invented to occupy the time and secure the expert status of professional theologians.

In plain language, then, story is necessary to identify persons. To be introduced to someone, we first need a name. So Hall introduces us to a woman named Ruby. Of course, there are hundreds of women named Ruby. To know this particular Ruby, we need to know something about her setting: where she is from, what she does for a living. And so we learn Ruby "was a truck-stop child" born "somewhere near L.A.," and that she is now a truck-stop waitress who has "poured a lot of hot coffee in [her] day." Notice what is happening. We are already telling, or on the verge of telling, a story. Ruby's name is somewhat particularized and two elements of narrative (setting and character) are already present.

But it is possible that there are any number of truck-stop waitresses named Ruby and born near Los Angeles. So to get a real idea of what this specific name "Ruby" stands for, we need the third element of narrative: incident or plot. And this Hall provides liberally, telling us Ruby was "born in the back of a rig," and that, though she is beautiful (known as "Ravishing Ruby"), she has nothing to do with men because she is obsessed with her father, a man called Smilin' Jack who abandoned her when she was fourteen. In short:

> Ravishing Ruby, a beautiful young girl now.
> Ravishing Ruby, she made a solemn vow.
> Waiting on Smilin' Jack, he'll come rollin' by,
> And she wants to see him,
> She wants to touch him,
> Either way, dead or alive.

So in a song under three minutes in length, Hall introduces us to a complex person, a gullible woman "who believes anything you say" (because she must believe Smilin' Jack's word that he will return), who longs for a certain man but has forsworn men in general, who has made her entire life into a sad parable of her preoccupation—"All the time she's been waitin' on him,/ She's been waitin' on you and me." By way of narrative we now know a particular woman who has lived a particular life, the one and only Ravishing Ruby.

Hall's story-song is diverting, so we tend to think of it as we do of all stories: as embellishments or decorations of a more basic identity. But there is no other way we can get to know Ravishing Ruby—this specific woman in these specific circumstances—than by her story.

Of course, our temptation is to believe that we can get at the real person by coming up with a fundamental or essential label. In our day and culture, these labels tend to be psychological. So we might begin to discuss Ruby as a woman in arrested development, marked by trauma, struggling to recover from a dysfunctional background.

The shortcomings of this approach are exposed with the aid of another Tom T. Hall ballad. "Turn It On, Turn It On, Turn It On" is the tale of a certain Johnny who rises one morning, loads his .44, and kills seven people before holing up in a farmhouse. Why?

> People said John was a slacker
> 'Cause he wouldn't fight in their war.
> A man wasn't much if he wouldn't fight
> Back in nineteen-forty-and-four.
> The doctor said John was just too sick to go,
> But the people said that he was a coward.

As Johnny hides in the farmhouse, he has "satisfaction in his eyes" and vows he won't be taken alive. Yet when the sheriff kicks down the door, John's gun misfires, and he is captured alive. He smiles at the sheriff and makes light of his situation, then later willingly pleads guilty. On the day of his execution he robustly consumes his last meal. Strapped into the electric chair,

> John said, "I ain't no coward
> And the people know that I won't run."

Then Johnny smiled up at the warden
And said, "Turn it on, turn it on, turn it on!"

Psychologically we might attempt to label and explain Johnny with theories about paranoia or a weak ego. More trivially, we might say he lacked self-esteem. But of course people with paranoia, weak egos, or no self-esteem do all sorts of things. Not all go on a murderous rampage. So we have to pay attention to John's particular setting, a setting in which a man who won't go to war and kill may be seen as not much of a man, and consequently may lose self-esteem, or suffer erosion of his ego, or begin to think everyone is against him. We must also pay attention to the incidents of John's life: he is a man who happened to be sick at a time when being sick got him labeled a coward. To prove his manhood in this setting and in light of these incidents, John must kill—and die—without fear.

In short, we are driven back to Johnny's story to get a genuine understanding of him. And we would need to know more about his particular story to conjecture why he responded with murderous violence. Someone else, born and residing in the same town but with a different father or mother, a different temperament, or whatever, may have responded with suicidal violence, or with no lethal violence at all, ended up an alcoholic, in the state asylum, or maybe more or less unfazed by the town's scorn. Consider, too, that psychologists of different schools will offer different labels as the explanation of John's actions. Whether he is said to suffer primarily from paranoia, a weak ego, or something else, John's diagnosis must in any case be justified with reference to his story.

In other words, no account of John and his identity can be offered that is richer or more essential than his story. As persons, we are contingent creatures, shaped and formed by a plethora of influences and circumstances. We are not exclusively at the mercy of drives or impulses that can be summarized and anticipated with the law-like accuracy of such events as the passing of Halley's comet. Maybe Halley's comet doesn't need a story. Persons do.

Of course, our labels are often helpful. They provide insight into stories and sometimes extend them. But a person is too complex, too divided in consciousness and allegiances, to be captured by any one label. We may try to overcome this complexity by applying a series of labels. Yet then we must explain the relation of these labels to one another, especially when they are apparently contradictory. For instance, we might plausibly say John had a weak ego and was sociopathic. But doesn't it take a sturdy ego to do something that so flagrantly violates social norms? We will now have to say what peculiar shape John's ego and sociopathy took. Justification of our series of labels will force us back to Johnny's story. In fact, the series of labels will probably tend to be connected and unfold exactly as a narrative.

Hoary, fanciful, and unscientific as it seems, narrative alone is capable of fundamentally describing the embodied contradictions that are persons. Even simple narrative, such as Tom T. Hall's country songs, can plausibly present characters as a mysterious mix of good and evil, baffling even (or especially) to themselves. So in "She Gave Her Heart to Jethro," Tom T. tells of a beautiful redhead who married a certain Jethro. She is unfaithful, cheating on her husband to the point that he goes mad. Hall never names the wife, perhaps, as he hints in the closing stanza, because he tempts and expects us to dismiss her with our name-labels.

The labels Hall anticipates are not psychological, but moralistic. Having set us up to name and dismiss the unnamed as "adulteress" or "whore," the singer reveals more of her story. Without excusing her, he claims "much can be said for this girl" and, in spare strokes, portrays her surprising fidelity as well as her prosaic infidelity.

> Some friends came and begged her to leave him.
> They said, "Jethro belongs in a home."
> She said, "My heart is Jethro's,
> But my God-given body is my own."
>
> Now some of her lovers were strangers.
> She gave everybody a whirl.
> She gave her heart to Jethro
> And her body to the whole damned world.

Of course, we might still insist that a single, judgmental label is most apt and descriptive, that it most fundamentally expresses the identity of this woman. We could suggest, for instance, that this woman stayed with Jethro out of guilt and thus her infidelity is the defining trait of her life. But in any event we are not escaping story. The question has become one of intentions. Does Jethro's wife stay with him because she always was and intended to be faithful to him in her own strange way, or merely out of guilt? To decide, we need to know more about how she has acted and what she has intended in any number of other relationships. In other words, we need to hear more of her story. Arguments over the best description of someone's identity are settled with reference to a story, indicating once again that story is as basic as you can get.

So far I have been concerned only with individual identities. But individual identities are, of course, never separate from communal identities. And it is also by stories—often by competing stories—that communities pass on their memories, and with them their communal identities.

One crucial sort of memories is memories about significant incidents or events. Stories most adequately convey the incidents that shape communities. Tom T. recounts, in "Trip to Hyden," a visit to a town where thirty-nine miners have just perished in an accident. The singer was disturbed by the almost carnival-like atmosphere at the tragic scene, where an old man mistook Hall for a reporter and kept "reminding me how his simple name was spelled." The undertaker "seemed refreshed despite the kind of work I knew he did." As far as this visitor is concerned, "It was sunny down in Hyden/But somehow the town was cold." He concludes with the observation of a local woman who declares of the miners, "They's worth more money now than when they's a livin'." In this telling Hyden appears to be a shallow, opportunistic community, unable to appreciate the magnitude of its loss and reduced to pitiful pandering. Others may tell a more flattering tale of the mine collapse and its aftermath; but the story must be told and will surely constitute a large part of Hyden's identity from now on.

A second crucial set of memories for any community is that about heroes, men and women who embody the highest virtues and hopes of the community. No community will endure if it fails to produce and honor heroes, or if it overidealizes its heroes and so invites cynicism and the collapse of its standards. Hall's "The Ballad of Bill Crump" is an example of the best sort of hero tale, about an ordinary man with faults ("he loved to sip that corn"), who yet employed his gifts for the good of community. Not forgotten, then, is Bill's ability to "make anything you could make out of a tree."

> He built the church, he built the pews.
> He built the cradles and the furniture for the school.
> Folks in Avery County say that he was better than good—
> Probably one of the reasons the Lord made wood.

Only now, with an incidental reference to the Creator of wood, do I need to return to the explicit theological claims from which I started. I said that narrative is necessary *for Christians*. Though I doubt it, there may be a way to envision and describe something like "persons" without recourse to narrative. But they would have to be "persons" outside community and history, autonomous and free of time. They definitely could not be persons as Christians conceive persons: created and contingent, called to know and to be reconciled to the Creator-Redeemer God through the particular, irreplaceable communities of Israel and the church.

In other words, the God Christians worship is a God who does not shun history and contingency. Ours is a peculiar, electing God believed to have chosen a particular people and finally to have worked most decisively through a particular man. We do not profess to be saved by cycles of nature or by a timeless ideal or abstract principle; we profess to be saved through specific characters in specific places and times. We cannot even begin to describe all of this, to account for the lives we try to live, without telling a story.

So Scripture presents God not by dwelling on conceptualized attributes, but by recounting stories of God's interactions with humans in their myriad and shifting circumstances. The Bible as a unity is in fact centered in and based on narratives (most significantly the accounts of the Exodus and of the Christ). Without these it would make no sense, and its bewildering, diverse parts would be irreconcilable. By saying as much I am not suggesting that all theologians should disparage the abilities to abstract and conceptualize, much less that they should all attempt to become storytellers. There is plenty of noble and needed work for theology to do in its stance as a second-order activity, reflecting on and adjudicating between the whole and parts of our canonical and postcanonical stories. But all of us as Christians will have to do with the necessity of narrative.

And if you still don't believe me, Tom T. has another song . . .

three

The Truth Is Out There

Why *The X-Files* Is Really about Epistemology

Some people think *The X-Files* is about UFO-chasing and urban vampires and government conspiracy. I think it is television's sharpest and most consistently rewarding exploration of epistemology.

Okay, okay, I hear the protests—but whaddya expect on commercial TV? Richard Rorty squared off against Alvin Plantinga? Of course, Fox-TV's highest-rated program features strong storytelling. It's got a chic, dark ambiance. It's got some mystery and suspense and PG doses of violence. And protagonists Dana Scully (played by attractive redhead Gillian Anderson) and Fox Mulder (played by attractive brunette David Duchovny) have potent sexual chemistry cooking at a slow simmer, the restraint of which only increases the excitement, to the point that the (very) occasional use of one's first name by the other has as much charge as a blitzkrieg bedroom scene. (Mulder and Scully may be popular culture's best argument that Marabel Morgan is right and chaste people really are sexiest—but that's another article.)

So, yes, the standard elements of sex and violence and curiosity appeal are there. But I still say the show is fundamentally about epistemology— about knowing, and how hard it is to know, and probing how we can know what we think we know.

The X-Files is one of the most discussed programs on television—not just in the United States, but in Australia, Norway, and Ireland as well—yet it is conceivable that some readers haven't seen the show. So here, in a theremin-scored interlude, is what you have been missing.

FBI agent Fox Mulder, an Oxford graduate in psychology, is one of the agency's best and brightest. But he is also—different, let's say. Mulder is convinced that his sister was abducted by aliens when he and she were little kids. Consequently, he is hooked on the bizarre, inexplicable cases most agents tuck away and forget in the bureau's "X-Files": unsolved crimes with evidence that points to the credibility of UFOs, reincarnation, were-wolves, psychic powers, and the stray episode of stigmata. The FBI powers-that-be, who regard "Spooky" Mulder as stranger than anything since J. Edgar Hoover last slipped into a skirt, sequester him in a basement office and try to ignore him.

The powers don't fire Mulder, though, because high-placed, enigmatic figures with monikers like Deep Throat and Cancer Man, obscurely linked to a secret and possibly governmental outfit called The Syndicate, won't let them. For some reason, they want this FBI agent alive and well and poking into lots of abandoned warehouses after midnight. So the bureau does the next best thing to firing Mulder and sics a fresh young agent with an M.D. on him. Dana Scully is assigned to tag along with Mulder, report on his activities, try to leaven his occult flights of fancy with scientific skepticism, and persuade him occasionally to track a garden-variety serial killer.

Still don't see the connection to epistemology? Well, whether or not you believe intelligent alien life really would travel millions of miles to ram tiny gadgets up human nasal passages, it truly is a crazy world out there. You can talk about the transition from industrial to postindustrial society, from modernity to postmodernity, or whatever you want to call it: Peter Drucker says we are living amid the most profound societal change in human history. You can talk about lessened confidence in government, the clergy, the media, and just about any other institution that tries today to set itself up as an authority on anything. Along that line, you can talk about how science, and the applied science of technology, was supposed to be the twentieth-century messiah, and then came atom bombs and oil spills and the Cancer-Scare-of-the-Month Club.

Talk about it all, and what do you get? For one thing, you get plenty of people suspecting truth is stranger and less predictable than it used to be. And you get bodacious ratings for agents Mulder and Scully.

Amid all this cultural upheaval, some folks are tempted right on into relativism of the crassest sort: everything's true so nothing's true. Not our intrepid agents. They stoutly believe, as the show's motto insists during opening credits, that "The Truth Is Out There," and weekly they coach us in a rough-and-ready critical realism fitted for the twilight zone of turn-of-the-century North America. That's right. Mulder (and not just Scully) is an epistemological objectivist. Mulder, after all, operates with a street version of the scientific method. He pays attention, records details carefully, avails himself of all sorts of high-tech equipment, posits hypotheses consistent within themselves and attempting to account for all the evidence, and he does his best to test those hypotheses. In this sense he is not unscientific, he is just allowing for a wider and more diverse band of "evidence" and causal agents than do more conventional scientists.

So, for example, people keep dying violently in the proximity of an odd fellow who has apparent motives for murder but never leaves any physical evidence whatsoever of harming a soul. The conventional cops think, *Can't be this guy, no matter how it looks, gotta look elsewhere.* But Spooky Mulder thinks: *Could be it's not him. But could be, too, that this suspect has psychic powers and knocks people off telekinetically. Let's investigate the hypothesis.*

Yes, Mulder—no less than his medically trained colleague, who is always trying to drag him back into more conventional boundaries—is an objectivist. And he is an old-fashioned, which is to say Cartesian, objectivist. Like Descartes, Mulder and his creators believe doubt is the royal road to truth. Descartes shut himself up in a hot room and tried to question everything until he arrived at something he could not doubt, and then rebuilt from there. Similarly, Mulder discounts all sorts of taken-for-granted wisdom; another of the show's mottoes is the doubt-enhancing "Trust No One."

After sweating it out, Descartes thought he actually had arrived at indubitable and foundational truth. Mulder, and Scully too (after seeing all sorts of weird mayhem, and her sister killed in her stead), really do trust no one—except each other. From this precarious foundation, they are trying to construct a world of knowledge that can include liver-eating mutants and fluorescent bugs that suck all the liquid out of your body. (No wonder Mulder apparently never goes to bed but only dozes on the couch in the blue glow of his TV.)

Now, lest you think I'm the only one who believes *The X-Files* is prime-time epistemology, let's be good objectivists and refer to authorial intention. Executive producer Howard Gordon affirms that Mulder and Scully are "tour guides" to the current "chaos that we're having to navigate." More to the point, *X-Files* creator Chris Carter refers to a poster hanging in agent Mulder's basement exile, "The 'I Want to Believe' poster in Mulder's office sums up a personal longing. I'm a skeptic, and I want to be challenged. I want to believe in something. That's the heart of the show and what infuses the characters."

But wait, creator Carter goes on. He goes on beyond Descartes, to, well, Alvin Plantinga. That is to say that he affirms faith, and not doubt, as that which lies at the bottom of all knowledge. That is apparently what he has in mind by having Mulder wanting to "believe" rather than flatly to "know." Listen to the non-Cartesian Carter speak, then: "To me, the idea of faith is really the backbone of the entire series—faith in your own beliefs, ideas about the truth, and so it has religious overtones always."

Whoa! So *The X-Files* can take not only flying saucers and killer computers seriously, but religious faith too? Even, say, Christianity? Yes. In one especially interesting third-season episode, entitled "Revelations," a little boy manifests stigmata, with blood inexplicably welling out of his hands and side. There's a twist. This time Mulder is the materialist skeptic, suspecting hysteria or some such. It's Scully, reared a Catholic and wearing a cross around her neck, who insists they consider the possibility that God is displaying the wounds of Christ on this bewildered child. She is so shaken by these events that, at the end of the program, she retreats to a confessional for the first time in years. In the show's trademark darkness, she tells the priest she is afraid, afraid most of all that "God really may be speaking. And no one's listening."

Before you solicit Donald Wildmon's endorsement of the show, I should add that "Revelations" loses momentum with a hokey subplot that has Satan's emissary stalking and trying to kill the boy. And at one point our heroes confidently refer to Saint Ignatius as a biblical character (shouldn't have trusted a Sunday-school teacher on that one). And, remember, "Revelations" is just one episode out of dozens: next week we're back in the middle of labyrinthine conspiracies beyond Oliver Stone's fever dreams, where the "other," whether extraterrestrial or bureaucratic or merely the quiet guy across the street, is always malevolent.

That, finally, is the real problem with *The X-Files*. Yes, it explores the unexplainable, the wondrous, the awesome with rarely faltering storytelling panache. In the way only good storytelling can do, it turns the world as we think we know it inside out and renders it oddly anew. (Thus actress Gillian Anderson, perhaps learning from the travails of her character, told David Letterman that her hometown of Grand Rapids, Michigan, is both "normal" and "strange.") For that we should be properly grateful. But ultimately, it seems, in the world of *The X-Files* the ineffable is evil—and viciously so. The truth is out there. But it is swaddled in darkness, and it wants to destroy all things bright and beautiful.

That said, I stand by my initial assertion. *The X-Files* is television's sharpest and most consistently rewarding exploration of epistemology. And it's almost as much fun as reading Rorty or Plantinga.

four

Nothin' But Us Liberals Here

Why Christianity Is Not Free in America

Is religion free in America? In *The Myth of American Religious Freedom* (Spence, 1999) Kenneth Craycraft would argue that the fact that the question itself seems absurd, even to most orthodox Christians, is an indication of how captive traditional or classical Christianity is in these United States. Craycraft, a Roman Catholic theologian now studying law at Duke University, says the only religion that is truly free in America is the privatized and dehistoricized faith of liberalism. Thus the United States has not "solved" the problem of religious freedom, at least not for believers in the God revealed through Israel and Jesus Christ, but has brilliantly imposed a single faith (Enlightenment-based liberalism) on all other faiths.

Station break: I paragraphically pause to let these assertions sink in. Rummage the refrigerator or run to the restroom, but hold those thoughts.

Now I am back, to add this: Craycraft is right on every count outlined above. Of course, this statement may make you want not just a station break, but to change the channel. But don't touch that dial. Craycraft's

interesting

[44]

argument is too important, too consequential to ignore, even if it certainly is unsettling.

I cannot, in this brief space, trace the book's argument in detail. And the middle chapters especially demand close reading, as well as ongoing debate among specialists, for their adjudication. These chapters unfold religious freedom as it was understood by the seventeenth-century philosopher John Locke, and as it was put into practice by political luminaries who followed in his philosophical footsteps—the American founders Thomas Jefferson and James Madison. Particularly as regards Jefferson and Madison, details of Craycraft's case hang on his assessment that in some key places they wrote ironically—that is, that they intended something other than what their words say simply on their face. Irony is easily misinterpreted, and since it is safe to say that neither Jefferson nor Madison wrote broad comedy, we will have to leave evaluation of these subtleties to historical specialists.

The Unfaithfulness of Athanasius and Calvin

What we can do in this space is unpack the main points of the book, outlined in the first paragraph above. It may be best to begin with some words about liberalism. The liberalism with which Craycraft contends is much broader and deeper than the usual application of the dreaded "L-word" in contemporary American politics. Rather, Craycraft refers to the political philosophy formed in the seventeenth century, based on the work of such thinkers as Locke and Hobbes. As he puts it, the "central audacious presumption of modern liberalism" was "that it had found a set of objective neutral principles, by which objective, universal judgments can be made." Largely in response to (and reaction against) traditional, revealed religion, the original liberals thought they had discovered a way to escape historical particularities and their attendant "sectarian" identities.

Locke, Hobbes, and their followers presupposed a universal reason that resided in every sane and reasonable individual, prior to and beyond any distinctive religious convictions. This universal and secular reason would be the ground and final court of appeal for public matters such as government. Religion, then, would be relegated to the private sphere. It is only the individual's business, and not that of the state—*or, note well, the church.* As Locke wrote, "The Care . . . of every man's Soul belongs unto himself, and is to be left unto himself." For Madison, the religious authority of the church reduced people to "slavery and Subjection," since in his estimate "in no instance" have churches "been guardians of the liberties of the people." And Jefferson inveighed against creedal or confessional Christianity, exactly because each assumes doctrines that are considered exclusively true quite apart from any given individual's opinion of them. So Jefferson called Athanasius and Calvin "impious dogmatists" and "mere usurpers of the Christian name."

But of what faith were Athanasius and Calvin impious usurpers? Exactly of Jefferson's Lockean liberal "Christianity," which determinedly set aside the revealed faith handed down by the church through history, and replaced it with a "tolerance" based on the universal reason professedly resident in every reasonable individual. For liberals, then, every person chooses his or her own faith. Liberal religious freedom is freedom of the allegedly autonomous individual (not the church); it is freedom of the individual to hold religious convictions as private opinions. In this regard the "conservative" pundit George Will is pristinely liberal when he writes that "religion is perfectly free as long as it is perfectly private—mere belief—but it must bend to the political will (law) as regards conduct." In fact, Will is not an anomaly. In terms of this classical liberalism, those most often referred to as liberals in current discourse would better be designated "admitted liberals" and those referred to as conservatives better designated "undeclared liberals." Or, if that is too pointed, we might more accurately refer to those now usually called liberals as "late modern liberals" and those called conservatives as "early modern liberals."

Craycraft's concerns with this state of affairs are explicitly based on his devout Roman Catholicism. But I think all believers in classical Christianity, including evangelical Protestants, must share his central concerns. Put quite bluntly, liberalism presumes a Pelagian Christianity. It endorses a faith that each individual autonomously chooses, and by his or her choice validates, for himself or herself. Yet as Augustine argued against the heretical British monk Pelagius, at the center of Judaism and Christianity is the truth that human beings did not choose God. God sought and chose Israel; it did not choose God. And God seeks out and calls Gentiles into the "commonwealth of Israel" through Jesus Christ (Eph. 2:12). "We love because he first loved us" (1 John 4:19). The essence of grace is that it is unmerited and even unsought, uninitiated by humanity. And whether Calvinist or Arminian, classical Protestants (along with Catholics) profess that only God's grace itself allows and enables individuals to hear and to accept God's saving claim on our lives.

Chosen Rather than Choosing

Consider what this means. It means that God has objectively acted, in specific ways, with the people of Israel and in the person Jesus of Nazareth. Through these particularities of revealed faith, and with the blessed enablement of the Holy Spirit, we know God and are saved from sin and death, and we learn how human beings can live most truly—exactly as and because they really are creatures of the God known in Israel and Jesus Christ. That is the most basic and important truth we can know about ourselves as human beings, and it is not something (*contra* liberalism) we know from the universal, "neutral" reason available to every individual simply by virtue of being a human being.

It is also a truth that remains truth apart from any given individual's response to it. Moses' choosing to go back to Egypt did not make God's call to rescue Israel true. The call and its truth would have remained even had Moses rejected it. And in fact, as the Scriptures recount, it was not really Moses' "choice" to return and confront Pharaoh. A rather pesky and demanding God sought Moses out and told him what to do. Moses had all manner of excuses and objections, but, well, God is God—"I Am Who I Am, I Will Be Who I Will Be." It was against his own choice and best judgment that Moses went back. If the Israelites asked, he was told to inform them "I Am Who I Am has sent me to you" (Exod. 3:14). The same dynamic—God initiating, persons responding (not always enthusiastically) continues through the rest of scriptural and later Christian history. Think of prophets like Ezekiel and Jonah struggling against their calls, which sometimes were genuinely dangerous and humiliating. Think of Paul fighting and even trying to destroy the faith of which he later, against his own designs, became the premier apostle. Think of Luther sputtering to his interrogators, "Here I stand; I can do no other." Think of C. S. Lewis's confession that he was dragged kicking and screaming into the church. Think, perhaps, of the relentless pursuit of the "hound of heaven" in your own life. Grace would not be grace if it did not often surprise, confront, challenge, and even frighten us. It would only be a human projection and illusion.

Yet it is exactly the grace of orthodox faith that liberalism disallows and declares illegitimate, if not flatly "mad" (as in the words of contemporary and self-confessed liberals John Rawls and Richard Rorty). Craycraft fittingly cites political philosopher Michael Sandel, who has said that the liberal envisions the ideal and genuine human person as an "unencumbered self," one free and independent of "aims and attachments it did not choose for itself." This unencumbered self is (allegedly) cut loose "from the sanctions of custom and tradition" such as the Christian faith, very much based in history. Liberated from "moral ties antecedent to choice, the liberal self is installed as sovereign, cast as the author of the only obligations that constrain." This is indeed what liberalism calls freedom. Orthodox Christianity calls it idolatry.

Getting Elected in the Land of the Free

These are crucial and far from "merely theoretical" theological objections, but that is not all. Not only does liberalism nullify grace at the root, it further distorts the grace of apostolic faith by privatizing it. Recall that liberalism's religious freedom is freedom of the autonomous individual, not freedom of the church. Craycraft's Catholicism makes him more alert to this fallacy than are many evangelicals, but once again I think the point transfers to all confessional or creedal Christians.

For clarity's sake, I will use two Roman Catholic examples from Craycraft. The first is John Cardinal O'Connor's 1990 declaration that "Where Catholics are perceived not only as treating church teaching on abortion with contempt, but helping to multiply abortions by advocating legislation supporting abortion or by making public funds available for abortion, bishops may decide for the common good such Catholics must be warned that they are at risk of excommunication." Cardinal O'Connor's statement met with a firestorm of criticism. Here was a breach of liberal faith, which allows religious convictions only as private opinions, and then only so long as those opinions have no public effect at odds with the state. "In other words," Craycraft observes, "the Catholic Church will be tolerated only insofar as it makes no demands on its members, especially regarding the exercise of their conscience in the legislative chamber."

As I say, Protestants may not so immediately sympathize with this concern, what with our own heritage of resisting "papalists" and their church. But the abortion example cuts deep, since evangelicals cannot and do not accept abortion as unobjectionable and harmlessly relegated to private, individual opinion. Some evangelicals have even been known to doubt the Christianity of pro-abortion politicians, which is to say that they have in their own way already excommunicated these legislators. So even if, due to what I—not alone among Protestants—consider a disastrously weak ecclesiology, evangelicals are not apt to consider abortion in terms of church discipline, our conviction of the objectivity of God's work and will undercuts relegation of the faith in the realm of private opinion. We understand God as objectively God, Creator and Redeemer of the cosmos, not as a household god concerned only for "personal morality." Our weak ecclesiology has in the past unfortunately made us talk that way, but abortion and other developments have given the lie to such misstatements. We emphatically do not understand and profess faith as private opinion or as true only for ourselves.

Which brings up Craycraft's second Catholic example, that of John Fitzgerald Kennedy as a candidate for the Presidency. Evangelicals in 1960 were, of course, among those most acutely concerned with Kennedy's Catholicism, and probably among those most acutely relieved when he insisted his faith would have nothing to do with how he governed were he elected. But again, evangelicals are in a different frame of mind since 1960, when many still intuitively (if mistakenly) regarded America as a Protestant Christian nation. It bears revisiting how Kennedy the potential President distanced himself from Kennedy the Catholic Christian. He said that in America the separation of church and state is "absolute," that America is a place "where no Catholic prelate would tell the President (should he be a Catholic) how to act and no Protestant minister would tell his parishioners for whom to vote." He said, "I believe in a President whose views on religion are his own private affairs" and insisted, "I am not the Catholic candidate for President. I am the Democratic party's candidate for President who happens to be Catholic."

Let us make some substitutions of phrasing more applicable to Protestant conservative evangelicals. Imagine a conservative evangelical candidate who, willing to make religious accommodations to increase his likelihood of attaining office, declared, "No pastor or Christian leader can tell church members that legalized abortion or state-sanctioned homosexual practice is wrong. No church or Christian organization should discourage its members from voting for politicians who would legally encourage abortion or homosexual practice." Or answering, when asked whether or not he was a believer by, say, the National Religious Broadcasters, "I have nothing to say publicly on that matter. Those are my own private affairs." Or insisting, "I am not the evangelical candidate for President. I am the Republican Party's candidate for President who happens to be an evangelical." Even if some evangelicals finally voted for such a candidate, I doubt many would want to vouch for the authenticity of his evangelical faith. That faith is simply (and correctly) not seen as a merely private matter with no public ramifications. If you are an evangelical Christian, you consider yourself to have been included in the body of Christ by the sovereign Lord of the universe. That is necessarily the most significant, determinative aspect of your self and character. From an evangelical vantage point, one does not "happen" to be a Christian in the way that one "happens" to have blue eyes or prefer mustard over mayonnaise.

But of course, to get elected on the terms of American religious freedom, JFK had to present himself more as a faithful liberal than as a faithful Catholic and Christian. The veracity of Craycraft's case is proven by the reality that a Catholic or an evangelical would still, to be elected, have to demonstrate that he or she would in office act more determinatively as a liberal than as an orthodox Christian. What, exactly, we should do about that well exceeds the purview of this essay and even, in large part, the purview of Craycraft's book. But first the scales must fall from our eyes, and we must see the liberal myth of neutrality for what it is. This outstanding book will hasten the process, though the process will necessarily remain painful and disorienting. After all, Jefferson and Madison succeeded. We are all liberals here.

PART 2

Inside Christian Borders

five

The Ivory Tower Comes to the Windy City

In Defense of Theology

The following essay developed out of Christianity Today's *request that I introduce its readership to the American Academy of Religion and Society of Biblical Literature. The joint annual meeting of these societies is the most important gathering of theologians and religious scholars in North America, and one of the most important in the world. Why should pastors and lay folk care about the often abstruse discussions of these meetings? More generally, why should the "working" church care about academic probings of faith at all? Much has changed, of course, since 1988—the date of the meeting I focus on here. But these deeper questions remain, and the AAR/SBL annual meeting—as well as the seminar rooms of most of our seminaries and graduate schools of religion—certainly remain places in which many non-scholars would be bemused, offended, intimidated, or all of the above. Here I hope to persuade such folk that academic theology (however troubling and misguided it sometimes can be) is pertinent to the ongoing life and mission of the church.*

It has been a while since a theologian was on the cover of *Time*.

That thought crosses my mind as I sit in my office on a fall day flipping through the 304-page catalog for the 1988 meeting of the American Academy of Religion (AAR) and Society of Biblical Literature (SBL). In Chicago on November 18–[22] there will gather thousands of theologians, biblical scholars, professors of comparative religion, historians, and philosophers of religion—Christians, Jews, Muslims, agnostics, atheists, Buddhists, Hindus, and probably a few of the forgot-what-I-believed-somewhere-along-the-way-but-had-already-spent-a-fortune-on-graduate-studies-in-religion variety. You just don't know exactly. After all, one of the first persons to declare God dead back in the sixties, Thomas J. J. Altizer, was an English teacher who apparently decided grammar and *Moby Dick* were not big enough game any longer.

At any rate, the only guarantees about AAR/SBL are that a real array of religious thinkers will be on hand and that at least two tons of pipe tobacco will go up in smoke. Between puffs, these scholars will sample a smorgasbord of sessions, with special selections for liberation theologians, for evangelicals, for gay and lesbian theologians, for thinkers enamored of the theology of the nineteenth century, for disciples of Paul Tillich, for Wesleyans, and even—my catalog tells me—for students of Ugarit (who will be presenting papers on "RS 1929.1," "*Keret*, Tablet 3, Column III," and the creatively titled "Reading *KTU* 1.2 IV = *CTA* 2.4 = *UT* 68").

It is said in Joshua 10:12–14 that the sun stood still "and did not hurry to set for about a whole day." I guess the presupposition for AAR/SBL's November meeting is that for four days God will stand still and let a few thousand acute observers, hunkered down in a Chicago hotel, get a better look at him—or, depending on whom you ask, her/it/them.

My main objective is to watch and listen to both the theologians (knowers of God) and the theologian-logians (knowers of knowers of God), and scurry back with a report about the state of their art, or science, or whatever it is these days. Theology no longer holds the lofty position of "queen of the sciences" within the academy. I am wondering how comfortably it is now fitting within the ivory tower. What exactly are theologians up to? Are they saying anything that is relevant to the church, and if so, is the church listening?

So my pencil is poised, calendar at hand, to rough out a schedule for this four-day extravaganza. The catalog is not exactly a Christmas wish book, but it is revealing of some treasures. There are always several sessions going simultaneously, so some hard choices are unavoidable. Being a fan, I would like to hear "Love and Death in the Films of Woody Allen." But how do I juggle that and "Are They Just Cows? Agricultural Biotechnology, Bovine Somatratopin, and the Common Good"?

I'm getting dizzy leafing through the catalog. My mind wanders, and I imagine what my church-going relatives from off the farm in downstate Illinois would think of this religious convention. What would they make of a room filled with men and women whose hands are powder white and callus free, expostulating that "fundamentalism is most broadly delineated as a universal urge to react, to protest, against the modernist hegemony" or that "four exegetical questions can be answered in a comprehensive way if 1 John 2:12–14 is understood as an example of the figures of thought called *expositio* and *distributio* used in combination with a variety of other stylistic figures"?

I can almost hear my outspoken cousin let off steam: "What has all this stuff got to do with anything? It has nothing to do with the real world. I can't understand every other word they say. And they're so highfalutin'. None of it's any use to the church."

Twisting slowly in and out of my reverie, the catalog heavy on my lap, calendar still gaping open in anticipation, I can't agree with my voluble, dreamy relative. Though we may not always understand the specialists' lingo or concerns, I have the feeling that it translates into something that is actually quite essential. But I have to admit, it has been a while since a theologian appeared on the cover of *Time* magazine.

Unless you count Jim Bakker.

Entering the Ivory Hilton Towers

Now the weeks have passed and I really am at Chicago's Hilton and Towers, paddling my way through the sea of tweed and clouds of pipe smoke. I have heard a sociologist of religion declare that Jim Bakker is our premier postmodernist theologian. The meaning was obscure, and I can't fully elucidate it; but then you pick up a lot of murky references meandering through the hallways, in and out of sessions. The snatches, clinging like lint to the memory, include "messianic materialism," "separate ontologies," something about whether or not a particular Babylonian word should be translated "navel," and a man calmly insisting we must get at the "compulsive and anal tendencies of the text."

It can get exotic. And overwhelming. The hotel is packed: Convention organizers say a record 5,533 attendees have shown up. Scholars swarm up and down the Hilton's ornate open staircases. Straggly lines of scholars maintain a vigil before the registration desk, kicking suitcases, shifting overcoats and caps from one arm to the other, shouting greetings across the lobby to suddenly sighted friends. Knots of scholars have mounted a relentless assault on the half-dozen elevators; every few minutes a bell sounds, doors open wearily, one knot surges off the elevator and another bobbles uncertainly on, losing a member here and there.

Going downstairs with the masses, you navigate between pockets of scholars who sit on the steps like boulders in a stream, trying to decipher schedules and maps. (No easy proposition, since meetings are situated over six floors of the labyrinthine hotel.) In the basement there is buried a massive exhibit hall with a bare concrete floor where nearly seventy publishers display their books and hundreds of scholars browse with all the relish of children in a toy store. (I'm feeling childish myself.) It is lunchtime, and the hotel's restaurants are full, too. Even the snack bars bustle with men who now eat hot dogs, squeezing mustard into their beards, and in half an hour will argue about Whitehead's epistemology.

Sleepwalking in an Exotic World

I need some air, and so I hit the street. It is a misty Saturday, the sidewalks are damp and Michigan Avenue buzzes with shoppers. I pass one, then two small restaurants, both crammed. Inside a third, I learn that no tables will be open for thirty minutes. So I veer off Michigan, make my way to State Street, and turn north again. Eventually I land in Ronny's Grill and find a spot for me and my cheeseburger. But Ronny's is crowded, too, and a long-haired stranger in a pullover sweater takes a seat across the table. I eat and thumb through a book I just bought. The stranger himself extracts a book from a sack, a Taoist volume on the strategy of war.

He is glancing furtively at the name tag pinned to my lapel, taking in the religious connotations. I sense he wants to talk, and soon he initiates a conversation. He says he is exploring all sorts of spiritualities and religions, "trying to discern where the world is going." He works as a computer programmer "to make money." But his heart is in the search. In fact, he has published in astrological magazines ("technical pieces—I'm no inspirational writer"). Standing beneath Ronny's garish yellow sign after lunch, my companion eagerly unloads a few last words about his interpretation of the Hebrew word *Elohim,* being the first-person plural and feminine. The implication is clear: *Just what does that say about God?* We part, heading opposite directions in the grayness of the city and our theological notions.

On the route back to the hotel I pass the Fine Arts Theatre and stop to read the posters, idly wondering if a movie would be a good diversion that night. Ken Russell's *The Lair of the White Worm* is showing. It is something about snake worshipers who inhabit a Victorian mansion and draw a young woman into their grasp for a night of fun. Roger Ebert, scaling the oxymoronic heights only movie critics can reach, deems it "delightfully kinky."

A few moments later, sucked into the Hilton's revolving doors, I am thinking that, yes, AAR/SBL gets exotic, but is it any more exotic than the world we all live in and so often sleepwalk through?

Polite Englobbing

Martin Marty is the 1988 president of the American Academy of Religion. He is a church historian at the University of Chicago and, since this year's meeting is in Chicago, has had a lot to do with its organization. Marty is a diminutive, bald-headed man, but what he lacks in size and hair, he makes up for by being nearly omnipresent and omniscient. He is everywhere at the conference, speaking at this panel or that, listening earnestly to bright young stars such as Elaine Pagels, beaming and swaying in his seat while a black choir raucously sings the gospel.

When he does speak, it is always worth listening. At a session on "Religion and the Public Schools," Marty stresses the difficulty of teaching religion in pluralistic America. "What is the consensus from which public school teachers should teach? Is it Judeo-Christianity? If so, do you emphasize the Judeo or the Christianity? If Christianity, do you emphasize Protestant or Catholic Christianity? If Protestant, which Protestant? If Baptist Protestantism, then whose interpretation—Jesse Jackson's or Jesse Helms's? Mark Hatfield's or Jerry Falwell's? Jimmy Carter's or Pat Robertson's?"

Despite all the pitfalls, Marty thinks religion should be taught. He concludes with a story, saying that when he was associate dean at the University of Chicago's divinity school he was charged with raising funds and once asked how he could go around begging money for the study of religion in a world where children were starving. A colleague said religious education was like sex education—if you don't teach it, the consequences are dangerous. The truth is, Marty says, if you get sex education or religious education right, it may make some other things come out right.

I go across the way to listen in on a famous German theologian. He is speaking in a cavernous exhibit hall, in a space cordoned off with blue curtains on aluminum poles. This session, like so many, is filled past capacity, and a couple dozen people are standing behind the chairs, thirty yards from the speaker. His accent is heavy and he is extremely soft-spoken, meaning I cannot make out much of what he says, but the gist is this: How do we talk about God and know God in our pluralistic world?

The next day I attend a session on "The Restructuring of American Conflict, Denominational Decline, and the Future." It is a discussion of sociologist Robert Wuthnow's new book by that title. Martin Marty is here again. He and Wuthnow are joined by George Lindbeck, who teaches at Yale, and Stanley Hauerwas, a Yale alumnus now teaching at Duke.

Appropriately, Wuthnow begins. He exposits on the declining significance of denominationalism and the growth of special-purpose groups in religion. Then he talks about the resurgence of fundamentalism, noting the degrees of difference between fundamentalists. Some are white supremacists; others stoutly oppose racism. Some now major on pro-life issues; others do not. He moves on to evangelicalism, cataloging differences among that clan, then to secular humanists, doing the same thing. Eventually he steps back to see the wider, national picture, observing that liberals take a strong stand on the Constitution's clause forbidding the establishment of religion, while conservatives focus on the free exercise clause. Neither side speaks persuasively to the other, so we can expect continued conflict.

Marty responds first. He is glad Wuthnow is pressing the issue. It is important to recognize that religion is often used to legitimize an ideology, and we are certainly seeing plenty of this today. He agrees with Wuthnow that denominations are increasingly less significant. Now, instead of simply being split from other denominations, the denominations are splintering from within. So the issue "is in one sense about knowing what trench you're in and who you're going to shoot at."

The crisis of the day is the collapsed middle. Marty says the majority of the population is fluid between extremes, gravitating toward a moderating position. But now, he laments, the center does not hold. He facetiously suggests that given our present, difficult situation, the most crucial difference is not between liberal and conservative religionists, but between the mean and the nonmean. The desperate question is, Who will fill the center? Fundamentalists, Catholics, evangelicals, liberals—Marty thinks no one group is going to run the country by itself, so *how* do we fill the center? At least if people were nicer we might move toward some healthy compromises.

Lindbeck, white-haired and white-bearded, next steps to the lectern. His candidate for the middle is what he calls Anselmian Scripturalism, a not easily explained position that looks to Scripture to provide a worldview, without necessarily accepting its historicity on details. Lindbeck insists this perspective is acceptable to moderns and, if conveyed to the masses, would be congenial to their biblical piety. So Lindbeck disagrees with Marty's prescription—a fluid public theology—but agrees with his and Wuthnow's diagnosis that we are in dire straits.

Now it is Hauerwas's turn. He alternately cups his beard and his own shiny pate; then, speaking in a robust Texas accent that belies his philosophical and theological sophistication, declares that Wuthnow, Marty, and Lindbeck are all wrong. Wuthnow comes to the crucial question: Given all this division, what do we do to recover a *nation* that is strong and free? Hauerwas thinks that is the wrong question for Christians; for them the right question is how to recover a *church* that is strong and free. As far as Hauerwas is concerned, American Christianity set out to be a religion that would sustain a liberal democracy, and now we've got the mess we wanted.

Hauerwas goes on to complain that theology has been rendered harmless by desiring to become just another academic discipline. "The Southern Baptists have this to say for them: their theologians still think their work should influence the church, and the church still cares what its theologians say." Then he fires a broadside at Marty: "We don't need more nice Christians—we've already got too many nice Christians."

Marty and Hauerwas go to it. Marty, playing a different tune than he did the day before—or at least another verse—says there is much from which to build a vital center. The people of this country have common suffering, common stories, common propositions. He cites the national mourning, enabled by television, after the space shuttle *Challenger* blew up.

Hauerwas, a pacifist, replies that if anything drew the country together, it was World Wars I and II, "And for Christians, that's just not right."

Well, replies Marty in so many words, I agree with that, and Hauerwas shakes his head. "It's so hard to disagree with Marty. He just keeps . . ." Hauerwas searches for a word adequate to his frustration ". . . englobbing you."

This argument is solved like many in the academic setting: time runs out. Afterward the panelists shake hands and clap each other on the back. It is all quite civil but not, in my judgment, ultimately englobbing. I can't shake off the sense that the differences expressed are not any smaller for the politeness of their expression. These men are not just politely agreeing to disagree, but politely agreeing to play in different ballparks, with unsettled rosters and under different rules. No wonder it's hard to find an umpire.

Pluralism in the Elevators

The third day, Monday, will be my final day at the convention. I decide to go for maximum variety. I go to a liberation-theology session and hear, "Objectivity many times simply covers over the subjectivity of those who hold power." I listen to a stimulating talk on Jacques Ellul. For lunch I eat chicken with two or three hundred Baptist professors of religion, in a sprawling ballroom with low-slung chandeliers and false balconies. (Later I find out, from convention organizers, that during AAR/SBL there were about twenty-five luncheons like the one I attended; forty-five to fifty receptions, with *hors d'oeuvres* and drinks; twelve dinners; and thirty breakfasts. At least I could tell my cousin that theologians are useful for keeping cooks and waiters employed!)

After lunch I wend my way through the now-thinning masses, past the marble-veneered walls, the museum-sized paintings, to the elevators and up to the eighth floor. There awaits the epitome of diversity.

In one room, with participants crowded out the open door, evangelicals are discussing George Marsden's history of Fuller Theological Seminary. Directly adjacent, the feminists are meeting, and on the other side of that "The Gay Men's Issues in Religion Consultation." I check out the gay men's seminar first.

There are no chairs remaining, so I take a seat on the floor. The lecturer is saying that America is in decline, and that when proud nations lose their power internationally, they may seek new ways to exercise their power at home. Lesbians and gays have made gains in civil rights because of the nation's largess; if things take a turn for the worse, there may be more harassment and even persecution. Considering the enduring historical popularity of scapegoats, this sounds like an all-too-plausible argument.

I skip over to the women's group and stumble onto two provocative papers. One, called "Towards a Hermeneutic of Childbirth," challenges the predominant associations of pregnancy and childbirth with sickness, fatness, and so forth. Then the radical feminist Naomi Goldenberg is introduced, with an air of eager anticipation. She is a small, enthusiastic woman, with large, horn-rimmed glasses and closely cropped black hair, and I soon understand why everyone seemed ardent to hear her.

She starts with a witty apocalyptic commentary on the tale of Chicken Little, then proceeds, for the next half-hour, to strew gleaming insights indiscriminately, like a gardener sowing cheap seed. There is one on the mechanization of relationships, the television and computers that push us toward "private cocoons in front of flickering screens;" an aside on the "prison architecture" of most universities; a quick exegesis of the B-movie classic *The Blob;* and more. I am enjoying all this tremendously, so Goldenberg's conclusion is a real disappointment. She avers that we (women especially) must reject the distant, transcendent God of the biblical faiths just as Chicken Little should not have sought the advice of the king. (A move, you will remember, that resulted in the fox's having Chicken Little for lunch.) In other words: Grow up, ladies, forget about God, and trust yourselves.

By the time Goldenberg is finished and I make it down the hall, the evangelicals are already dispersing. I stand briefly in their empty room, looking at the unoccupied and jostled chairs, the upended drinking glasses. Conferees from the women's session and the gay session shuffle by behind me, and once more the jarring pluralism of the entire meeting hits home. While the homosexuals worried over potential persecution, people in the movement they probably consider their greatest threat were convening two rooms away. And as those would-be-persecutors calmly discussed how well or poorly a seminary has served God and the kingdom, a brilliant woman next door pointed a finger at God and that kingdom as the central source of the Western world's problems.

Down and around the hallway, evangelicals, gays, and feminists helped one another mount the elevators.

Who Would Miss Them?

There were gathered, in a single building, the best North American minds in religion. What if (for whatever reason) the earth opened up and swallowed the Hilton—the marble cracking, staircases corkscrewing, the walls heaving out and down like divers, room imploding on room imploding on room? Just like that, the brightest theologians on a continent, disappeared, gone. Would it make any difference? Would the church or the country suffer for it, after a few obligatory days of television-facilitated national mourning?

After all, as theologians will be the first to tell you, theology is in a predicament. On the one hand, it must convince the academy it is academically respectable—objective, disciplined, adding to that great store of knowledge that dyed-in-the-wool academics refer to with mystical awe. On the other hand, theology must convince the church it is faithful and serving the faith—committed, bold, vital to the discernment of the sovereign God's will.

Add to this the dizzying array of convictions theologians present and promote. What theologian do you trust? What *school* of theologians do you trust? As Marty and Wuthnow observed, it is no longer a matter of simply disagreeing among denominations (though even that gives hundreds of options). Now there is profound disagreement within denominations. Methodists, Southern Baptists, Anglicans, Presbyterians, Lutherans, even Roman Catholics—all have suffered from major intramural strains in recent decades, and all remain far from cozy unity.

The litmus tests for true Christianity proliferate. And in many cases, the litmus test adopted by some who call themselves Christian is diametrically opposed by the litmus test of others equally certain they represent the genuine faith. Thus radical feminists say the true Christian works to eliminate patriarchalism, while some evangelicals virtually make the traditional, patriarchal family the sign of true faith. Liberation theologians say you are not loyal to the Bible unless you promote proletarian revolutions; establishment theologians say real Christians respect the rule of government. Gay theologians say those against the ordination of practicing homosexuals fail the spirit of Jesus; many other thinkers say they could not continue to worship within a communion ordaining practicing homosexuals. The list goes on. Some Christians use biblical inerrancy as the litmus test, others use nuclear pacifism, yet others an unqualified anti-abortion stance, and still others faithful submission to the declarations of the pope. Things have come to a pretty impasse.

And you must add to the theologian's burden my farm cousin's complaint that theologians simply don't talk the language of people in the pew, that they are stuck in their ivory towers.

All told, theologians may be among Earth's most beleaguered creatures. They are members of the only endangered species that has one group (academics) trying to throw it out of its roost (in the ivory tower) while another group (laypersons) stands below and yells for it to jump.

Let's start from the bottom and take the complaint that theologians are too esoteric and prideful. Theologians can be arrogant. In a technologically advanced society, knowledge is power, and theologians ply a certain kind of knowledge. They sometimes do act as if ordinary churchgoers are hopelessly naïve and need nothing so much as to be disabused of their humble faith. But, on the other hand, there is no solvent as effective for cant and pomp as humor, and certainly there was an abundance of that at AAR/SBL. Theologians can mock themselves, and that alone bounds their pride. What is more, they are keenly sensitive to their cruel contemporary predicament. Many want desperately to be heard by the church, and yet at the same time they believe they can best serve the church by doing respectable work within the academy. Is the Christian faith true to life and the world or not? If Christians cannot make compelling arguments to that effect, then we are as much as admitting we cling to a delusion. Theology may no longer be at the heart of the academy, but all Christians have an interest in seeing that it is not dismissed as a mere vestigial organ.

What about technical language? Again, there are grounds for criticism, since theologians often use fancy words when plain ones would do. But that is not always the case. Technical terms focus inquiry, sharpen concepts that enable arguments. Without them each concept introduced into a discussion would have to be laboriously described, then described again each time it was reintroduced. We readily accept technical language from doctors, realizing no one needs a surgeon who would ask a nurse for that thingamajig so we can slice off this whatchamacallit. We also don't berate mechanics for referring to fuel-injection or gear differentials, and it is short-sighted not to accept a similar precision in theology.

Consider next the bewildering variety of theologians and theologies. This feature of the theologian's predicament may tempt us to gloat, to say it proves we do not need to listen to theologians since they are in such discord. But again there is no place for gloating: the theologian's predicament is every Christian's predicament. AAR/SBL, in its radical plurality, is only a microcosm of the world we all live in. At least in that respect theologians are very much engaged with the "real world," a world bereft of common metaphysical presuppositions, with passengers who have had to abandon the great ship of shared meaning to the separate lifeboats of contested meanings.

All pursuit of meaning in this modern world (now postmodern, by virtue of this predicament) is fragmented and arguable. As demonstrated by the potentially shattering arguments over, say, abortion, the church and the nation need urgently to build a new ship of common meaning, or at least learn how to row our lifeboats in formation. In a world that has forgotten most of what it knew about shipbuilding, that can barely remember how to use oars for paddles rather than weapons, it makes little sense to kill off sailors. If there is any way through our predicament, surely theologians and philosophers are essential to finding it.

Tacit Holiness

The Importance of Bodies & Habits in Doing Church

Holiness is not a popular subject in contemporary theology. Among the vital and much investigated theological themes of the last few decades, one might list such topics as political liberation, religious epistemology, gender and gender language, and of course an overall preoccupation with methodology. But academic or "professional" theologians have devoted little attention to holiness. The same is true at the less rarefied level of seminary education. As John Alexander writes, seminary education, like secular education, has become a matter of information transfer. "If you told seminary professors that they were indistinguishable from professors in secular graduate schools, most would be delighted. They suppose God is a topic to be studied much as you would study geological formations on the moon. And from about the same distance." In fact,

The holiness of professors . . . is of little concern. And it doesn't occur to any-one that the center of the curriculum should be teaching students to be holy. No, we settle for transferring information into their heads. And usually it isn't even information about holiness. Seminaries rarely offer courses with information on Mother Teresa, let alone courses on how to *become* Mother Teresa.[1]

Thus Stanley Hauerwas in his essay "The Sanctified Body" proves him-self distinctive.[2] Here is a serious theologian willing to take up the subject of holiness. Even more, he is willing to suggest not merely that holiness be a subject of dispassionate study, but in fact that Christians should worry about becoming holy. In his essay Hauerwas makes it clear that he wants holiness, but holiness of a particular sort—a holiness that does not lose the "catholic character of the church" (p. 20). He doesn't say exactly what he means by *catholic,* but it is clear from his subsequent exposition that at least part of what he means is *catholic* in the sense of the church universal and whole, and accordingly a Christianity with a deep appreciation for the intrinsically corporate—both bodily and socially—nature of its holiness.

Of course, holiness has not been neglected in recent theology for entirely specious reasons. In the North American evangelical churches holiness has been grossly trivialized by its exclusive obsession with "personal" absti-nence from habits and pastimes that not even many Christians would con-sider vices. Under this paradigm the avoidance of social dancing, movie-viewing, cardplaying, alcohol, and tobacco becomes the primary mark of holiness. Though I suspect Hauerwas might be more patient with such behavioral codes than those who have had to live under them, the holi-ness he is after is decidedly not this individualized and privatized piety. Instead, Hauerwas most admires the sort of holiness exemplified in peas-ant Roman Catholicism. He means nothing pejorative by the appellation *peasant,* but appreciates the peasant as someone who "works every day at those duties necessary for us to eat, to have shelter, to sustain the having of children, and to carry on the basic practices necessary to sustain com-munities" (p. 21). Given their formation and material situation, "peasants may not be 'intellectuals,' but they have knowledge habituated in their bodies that must be passed on from one generation to another" (p. 21).

Consequently, peasant Catholicism does not focus on being a Christian or becoming holy by mere mental assent to beliefs or doctrines. Beliefs and doctrines are important, but peasants, not being intellectuals, are often not skilled at articulating or defending them—that they leave to bishops and theologians. The primary knowledge of peasant Catholics, then, is not ana-lytical, detached, highly rational, and systematized. It is instead the knowl-edge of embodiment and habituation, a knowledge intended "to have one's body shaped, one's habits determined, in such a manner that the worship of God is unavoidable" (p. 22).

Tacit Holiness

It helps me, at least, to better understand what is meant by embodied and habituated knowledge by referring to Michael Polanyi's concept of "tacit knowledge." Polanyi observed that a great deal of knowledge (even that of intellectuals) is not consciously known and used. An able physicist might, for example, analyze successful bicycle riding and the concomitant physics of balance. The physicist might then arrive at the formula that a person wobbling on a moving bicycle should curve in the direction of the imbalance to a degree inversely proportional to the square of the speed at which the bicycle is going.[3] The formula is correct in its own way. Indeed, people who right the balance of their bicycles do curve to a degree inversely proportional to the square of their speed. But does knowing the formula or being capable of its calculation make one a better bicycle rider? Surely not, as any number of six-year-olds might ride circles around the eminent physicist who has never before set feet to pedals.

And in fact no six-year-old I know of was ever taught to ride by first studying the physics of bicycling balance. Instead, parents put their children on bicycles, walk beside them, push, catch, and exhort with simple advice such as "Don't turn too sharply," "Keep up some speed," and "Watch out for that tree!" Eventually, via coaching, intuition, and actual trial and error, children consistently learn to ride bikes. What they have achieved is embodied and habituated knowledge—knowledge they likely cannot articulate or reflect on in analytical fashion, but very real and effective knowledge nonetheless. They are not thinking about the pedals or handlebars as they ride, but are tacitly aware of them, just as the blind person is tacitly aware of his cane as he concentrates on what lies ahead or as the pianist is tacitly aware of the keyboard as she concentrates on sheet music.

And many types of knowledge that involve our bodies are likewise tacit knowledge. Swimmers typically do not know the pulmonary physiology that makes their bodies float. As Stanley Fish points out in a marvelous essay, baseball players can rarely as illuminatingly talk about playing baseball as can announcers: "playing baseball" and "explaining playing baseball" are distinct activities.[4] And a friend who was formerly a dancer tells me that her instructor frequently insisted, "The worst thing you can do while you're dancing is to think about it."

What Hauerwas wants to do, then, is to remind us that Christian knowledge—firsthand knowledge *of* holiness and not merely *about* holiness—

involves the body and habituation. Like Polanyi, he challenges the assumption that we do not need our bodies for all kinds of knowing. Hauerwas's (and Polanyi's) move is postmodern in the regard that it rejects the (modernist) Cartesian assumption that to know something we must achieve "an absolutely clear and indubitable conceptual grasp of an object of knowledge."[5] In fact, not even analytical and scientific knowledge is known all at once, and comprehensively, or achieved apart from bodily senses. As theologian Colin Gunton glosses Polanyi, "Although knowledge involves concepts, no knowledge can be of such a kind that it is completely explicit or exhaustive." Consequently, we need to trade an "excessive regard for explicit [rationalized, formalized, abstracted and articulated] knowledge" for the recognition that "always 'we know more than we can tell.'"[6]

As regards holiness and so much else, peasants always know more than they can tell. They know holiness "in their gut" or "in their bones," bodily and tacitly, through the tutelage of habit. Such tacit holiness is reflected in classical writers on Christian spirituality like Thomas à Kempis, who said, "What good do you get by disputing learnedly about the Trinity, if you are lacking in humility and are therefore displeasing to the Trinity?" and, "I would rather feel compunction than know how to define it."[7]

The Illusions of Individualism

Of course, Hauerwas recognizes that many (if not most) Christians in modern, highly Cartesian, "developed countries" are far from embracing this sort of bodily, social, tacit holiness. Instead, as he puts it, we "believe our lives are the outcome of choices we have made" (p. 22). We are believers in individual autonomy, in the self-made man or woman who abstracts from his or her particular bodily, social, and historical situation, and with careful reflection on any number of options, decides to be who he or she wants to be.

But it is important to recognize that this understanding of self as individuated, isolated, and in control of its own destiny is, ironically, a social and historical creation. In the span of recorded history it is in fact a highly unusual and even unique interpretation of the self. As rhetorician Wayne Booth notes, the self as "individual" (literally "undivided one") is barely more than two centuries old. The individual was invented by a succession of Enlightenment thinkers and was reflected, in its most extreme but perhaps also its most widespread interpretations, in a view of the self as "a single atomic isolate, bounded by the skin, its chief value residing precisely in some core of individuality, of difference."[8]

Thus it remains popular—almost second nature—to think we get at our "true self" by peeling away social ties like the skin of an onion. The "real me" is not my membership in the worldwide church, my shared kin with Clapps around the country, not my connection—with three million other people—to the geography and culture of Chicago. The "real me" is my unique, individual, core self. The individual self values itself most for what is supposedly utterly different and unconnected about it. But, objects Booth, such an understanding of self is incoherent. Can we really believe that we are not, to the core, who we are because of our kin, our occupations, our political and social situations, our faith or philosophical communities, our friendships? And if our "true self" is whatever stands apart from those around us and is altogether unique about us, most of us are in trouble. The bizarre modern notion of the self means even the greatest geniuses have only minimal worth. "Goethe," says Booth, "was fond of saying that only about 2 percent of his thought was original."[9] Truly, as Philip Slater remarks, "The notion that people begin as separate individuals, who then march out and connect themselves with others, is one of the most dazzling bits of self-mystification in the history of the species."[10]

In fact, Booth continues, "People in all previous cultures were not seen as essentially independent, isolated units with totally independent values; rather, they were mysteriously complex persons overlapping with other persons in ways that made it legitimate to enforce certain kinds of responsibility to the community." In these settings persons were not "'individuals' at all but overlapping members one of another. Anyone in those cultures thinking words like 'I' and 'mine' thought them as inescapably loaded with plurality: 'I' could not even think of 'my' self as separated from my multiple affiliations: my family, my tribe, my city-state, my feudal domain, my people."[11]

In light of Hauerwas's concern for a bodily and social holiness, as opposed to an individuated holiness, it is worth asking: Are the biblical cultures part of the "previous cultures" Booth here remarks on? Scholars have again and again noted the Hebrew conception of "corporate personality," the understanding that families, cities, tribes, and nations possess distinctive personalities and that individuals derive identity from and so might represent these social bodies.[12] We need no new frame when we extend this picture into the Greco-Roman world of New Testament times. Writing on the concept of personhood in the New Testament setting, Bruce J. Malina notes, "the first-century Mediterranean person did not share or comprehend our idea of an 'individual' at all." Rather, "our first-century person would perceive himself as a distinctive whole set in relation to other such wholes and set within a given social and natural background."[13]

Thus when Paul spoke of the church as a "body," he borrowed the metaphor from a fable widely used in several cultures of antiquity. Just as

"Israel" could serve as the name either of an individual (Jacob) or a community (the nation), so could Paul use "Christ" to refer to an individual (Jesus the Messiah) or a community (the church). In the words of New Testament scholar Charles Talbert, "'Members' . . . is Paul's term for the parts of the body through which the life of the body is expressed (see 1 Cor. 12:12, 14–26; Rom. 6:13). Paul is saying then that individual Christians in their corporeal existence are the various body parts of the corporate personality of Christ through which the life of Christ is expressed."[14]

All this confirms Hauerwas's adaptation of Dale Martin's work on *The Corinthian Body*. At the beginning of his book, Martin in fact sets his interpretation of the biblical self in direct opposition to the Cartesian, individuated self. Martin writes that Paul (and the ancient world in general) simply knew nothing of such dichotomies as matter versus nonmatter, corporeal versus psychological, spiritual versus physical, and so on. It was Descartes who practically "invented the category of 'nature' as a closed, self-contained system, over against which he could oppose mind, soul, the spiritual, the psychological, and the divine." Descartes removed to the nonphysical realm all those aspects of reality that exercise volition and true freedom—that is, God, and the soul or mind or "I" of the human self. He wrote that "that 'I,' that is to say, the mind by which I am what I am, is wholly distinct from the body" and thus categorized the human body with other nonvolitional entities, namely those comprising what he called nature. "It was this disenchanted, machine-like nature that could be legitimately examined and manipulated scientifically."[15]

Thus, taking into account Descartes and a long line of Enlightenment thinkers who followed him, it seems clear that modern individualism emphasizes the noncontingency and hence the self-determination of the nonphysical, essential self. The body, as well as all other things nonvolitional and merely physical, is nonessential and instrumental, to be directed and used by the deeper, real self. Control, then, is a much-prized modern value. Rationalism bolsters this sense of control by removing us from the limits and vulnerabilities of the body, something we clearly did not autonomously choose, and which possesses a nastily persistent vulnerability to sicknesses, injuries, and deaths we cannot predetermine.

It is exactly this sense of control and self-determination that Hauerwas fears sets Christians in "advanced" countries off from peasants. Contemporary professionals especially, heir to the "endemic individualism and rationalism of modernity" (p. 23), believe themselves to be their own masters. But this sense of control and self-determination is, as I have indicated, historically anomalous. Even nonpeasants, in all times prior to ours, did not imagine that they controlled their destiny. Professionals, and the modern middle class they so much comprise and influence, are enrapt by an illusion of individualistic self-determination that ironically makes them less free than peasants. As Hauerwas puts it, "Peasants know there are masters and accordingly develop modes of resistance. Professionals think they are masters, which of course makes them completely incapable of defending themselves" from the actual masters of their destiny (p. 22, n. 5). You cannot effectively resist masters you do not recognize as such, and we modern individualists are constantly taught and coached to buy into the illusion of self-determination, but not to notice that we are so taught and coached by a pervasive mass, technological, liberal, consumer capitalistic system.[16] Like Hauerwas, the Catholic writer Robert Inchausti worries about the modern, professionalized middle class whose very

> longing for a more profound existence makes them prey to salesmen and commercial visionaries who sell them dreams without inspiring them to the discipline necessary for authentic transcendence. They become consumers— systematically miseducated, underestimated, financially pampered, and morally exploited. They are nonpersons who are celebrated by the media as existentially free but whose history, ethnicity, personality, and moral seriousness have been marginalized, if not entirely debunked, by a world socioeconomic order that runs according to its own impersonal rules and agenda."[17]

In such a setting Hauerwas is right to think that the church faces a considerable challenge in becoming a "disciplined body of disciples" (p. 23). He is also correct to recognize the professionalized middle class as a special challenge to a disciplined church, since professionals and consumers "assume the church has no right to tell them what to believe or do. They assume what they know as a banker or lawyer or university professor gives them critical perspective on Christianity. Too often they get to make up the kind of Christianity they like" (p. 22, n. 5). How, then, to recover a disciplined, embodied, and habituated church in a setting so much more congenial to an individualized, rationalized, self-determining consumer "Christianity"?

Suffering and the Embodiment of Holiness

I have, of course, already begun to answer this question. To recognize that the isolated, self-creating self is a creation of modernity, and in fact historically anomalous, is to see that this rendering of self is at least open to challenge. That challenge can in turn lead to closer reflection on whether or not it is at all coherent to believe in—let alone try to be—a "self-creating self." Further, I have mentioned Hauerwas's appropriation of the work of Dale Martin, which suggests that biblical anthropology countenanced no such conception of the self. For Christians, this is a serious recognition indeed. What if Martin is right that for the apostle Paul "individual bodies have reality only insofar as they are identified with some greater cosmic reality," so that "Christian [physical] bodies have no integral individuality about them" but in truth have their "identity established by participation in a larger entity" that is the "body of Christ"?[18] Then Christians may have little investment in trying to construct for themselves modern, Cartesian selves. We may rather turn to the difficult hermeneutical and practical tasks of becoming Christian selves via our participation in the church as the disciplined, habituated, and habituating body of Christ.

For an example of this task, Hauerwas resorts to Arthur Frank's account of illness and suffering in *The Wounded Storyteller*. Following Frank, Hauerwas notes, "Sickness makes it impossible to avoid the reality of our bodies" (p. 29). However much we as good moderns might like, generally, to ignore our contingency and vulnerability by Cartesian abstraction, "When I am sick I am not a mind with a suffering body, but I am the suffering body. Illness may then be the only time that we have the opportunity to discover that we are part of a story that we did not make up" (p. 29).

Of course, this is the case only when we are seriously ill and cannot escape or eliminate our suffering by the ministrations of modern medicine. When my headache can be extinguished by a prescription or my jutting jaw resculpted by plastic surgery, I am only encouraged in the modern myth that Cartesian science can enable me to escape or eliminate affliction and remake my self at will. Accordingly, as medical ethicists have often observed, modern medicine has concentrated on curing patients to the serious neglect of caring for patients. This medicine, in Hauerwas's account, demands a body that "is characterized by self-control, through which it seeks predictability by employing therapeutic regimens. Such regimens organize the body in the hopes that contingency can be avoided or at least compensated" (pp. 30–31). Modern medicine thus helps us deny contingency by striving to eliminate its undeniable manifestation in acute suffering, that is, by offering cures (the more immediate the better), and by largely removing incurable suffering to (and hiding it in) institutional settings. Hence the likelihood that most of us will die in hospitals, not in our homes.

The state of such medicine is all too accurately satirized in Sidney Lumet's 1997 film *Critical Care*. Lumet depicts a young Dr. Ernst, just finishing his residency. Ernst longs to study under a senior doctor who uses computer monitoring and advanced technology to "treat" his patients from a centralized laboratory, dispatching nurses to administer drugs and other therapies, and dreaming of the day when he will never have to actually see or touch a patient's body again. As the story progresses it becomes increasingly clear to Dr. Ernst that he is caught up in a corrupt practice of medicine in which doctors, lawyers, and insurance companies vie to garner more money and prestige. All this is done at the expense of patients who are no longer identifiable persons but merely cited by their bed numbers—hospitals make money, after all, by filling their beds. Only when he is forced through circumstances does Dr. Ernst realize that he has stopped paying any mind to the patients, to the people who are suffering under and to some extent because of his care. At the film's end he is leaving the hospital when a rollerblading teenager crashes in front of him. As he rushes to the boy's aid, a mentor doctor shouts across the parking lot that he'd better be careful. He might get sued—and he doesn't even know if the boy has insurance. Ernst begins to tend to the boy anyway. When the boy asks, "Are you a doctor?" Ernst, with a pause, realizes that finally he can say with real truth, "Yes, I am a doctor."

What the film, coupled with Hauerwas's and Frank's reflection, suggests is that even the most idealistic, well-intentioned physician can be only as good as the practice in which he is bodily and socially embedded allows. If serious illness can still force us to admit our vulnerability and contingency, Christians should be among those who imagine that medicine can still be about caring and bearing suffering, and not merely, or even especially, about curing. As persons who believe they are creatures of the God of Israel, and not of their own creation, Christians need not pretend to control their own lives and deaths. As Hauerwas writes, "This requires that we understand that heroism is not to be identified with those who can 'do something,' but rather is to be found in those who persevere through suffering. What such a body offers is not victory, but testimony. Our healing is not the overcoming of our illnesses, but rather our ability to share our going on with one another through the community stories create" (p. 33).

Consequently the church should be concerned with a renarration and reembodiment of illness and the objectives of a genuinely Christian medicine. Pastors and Christian patients should not, for instance, regard bedside prayers as desperate pleas to be thrown up once doctors admit there is "nothing more to be done." Instead, such prayers are part of enabling the patient to own her illness and her fragile body, to have herself and her loved ones depend on the care of the church, and to witness to a hope that does not finally despair even in the face of death. Occasions of such suffering are also times of profound tacit knowledge, of knowing more than we can ever tell. Who, after all, standing at the bedside of a gravely ill person, has not been at a loss for any adequate words? Surely the sick body "eludes language" (p. 29). Yet at the same time bodily presence at the bedside—and the patient's allowance of it—communicates care and solidarity. Very often our deepest and best communication is the holding of a hand or the rubbing of a shoulder or the drying of a tear. In such acts we embody the way and the spirit of holiness.

The (Double) Body at Worship

Illness shatters the illusions of independence and noncontingency constantly promoted by mass, technological, liberal, and consumer capitalist society. Yet in looking to serious illness, Hauerwas is concerned to recover truths about our whole lives, not merely about who or what we are when we are sick. Hauerwas wants Christians to notice this, intellectually and in such practices as health care, and to carry these lessons into other realms of our existence. Hard as it definitely is to bear suffering or to stand by the suffering of others, it may be even more of a challenge to take an awakened awareness of creaturely contingency out of the hospital and back into the rest of our lives. The truth, in the Christian confession, is that we are always contingent and dependent, whether in sickness or in health, in poverty or in wealth, in death or in life.

I agree with Hauerwas and now want to emphasize a reality that is more regular and formative of Christian character. Even when Christians are not sick, we are routinely called to worship. Nowhere, I think, should we be so profoundly habituated in our creaturely dependence on God and God's grace as we are at worship.

Worship, most fundamentally, is not something we initiate or create. We are gathered to common worship at the initiative of the Father, through the saving deeds of the Son, in the power of the Holy Spirit. In common or corporate worship we celebrate and rehearse, at least weekly, the work of Yahweh in the story of Israel and Jesus Christ. Had not God first acted in Israel and Jesus, we would have no creation and redemption to celebrate, no Christian story to rehearse. And if God the Spirit did not call Christians to gather, we would not leave our beds each Sunday morning—each "little Easter"—to be and to act as members of Christ's body and of one another.

In worship, then, we act out of contingency. We recall that our very being is contingent; this is exactly what it means to be "creatures" as opposed to self-made men and women. We bless God for our creation, our redemption, and our sustenance in the faith. And our whole selves—body, mind, and soul—are required for genuine worship. We gather bodily to pray, to sing praises, to lay hands on the sick, to baptize, and to celebrate the Eucharist. And all of this is initiated and enabled by God. So we profess our contingency in word and also in our very physical presence, one to another, at worship. No single one of us, no "individual," constitutes Christ's body. We do so only by gathering and sharing and depending on the gifts God has given the community called church. Not all are teachers, not all counselors, not all prophets or priests. We need one another to be what we are, the body of Christ. God's Spirit gifts each of us not for any individual's sake, but "for the common good" of that body (1 Cor. 12:7).

So Christian worship is the preeminent practice of the kind of holiness Hauerwas seeks—a doubly embodied holiness, corporate both physically and socially. Consider the sacrament of baptism. Baptism immerses our physical bodies in the body of Christ. In so doing, it initiates us into a social body in which "there is no longer Jew or Greek, there is no longer slave or free, there is no longer male and female; for all of you are one in Christ Jesus" (Gal. 3:28) and it grants us Gentiles a new citizenship in the commonwealth of Israel (Eph. 2).

In baptism, as in other sacraments, physical and social bodily involvement is crucial. The baptizand's physical body, not just his or her mind or soul (whatever that might be), must be touched and wetted. And the baptizand must be surrounded and joined by the social body of the church—private baptisms are an oxymoron imaginable only in the distorting wake of modern individualism. The social body vows (as in my own Episcopal tradition) to "do all in your power to support this person in his or her life in Christ." In these and other ways it necessarily participates in the individual's baptism. Certainly baptism involves words and rational assent. But the words of the baptismal formula and our rational assent are never separated from bodily and tacit knowledge. In fact, the tacit knowledge of baptism both enriches and in some ways goes beyond intellectual knowledge. Baptismal water, for instance, teems with tacit significance. It palpably hints at creation (water is life-giving), creaturely mortality (water drowns and disintegrates), cleansings, new life, and much else. So, as Polanyi would have it, the one who has been baptized can never tell all he or she knows through baptism, through the actual participation of the physical and social body in this rite. Accordingly, one can no more truly "know" baptism without bodily participating in a baptism than one can really know the ecstasies of sex by simply reading a therapist's manual. It is never simply or even primarily a matter of intellectual or soulful consent. As the church father Tertullian remarked,

> [In baptism] the flesh is washed in order that the soul may be cleansed; the flesh is anointed in order that the soul may be consecrated; the flesh is signed in order that the soul may be fortified; the flesh is overshadowed by the imposition of the hand in order that the soul may be illumined by the Spirit. . . . Therefore, those things which work together are not able to be separated in reward.[19]

Similarly, the Eucharist for its enactment requires double embodiment, both physical and social corporateness. For it, too, the body of Christ must gather and the physical bodies of the members of Christ must go through certain motions and assume particular positions. Kneeling and standing at the appropriate junctions, cupping one's hands to receive the bread, crossing one's self—all of these are bodily gestures communicating and reinforcing a wealth of tacit knowledge. To kneel, for example, is to admit our submission more powerfully and completely than any words alone might; to stretch out empty and receptive hands for the bread of life is to practice our contingency fully and dramatically. So the Eucharist leads us to say that corporality is the very mediation where faith takes on flesh and makes real the truth that inhabits it. "It says this to us with all the pragmatic force of a ritual expression that speaks by its actions and works through the word, the word-as-body. It tells us that the body, which is the whole word of humankind, is the unavoidable mediation where the Word of a God involved in the most human dimension of our humanity demands to be inscribed in order to make itself understood. Thus, it tells us that faith requires a *consent to the body*."[20]

With the faithful consent to the body that is worship, we can begin to have healed the Cartesian separation of matter and nonmatter, of the corporeal and the psychological, the physical and the spiritual.

Unfortunately, much Protestant worship only serves to reinforce such Cartesian dichotomies. If the Eucharist, for instance, is mainly a Zwinglian matter of the individual's remembering and thinking about Christ's sacrifice, then the gathering with other Christians is secondary, dependence on God's initiatory grace is downplayed, and a rationalistic, nonbodily human action is made central. A merely memorialist Eucharist is double disembodiment, separating the worshiper both from the social body of the gathered church and from his or her own physical body. Such worship may, in fact, be more a Cartesian sort of disembodied *observation* than it is actual *participation* in the body of Christ. This is yet another cause to join Hauerwas in his concern for a genuinely catholic Christianity. A full and real holiness is tacit holiness, necessarily habituated and (doubly) embodied. If some forms of Protestant worship fail to be less than catholic in this regard, then they are actually misshaping the Christian formation of their practitioners. And that is a serious matter indeed.

seven

The Grammar of Thanksgiving

Grammar is about how things work—how we put words and phrases together properly, in due order and correct relation to one another, so that they make sense. Traumatic memories of nitpicky and anal retentive third-grade teachers aside, grammar matters. Without some modicum of grammar, you couldn't at all say what you mean or get what you want—even when you wanted something so simple as a bag of groceries. And in a sense, "grammar" applies beyond words and punctuation. It's fair to say, for instance, that car mechanics must know the grammar of engines—that carburetor heads shouldn't be fitted on top of radiators, or axles connected to rear view mirrors. In recent years, theologians have profitably explored the grammar of Christian doctrine and ethics. How, for example, is the Son related to the Father and to the Spirit, in a careful grammar of the Trinity, and how does that make a difference in worshipful lives?

It is in this spirit that I want to reflect on the grammar of Thanksgiving. Since the Civil War, Americans have celebrated the fourth Thursday of every November as their primary national feast day. I am an American citizen. But, by baptism and in the maintenance of grace, I am first of all a Christian and an adopted citizen of "the commonwealth of Israel" (Eph. 2). So I am possessed by a first language and grammar—that of the Christian faith—that trumps my American citizenship. How might a Christian, exactly as a Christian, best read and apply the grammar of Thanksgiving?

Perhaps it is appropriate to note, first of all, that the Thanksgiving holiday is grounded on a story of origins. Stories of origins are extremely significant, because they tell a people who they first were, and accordingly what they should continually strive to be. The American Thanksgiving story has it that a hardy band of Pilgrims landed at Plymouth Rock, faced an empty wilderness, tamed it with their bravery and agricultural prowess, then settled into a feast of Thanksgiving. To this primordial feast they invited some of the friendly nearby Indians, sharing generously from their bountiful stores of food. As one holiday greeting card puts it, "*I* is for the Indians we invited to share our food." Or, in more detailed terms, a school handout notes, the Pilgrims "served pumpkins and turkeys and corn and squash. The Indians had never seen such a feast!"

Among other things, this story underwrites the myth of America's extraordinary generosity. As Pilgrim Fathers shared and cared for the needy in their midst, so America now offers lavish sums of foreign aid to the needy, less "developed" nations of the earth.

Right here I am afraid Christian grammar challenges the typical American Thanksgiving grammar and demands, for a proper Christian reading and practice of Thanksgiving, important grammatical reorientation and correction. That is the case because the Pilgrims and pumpkins story is not truthful, and in fact underwrites an ongoing lack of truthfulness about American generosity. In terms of foreign aid, the United States is not one of the most generous nations in the world, and on a per capita basis provides less foreign aid than most any other "developed" country. The erroneous belief that Americans are the world's greatest benefactors is reinforced by a distorted founding story.

The fact, attested to by the colonists' own journals, is that Plymouth Bay was not a barren and unsettled wilderness. Native Americans had for generations lived there, burned away underbrush, cleared fields, and carefully cultivated crops such as corn. It was not the Indians who had never seen a feast of corn, pumpkins, squash, and turkeys, but the Pilgrims, since all these foods were indigenous to the Americas. The Pilgrims founded New Plymouth in and on the Native American village of Patuxet, recently decimated by plagues borne to the new land by Europeans. "In this bay wherein we live," journaled one colonist among the original 102, "in former time hath lived about two thousand Indians." Even less appealingly, and again as attested by their own records, the Pilgrims were grave robbers. They desecrated Indian burial sites to retrieve foodstuffs left with the dead.

The Pilgrims of course did not cause the plague (though they unfortunately praised God for its decimation of the "savage" population). Nor were they, in comparison to other colonists of their day, especially harsh and immoral. Plymouth, unlike most colonies, actually paid the original inhabitants for most of the land it took. But it was fundamentally the Indians who shared with the Pilgrims, from fields already planted, from stores of corn and beans already stocked, and from agricultural technology hospitable to the new world. Thus the typical Thanksgiving story of origins turns the truth on its head, and does not help current-day Americans to be honest with themselves about their own level of national generosity.

Compare this grammar of sentimentalized falsification with the Christian story of origins. The early chapters of Genesis do not imagine the inhabitation of the Garden of Eden as a purely praiseworthy event. There is much beauty, and Adam and Eve are declared good, but the account of their rebellion, and the subsequent murder of one brother by another, is also included. The rest of the Old Testament, though it can occasionally idealize its heroes, frequently shows our fathers and mothers in the faith—from Abraham to Jacob to Rahab to King David and beyond—in their worst as well as their best light.

In the shorthand terms of the Christian grammar, human beings are the good creatures of a loving God, but have subsequently fallen into sin. If that is the truth about human existence, Christians need not oversentimentalize and falsify any national story of origins. In fact, we will be profoundly suspicious of any story of origins that presents utterly pure and blameless founders, or severs the act of thanksgiving from the act of repentance.

Traditional Christian worship, true to such grammar, has always closely related thanksgiving and repentance. So the *Book of Common Prayer*, for instance, immediately precedes Holy Communion with confession and forgiveness of sin. Reconciled to God and one another, the Body of Christ can in full joy and earnest celebrate the Eucharist (literally, the Great Thanksgiving): "It is right, and a good and joyful thing, always and everywhere to give thanks to you, Father Almighty, Creator of heaven and earth."

Intriguingly, a case might be made that earlier celebrators of the American Thanksgiving were enough shaped by Christian thanksgiving that they avoided the grammatical error of separating thanksgiving from repentance. So when George Washington declared November 26, 1789, a national day of thanksgiving, he urged all Americans to "unite in most humbly offering our prayers and supplications to the great Lord and Ruler of Nations, and beseech him to pardon our national and other transgressions." And Abraham Lincoln regularized the fourth Thursday of every November as Thanksgiving Day in 1863, smack in the middle of the Civil War, expecting thanksgiving to include petitions for national reconciliation. This was after all the same Lincoln who saw the war as a terrible judgment on both the south *and* the north.

I mention Washington and Lincoln to indicate that something crucial, from deep Christian grammar, carried over into their thanksgiving, but certainly not to endorse their civil religion and promote worship of its vague deistic god. Contrary to such civil religion, Christian celebrators of the American Thanksgiving again do well to remember the Pilgrims truthfully and accurately—and this time more to the Pilgrims' credit. Because, however imperfectly they carried it out, the Pilgrims worshiped the triune God of Israel and the church. At real cost and peril, they fled first England and then Holland—finally the "civilized" world as they knew it altogether—in search of a place where they could most fully and unstintingly live true to their faith. Nor was that faith, like that of today's American church, compartmentalized and privatized: the Mayflower Compact opens by declaring that the Pilgrims "Covenant and Combine ourselves into a Civil Body Politic."

Thus a celebration of Thanksgiving guided by Christian grammar can be enthusiastically grateful for much: for our creation and redemption by a loving God, for the abundant comfort and food so many of us as Americans enjoy, and for the deep faith of our Christian forebears, the Pilgrims. Indeed, Christian grammar will enhance and embolden our thanksgiving, because we will not have to lie to ourselves about our brokenness and sinfulness, and disguise the American story of origins with incredible innocence. And it will strengthen our faith because it will push us to think of the Pilgrims as they thought of themselves: as Christians, first and foremost.

Those early American Puritans are now dead, but still alive in the communion of the saints, and in that communion they may well hope for considerable adjustment in our appropriation of their memory. As theologian Darrell Jodock writes, "The Puritans were powerless; the contemporary United States possesses enormous power and influence. The Puritans saw themselves beginning anew; a two-hundred-year-old nation is hardly beginning anew. The Puritans shared a single religious outlook; contemporary citizens do not. Though not exactly equal, the Puritans were all of poor to middling means; enormous inequities now characterize our society. If the Puritans were to describe the contemporary United States, might they not find it more like the Egypt of the Pharaohs than the Israel of the exodus?"

eight

Let the Pagans Have the Holiday

It is time to recognize that a new tradition has been added to Christmas. As surely as trees and lights and reindeer, December now brings Christian complaints about the secularization of the holiday. T-shirts and posters and preachers declare, "Jesus Is the Reason for the Season," but their protests are drowned in the commercial deluge.

Christmas is ruled not from Jerusalem or Rome or Wheaton or any other religious center, but from Madison Avenue and Wall Street. In a revealing symbolic act, President George Bush some years ago inaugurated the season not, mind you, in a church, but in a shopping mall. There he bought some socks and reminded Americans their true Christmas responsibility is not veneration but consumption.

To some, Christmas also seems less Christian because many of the nation's institutions are less and less willing to prop up the church. So some disgruntled believers—misguidedly, by my estimate—do battle with various courthouses that no longer allow crèches on their lawns.

Sometimes outsiders glimpse our own dilemma more acutely than we can. In 1992 Rabbi Lawrence Hoffman wrote an article in *Cross Currents* entitled, "Being a Jew at Christmas Time." In it he observed, "There is nothing wrong with sleigh bells, Bing Crosby, and Christmas pudding, but I should hope Christians would want more than just that, and as Christmas becomes more and more secularized, I am not sure they get it." He went on: "In the end, the problem of Christmas is not mine any more than Christmas itself is. The real Christmas challenge belongs to Christians: how to take Christmas out of the secularized public domain and move it back into the religious sphere once again."

The rabbi is right on both counts. For Christians, Christmas definitely loses something—in fact, loses its core—as it gets more and more secular. But the solution is not to worry over courthouse crèches: The real Christmas challenge belongs to Christians. The church and not city hall is charged with witnessing to the gospel and remembering to the world the birth of Jesus Christ.

Seasonal Humbug

Here I want to suggest that Christians may best reclaim Christmas, indirectly, by first reclaiming Easter. Ours is an ironic faith, one that trains its adherents to see strength in weakness. The irony at hand could be that a secularizing culture has shown us something important by devaluing Christmas. In a way, Christians have valued Christmas too much and in the wrong way. I defer again to Hoffman, who writes,

> Historians tell us that Christmas was not always the cultural fulcrum that balances Christian life. There was a time when Christians knew that the paschal mystery of death and resurrection was the center of Christian faith. It was Easter that really mattered, not Christmas. Only in the consumer-conscious nineteenth century did Christmas overtake Easter, becoming the centerpiece of popular piety. Madison Avenue marketed the change, and then colluded with the entertainment industry to boost Christmas to its current calendrical prominence.

The Bible, of course, knows nothing of the designated holidays we call Easter or Christmas. But each holiday celebrates particular events, and there can be no doubt which set of events receives the most scriptural emphasis.

It is well known that all four Gospels build toward and focus on the events leading up to and including what we commemorate at Easter. One-quarter to one-half the chapters in each of the four Gospels deal with Easter events. Clearly, the gospel traditions see these as the crucial episodes, the events that identify and ratify Jesus as God's Messiah. In fact, two of the four Gospels (Mark and John) have no birth, or Christmas, narratives. This means certain of the earliest Christian communities knew no Christmas (at least, not from their basic texts). To put it another way, we could be Christians without the stories of Christmas, but not without the stories of Easter.

The rest of the New Testament does not deviate from this pattern. The earliest recorded Christian sermon (in Acts 2) proclaims the Easter message of the world's Savior crucified and then raised by Israel's God. And what can we say of Paul, who nowhere speaks of Jesus' birth, but everywhere heralds "Jesus Christ, and him crucified" (1 Cor. 2:2) and warns that "if Christ has not been raised, then our proclamation has been in vain and your faith has been in vain" (15:14)?

To this day, Christian worship is marked by Easter more than by Christmas. Consider the sacraments. Baptism is baptism into Christ's crucifixion and resurrection. As Paul writes, "We have been buried with him by baptism into death, so that, just as Christ was raised from the dead by the glory of the Father, so we too might walk in newness of life" (Rom. 6:4). Celebrating the Eucharist, or Communion, includes rich themes drawing both from Christ's passion and his resurrection. And of course, we gather to worship on the day of the Lord's rising, so that Christians for centuries have thought of each Sunday as a "little Easter."

The recovery of Easter as our pivotal holy day may best be served by a recovery of the Christian calendar, complete with the cycle of seasons that recall the gospel from Advent to Christmas to Epiphany to Lent to Easter and Pentecost. The calendar, like the gospel narrative, builds toward and pivots around the focal events of Christ's passion and Easter. Recognizing the liturgical year is a large step toward seeing Easter as the main Christian holiday.

Christmas Reenvisioned

In calling Christians to return to the Christian calendar and return Easter to its rightful prominence, I am not implying that the events of Christmas are trivial or untrue. The nativity stories help us to remember key and glorious truths, such as the Incarnation. But surely Easter, and not the Christmas on which we modern Western Christians focus most of our attention, is the "fulcrum that balances Christian life."

Christmas celebrated without the events of Easter overshadowing is too easily sentimentalized and secularized. A baby in a manger, angels hovering overhead, cattle lowing nearby—surely this idyllic world needs no redemption. A dechristianized Christmas is the ultimate Pelagian holiday; for at what other time of the year can we seem so certain that, merely with good feelings and good will, humanity can save itself? Annually, in fact, newspaper editorials and television commentators say exactly that, pleading that all the world needs is to spread Christmas cheer through the year.

But Easter—Easter is on the other side of a cross with nails, of confrontation and beatings and death, and then, only then, resurrection and new life. Christmas we can too easily teach to our kids (and ourselves) without blinking, free of strain or discomfort (provided we gloss, as we usually do, such details as Herod's slaughter of the innocents). Easter is harder, for it requires facing death, the shortcomings of the disciples, the bloody lengths God must go to in order to rescue a confused, hateful world from itself.

All of this is to say we have worried about Christmas too much. Christians in an indifferent and even hostile society need to learn cultural *jujitsu*— to sometimes let the culture push at points where it wants to, and there collapse of its own momentum. This is especially important in our cultural situation, where resistance is so easily itself turned into a marketable commodity. T-shirts and bumper stickers proclaiming "Jesus Is the Reason for the Season" make the message itself into a consumer item.

So let the pagans have Christmas as their most significant holiday. Easter is the central *Christian* holiday. And when we are known for our Easter, then we will have our Christmas back.

nine

Shame Crucified

The week before my wife and I closed on our first home, the most powerful emotion I felt was shame. Not anticipation or euphoria or pride, but
shame.

It went like this: We had read books on home buying. We had schooled
one another in ARMS, FRMS, points, and title insurance. We had debated the
pros and cons of living in one community over another. We had found a
real estate agent, diligently looked at properties, discovered a house, placed
a bid, and applied for a loan.

Then the loan officer called and said she did not know if our finances
were adequate for the modest home we wanted.

For a few days we lived in suspense—and I, in shame. Voices from deep
inside asked and accused:

"What kind of man can't provide for his family?"

"What have I done with my life?"

"Am I incompetent and irresponsible, a failure and a fool?"

The voices were not muted until the loan was approved.

Psychologists say shame is the sense that we have radically disappointed others, failed to live up to standards of acceptability. We stand exposed, bound, and immobilized.

Shame reduces us to muteness, alienates us from those at hand, makes us acutely aware of ourselves as deficiency incarnate. When we are ashamed, we bow our heads—not to pray but to hide. Letting someone look us in the eye is especially painful because their gaze seems to pierce to the soul—the deepest and real self now feared to be rotten and worthless.

I am afraid such experiences of shame are not unusual for me. Or, apparently, for other people. Pop psychologist John Bradshaw, whose books sell into the hundreds of thousands, takes shame as a prominent theme. He and other gurus in the still powerful codependency movement see unhealthy dependence on others rooted in identities based on shame.

In an officially independent and individualistic society like America, why are so many people ashamed?

Based on the work of social critics such as Christopher Lasch and psychologists such as Gershen Kaufman, here's my guess: Ours is a shame-based culture ashamed of shame. Success, particularly the tangible success exemplified by health and wealth, is the measure of our worth. Despite our professed independence, we do care what others think of us. We want to appear worthy, to possess and brandish the trappings of success.

But since we imagine ourselves independent and self-sufficient, we won't acknowledge our desperate desire to be seen as worthy. Nor do we want any reminders that worthiness measured by tangible success is a precarious worth, based on such vagaries as the stock market, a body free of cancer cells, the weather, or Saddam Hussein's ego. Thus we have little place for failure or the admission of vulnerability and need of others. We are, in fact, extremely liable to shame and even more ashamed to admit it.

After all, our most cherished myths herald the "self-made" man or woman. And with Vince Lombardi we profess, "Winning isn't everything—it's the only thing." We elect presidents who play on the potent cowboy images of the loner who rides into town to clean it up single-handedly. Pat Schroeder of Colorado sees her presidential campaign crumble after she weeps publicly. And the best-selling books of rosy futurist John Naisbitt refuse, on principle, to consider inadequacies or injustices in the world.

Shame thrives under the conditions our culture inspires. Shadows, illusive appearances, an atmosphere of deception, denial, and mistrust—they all make a murky swampland ideal for shame's growth. At least the Bible sees it that way, and perhaps it can illuminate a path out of the swamp.

Naked and Exposed

Eve and Adam lived in harmony with one another and God. In an atmosphere of trust and truth, they "were both naked, and were not ashamed" (Gen. 2:25). Here nakedness, or exposure and vulnerability, was no threat.

Vulnerability presents a problem only when we cannot trust others. Then we fear they might take our vulnerability, our admission that we need others and depend on something outside ourselves, and use it against us. Exactly that fear shattered the peace of Eden. Once God was betrayed and trust was broken, Adam and Eve were at odds with God and one another.

Then "they knew they were naked; and they sewed fig leaves together and made loincloths for themselves" (Gen. 3:7). It seemed necessary to cover and protect the self, even (or especially) from God. In Adam's words, "I was afraid, because I was naked; and I hid myself" (Gen. 3:10).

In shame's train comes a preoccupation with appearance. Adam and Eve must now calculate and control how they present themselves. Life will now be filled with stratagems and second-guessing. Things cannot be as they seem: "What did he really mean by that gesture?" "What's in this bargain for her?"

Shame also brings terrifying self-doubt. Eve and Adam are no longer sure they are worthy as they are, unadorned and naked. Hiding from each other and from God is a way of hiding from themselves, guarding their nakedness from another who might speak honestly about what he or she sees. And notice how quickly man and woman, now doubting their own worth, try to direct attention away from themselves by pointing the finger at someone else (Adam at Eve, Eve at the serpent).

The irony of shame is that hiding and covering our vulnerability only increases it. The higher our lies are stacked, the more likely they are to topple. The games we play grow so complex that we are bound to slip up. Life for ashamed people who cannot admit shame is a complicated and tense affair. Yet, unable to admit and deal with their shame, such people can only use shame to try to stay one step ahead. Shame fuels pecking orders and status symbols.

Once again the Bible throws light on the darkness of our condition. Consider the story of the adulteress dragged before Jesus as recorded in John 8:2–11. Here the lawyers and Pharisees use shame as a weapon. They hope to trick Jesus into saying or doing something that will shame him. Their ploy depends, for its effectiveness, on the elevation of the lawyers and Pharisees at the expense of Jesus—and the woman. She is doubly degraded. Not only is she a publicly exposed adulteress, but she is only being used to get at Jesus.

Having used their power to insulate themselves from shame and focus it on the woman, the Pharisees and lawyers barge into Jesus' presence with all the misplaced confidence of self-righteousness. Significantly, they come as a group, representing the prestigious law and temple. But Jesus shatters the solidarity of the shamers: "Let anyone among you who is without sin be the first to throw a stone at her" (v. 7).

Poet Sharon Olds images shame as a circle, spotlighting and isolating a vulnerable self. Here the Pharisees and lawyers suffer what Olds calls "the horror of circles." To follow up on Jesus' challenge means singling yourself out as "the first" and so being exposed. To step forward into the middle of the stoning circle makes you liable to shame, since no one can honorably claim to be free of sin.

Its solidarity broken, the crowd filters away from the circle "one by one" (v. 9). The Pharisees use shame to hurt and destroy. Jesus uses shame to affirm and rescue a degraded woman. He does not deny the shame of her sin, but he refuses to let shame have the last word or define her: "Neither do I condemn you. Go your way, and from now on do not sin again" (v. 11).

So Jesus points a way out of the vicious, horrible circle of shame. Following that way means refusing to hurt others with their shame. And, more dauntingly, it means admitting our own shame. But how can we afford that? We really are afraid we are worthless, that others would abandon us if they knew us as we are. So how can we admit shame without destroying ourselves?

Deep Reassurance

The beginning of an answer lies further along the way of Jesus, in the cross. Individualists that we are, we see crucifixion as a dreadful death mainly because of its terrible physical pain. Occasionally revivalists still describe the whip and nails and slow suffocation in excruciating detail. But what the early Christians most dreaded about the cross was its shame.

This form of execution was reserved for those least worthy of respect: slaves, hardened criminals, and rebels against the state. It was deliberately public, heightening its disgrace. *Cross* was a vulgar word in ancient Rome, not used in polite company. The formula for sentencing to crucifixion read: "Executioner, bind his hands, veil his head, and hang him on the tree of shame."

Even more dramatically, consider that the condemned were often killed before they were crucified. No longer able to suffer physical pain, but still liable to the shaming of their name and reputation, they were only then humiliated on a cross.

So the writer of the Letter to the Hebrews gets to the point by stating that Jesus endured the cross by "disregarding its shame" (12:2). Shame is also clearly a central concern of the gospel writers, perhaps most apparent in Mark's compact account of the Passion:

Shame binds: Jesus is literally bound (15:1). Shame silences: Jesus has little to say to Pilate and finally falls mute (15:5). Shame renders us acutely self-conscious and afraid others will reject us: Jesus is rejected by the crowd (15:13–14), mocked by soldiers and even those executed with him (15:16–32). Shame exposes: Jesus dies naked. Shame makes us powerless: Jesus "saved others" but "cannot save himself" (15:31). Shame is abandonment or fear of abandonment at its most intense: Jesus cries, "My God, my God, why have you forsaken me?" (15:34).

Once again, Jesus' enemies use shame in an attempt to destroy him. And this time they succeed. Jesus has been profoundly discredited, his mission shown for a sham, his followers scattered. For him, unlike the adulteress, shame apparently has the last word and finally defines him. He and his dreams are scorned and cursed.

Of course, that is not the end of the story. God's resurrection of Jesus vindicates him and his mission and restores his followers. The resurrection is deep reassurance—exactly the reassurance we need—that shame does not destroy. We have no hope in the face of shame without the resurrection.

But we also have no hope in the face of shame if we rush from the cross to the resurrection. Ours is a shame-based culture ashamed of shame. We *want*, to our detriment, to hear that the Resurrection obliterates the shame of the crucifixion. Our central self-deception is that successful individuals are autonomous and don't need others. So shame must be denied, for in denying it we are protected from trust in and vulnerability to others. Only the shameless man or woman needs no one.

Our hope is not that resurrection obliterates the shame of crucifixion. Our hope is that resurrection transforms and paradoxically elevates the shame of crucifixion.

The Gospels see Jesus' shame and weakness as his preeminent revelation of God's power—John considers it nothing less than his glory and "lifting up" (John 12:30–33). Paul insists that Jesus became a shameful curse for our sakes (Gal. 3:13–14). And Christ's followers await their own resurrection; in this time between the times we must bear the cross and its shame. If we are not ashamed of Jesus before humanity, he will not be ashamed of us before the Father (Mark 8:38).

So our hope is not that shame has ended. Our hope is that Jesus bore shame to the cross and shamed it. Shame was crucified, itself disarmed and publicly stripped of its ultimate malignancy (Col. 2:15). By enduring the cross, Jesus suffered shame's worst and yet was vindicated by God. The central, pivotal reality of all existence is now that our worth was secured on the cross. No shame, however just or unjust, however petty or spectacular, can "separate us from the love of God in Christ Jesus our Lord" (Rom. 8:39).

The cross creates a community of people who, no longer afraid of being defined and destroyed by shame, can admit their failures and allow their neediness. Forgiveness means being able to say you're sorry. Since we now know shame cannot destroy us, we need no longer deny it and foist it off on others.

In the church, I have begun to know the healing of my shame. I have not found anything flashy or spectacular about it—at least most of the time. Heroes don't go to church. In church we are given a courage rarely lionized—the courage to stand up and say, like the emboldened members of Alcoholics Anonymous, "My name is Rodney, and I'm a sinner. . . ."

Because only self-acknowledged sinners can admit and confront their shame, we can say, in a sense, that we go to church for training in being sinners. Such is the way through and beyond humiliation.

At the Intersection
of Eucharist and Capital

On the Future of Liturgical Worship

Some years ago, I was driving to work one morning. I stopped at an intersection across from the neighborhood Roman Catholic church. It was a nippy fall morning, and an elderly gentleman in a windbreaker and a beret stepped into the crosswalk in front of me. He was not moving fast, and I was a bit late, but was careful. My thoughts hurried ahead into the day but my car did not. It was totally stationary, not inching impatiently forward into the crosswalk. But, inexplicably, when the old fellow was smack-middle in front of my bumper, lined up by the hood ornament as if it were a rifle sight, he made the sign of the cross on himself.

You must understand that at this time I was at the end of a distressing rash of automobile accidents. None were more serious than fender-benders, but I seemed for awhile uncannily prone to missed stop signs or obstructed views at busy intersections. The police had noticed, and accordingly issued a sheaf of tickets. And in its turn the insurance company had taken note, and adjusted my insurance rates upward. Steeply. Now here was a stranger crossing himself, apparently praying for survival and even trying to hustle, as he labored in front of my car. My paranoia was based in reality. How did he know about my highly decorated driving record? Were there pictures of my rust-colored 1981 Toyota Tercel hanging in the post office, right alongside the mug shots of bank robbers, rapists, and other felons?

These were my first, disconcerted thoughts. But then the elderly gentleman glanced across the street at the Catholic church and I regained composure. His crossing himself had nothing to do with me, but everything to do with the shrine to Mary and the Christ Child in front of that building. His prayer was not a prayer of urgent petition, but of humble adoration.

Now the circumstances of this incident were highly particular and idiosyncratic. But with a little imagination it may say something of more general significance. An old man on foot, endeavoring the most venerable form of human transportation, remembers the enacted adoration of a two thousand-year-old religion. He confronts a young man in a car powered by an internal combustion engine, a mode of transportation hardly one hundred years old, not remembering but thinking ahead to the news stories of the moment, and a journalistic office filled with personal computers, fax machines, and other machinery at that date not even a decade beyond their invention. The old meets the new, the past meets the future, and there is plenty of room for misunderstanding. What is the present, really, but a kind of chronological traffic accident, the temporal intersection where past and future collide? The past, what has not died of it, and the future, what is already born of it, rush together into a succession of instants we call the present.

And the turn of a millennium seems to us an especially momentous intersection. Arriving at it, we inevitably look back and we cannot resist looking forward. Those of us who care about Christian worship—not least because we *are* Christian worshipers—have to wonder at this intersection: what is the future of our worship? If our present (like all presents) is something of a wreck, what will survive it? What will be salvaged from it and set back on the road into the future?

JFK and Constantine

Let me begin with one reality of the past that I think will not survive, and indeed in any effective sense is already behind us. I have in mind the church's concordat with western civilization that is often called Constantinianism. Constantinianism was that arrangement under which the major institutions of western civilization (political, medical, economic, military, and others) were presumed to be implicitly, if not explicitly, Christian—or at least "Judeo-Christian." The Lutheran theologian Robert Jenson does not overstate when he writes, "The Constantinian settlement is now manifestly at its very end. Western civilization is still defined by Christianity, but as the civilization that *used* to be Christian . . ."[1]

There are those who would disagree with Jenson's judgment, especially as it concerns the United States. They can point to still high rates of church attendance; flourishing Christian magazines, record companies, websites, and other media; and even to the spectacle of presidential candidates eager to declare their religious faith—all as evidence that this is not a post-Constantinian culture. Certainly no one can deny that many individuals and groups in the culture continue to profess belief in the God of Israel and the church. But it is crucial to notice that they do so exactly as individuals and "private" or even "interest" groups. As David Toole writes, "[J]ust note the fact that we no longer build Gothic cathedrals; instead we spend comparable resources building research hospitals. And in the same manner, physicians have replaced priests as figures of authority. Although we may still profess belief in a suprasensory world, as a cultural force such a world commands little attention."[2]

An excellent example of this cultural, or social and public, marginalization of Christianity comes to us from the field of presidential politics. It is true that presidential candidates still seem eager to profess faith, usually Christian faith. But consider how these professions are couched. In 1960, when John F. Kennedy ran for president, some of his countrymen noticed that he was Roman Catholic. Addressing these concerns, Kennedy vigorously insisted America is a place "where no Catholic prelate would tell the President (should he be a Catholic) how to act and no Protestant minister would tell his parishioners for whom to vote." He said, "I believe in a President whose views on religion are his own private affairs" and insisted, "I am not the Catholic candidate for President. I am the Democratic party's candidate for President who happens to be Catholic."[3] These remarks neatly encapsulate the status of Christian faith in our culture. It is a strictly private affair, not to be carried in any significant way into the public square or the marketplace. And it is accidental (Kennedy just "happens" to be Catholic) rather than essential to one's character.

What does all this mean for the status of worship in the future? It means that ritual worship is and will continue to be seriously prey to sentimentalization and trivialization. Some, such as those in the religious right, long for retrenchment: they want Christians of a certain sort back in public control. But of course their evangelically dominated America is now nearly a century behind us. The United States of the dawning twenty-first century is exponentially more religiously and ethnically diverse than the United States of the nineteenth century. Given that diversity, the restoration of some sort of conservative evangelical regime would require truly draconian legislative, judicial, and cultural measures. Confronted with such necessities of coercion, even the leaders of the religious right quail and say they have nothing of the kind in mind. So, barring catastrophic social and economic collapse, and the ascendance of a religious fascism, what we are really dealing with here is nostalgia. In the face of an uncomfortable present, it is a longing for a past golden age that, actually, in many ways never was. These Christians do believe, devoutly, in the reality of God and heaven—in Toole's "suprasensory world"—but that is finally and decisively a private affair between the atomized individual and God. The flags in sanctuaries, the talk of a "Christian nation," the patriotic Independence or Thanksgiving Day worship services—these are, if I may put it so harshly, emotional window dressing, sops to sentiment. Upon even slight examination, the dreams and visions of these ceremonies are not supposed to affect or significantly change the public and cultural world in which we live. So, for those inclined to retrench, worship is either a strictly private affair or a misty exercise in nostalgia.

Conservative evangelicals enamored of the religious right are not, of course, eager to acknowledge some of their liturgical activity as plain nostalgia. But others are not so reticent about admitting it. I have in mind those nominally associated with mainline Protestantism or Catholicism, who have nothing to do with the church except on occasions such as weddings and funerals or Easter Sunday. These folk do not pretend that God—at least the God of the institutional church—has much if anything to do with their everyday lives. But when it comes to, say, a wedding, the church can do it with so much more pomp and circumstance. The setting and the ceremony feel better, more appropriate to what is undeniably an important occasion. Yet, disconnected from the rest of life and any serious intention to live as if the words and symbols of the ceremony are true, the church wedding is itself not much deeper than the frosting on the bride's and groom's cake.

In this more unabashed sentimentality God is like the groundhog: we pay attention to him about once a year, and even then we're really only looking for a shadow. I think such hollowness, such half-hearted posturing is what protestors in the sixties had in mind when they complained about "empty ceremonies" and considered "ritual" a term of contempt. But to one degree or another many clergy and other "religious professionals" try to make peace with this state of affairs. I call their response a kind of sentimental capitulation.[4] They basically accept that the faith of which they are representatives no longer carries much cultural force, but are ready to respond to the occasional vaguely religious twinges or impulses with which they are presented. It would be much too severe to say such clergy take the treasures of the liturgy and throw them like jewels to the swine. But it would not be too much to say they drop these diamonds before faithless-albeit-decent persons who regard them as little more than costume jewelry.

I hasten to confess I have drawn this picture sharply and starkly, and that a softer, more nuanced, and certainly more charitable picture might be drawn. Most Christian and liturgical life is conducted somewhere between the typological extremes of retrenchment or sentimental capitulation. But I do think this picture isolates the basic trajectories. As Jenson puts it, the church "is in the midst of divorce proceedings from the culture."[5] In these awkward circumstances Constantinianism appears most visibly as sentimentalized vestiges. Faith is strictly privatized and in that regard no longer a "cultural force." In such a setting there are great, and often succumbed-to, temptations to dilute or denature or trivialize liturgical worship. To take the true measure of these temptations, we must not only understand the reality that is now behind us (Constantinianism), but also take account of the regnant reality very much alive and with us: the reality of advanced capitalism.

The Triumph of Advanced Capitalism

Modernity is many things, but among them it is that period in which religious faith was privatized and two great institutions were left to oversee the conduct of public life: the nation-state and the market. The nation-state is, of course, still very much with us. Yet though it was, in its maturation and extent, the earlier of these two modern public institutions, the nation-state's power has long been challenged by free market capitalism. And since the 1980s, it has been overcome. The North American Free Trade Agreement and General Agreement on Trade and Tariffs has assured its supremacy for the foreseeable future. We now live in an age of advanced, global capitalism. Out of the world's one hundred largest economies, fifty are now transnational corporations. Mitsubishi's total annual sales are greater than the gross domestic product of Indonesia, the world's fourth most populous country. Wal-Mart's internal economy is larger than that of 161 of the world's countries, including Israel, Poland, and Greece. Corporate, global spending on advertising now rivals worldwide military spending: In 1994, $778 billion was invested on weapons, but nearly $500 billion on advertising.[6]

Capitalism has grown to a point of such dominance in large part by what might be called the belligerence of the bottom line.[7] Here is what I mean: It is one thing to recognize the market as a marvelously efficient instrument for the exchange of material goods. The profit motive, or bottom line, can indeed regulate supply and demand more efficiently than any other mechanism humanity has devised. But it is another thing to commodify and recast all of life in light of the market. Then the market, the bottom line, belligerently steps outside a circumscribed realm, and moves into other realms that were formerly regarded as beyond or inappropriate to its influence. Our faith in the market has now become so fervid and all-encompassing that even body parts are for sale ($10,000 for a kidney in Egypt, $4,000 for a cornea in India). In 1980, the U.S. Supreme Court ruled that life forms are simply chemical products that can be patented and sold like any other "manufacture," and in 1988 the U.S. Patent and Trademark Office issued the first patent on a living animal, a genetically altered mouse.[8]

Less dramatically, we can see and hear the belligerence of the bottom line in our language, in the way we have redescribed so many activities as preeminently economic activities. So Christian worshipers have become "church-shoppers" and students have become "educational consumers." Hospitals and other medical institutions are converted into profit-maximizing corporations and "patients," most now with patchier medical care than they received before, are "health care consumers." "In this fashion," Ted Halstead and Clifford Cobb write,

> what economists call growth and the GDP records as growth is really just the shifting of functions from the nonmarket economy of household and community, where economists can't see them, to the market, where they can. The garden plot becomes the supermarket, home sewing of clothes becomes the sweatshop; parenting becomes childcare; visitors on the side porch become the entertainment economy and psychiatry. Up and down the line, the things people used to do freely for and with one another turn into products and services. The market grows by cannibalizing the family and community realms that nurture and sustain it.[9]

In its drive to become more and more nearly comprehensive, to provide a vision and inculcate practices that define the ultimate human good in terms of the market and its dynamics, I think we can say that advanced capitalism is itself a kind of *cultus*. For partisans of advanced capitalism, the eschaton has arrived: Francis Fukuyama, after the fall of the Berlin Wall, announced that the world has reached the "end of history." Advanced capitalism has its own, worldwide church, the transnational corporation. It has its own saints, the CEOs and stock-market speculators and entrepreneurs who, practically overnight, make millions and even billions of dollars. Its rituals include the post-Thanksgiving, first shopping day of Christmas, on which presidents ceremonially buy a pair of socks.

I am not being facetious. Just as the Christian *cultus* is about worship and its concomitant formation of a way of life, advanced capitalism is profoundly formational: it makes people suited to and equipped for a particular way of life. In the postwar boom days of 1955, retailing analyst Victor Lebow declared, "Our enormously productive economy . . . demands that we make consumption our way of life, that we convert the buying and use of goods into rituals, that we seek our spiritual satisfaction, our ego satisfaction, in consumption. . . . We need things consumed, burned up, worn out, replaced and discarded at an ever increasing rate."[10] So if Christianity, as a *cultus*, sees self-control as a virtue, capitalism understands it as a vice called sales-resistance. If Christianity would promote patience, consumer capitalism would promote instant gratification. For peace and joy, this way of life substitutes deified dissatisfaction—forming a character that is never content with an existing experience (or product or service), but must always ache for the newer and the improved.

Again, I do not here mean to say that capitalism and the market have no appropriate place in the affairs of humanity, or that Christians should try never to participate in the market—which would in today's world be an utter impossibility anyway. Instead, I am concerned with the market's invasion of every sphere of human activity, and want Christians to recognize that capitalism, so construed and practiced, is in many and crucial ways a competing *cultus*. As the pundit George Will, himself an unabashed acolyte of capitalism, has put it, "The [American] founders . . . wished to tame and domesticate religious passions of the sort that convulsed Europe. They aimed to do so not by establishing religion, but by establishing a *commercial* republic." Accordingly, religion is "perfectly free as long as it is perfectly private—mere belief . . ."[11] Thus capitalism (and the classical liberalism that is its political counterpart) has domesticated Christianity by privatizing it, by sundering Christian practice from Christian convictions and consequently reducing those thick, powerful convictions to "mere belief," a matter of personal choice and preference on level with hobbies or entertainment options or spectator sports.

Liturgical Renewal and the Absence of Discipline

It is this development that well accounts for much of the disappointment that has followed in the wake of the liturgical renewal. For those who care about Christian worship, the twentieth century has in many ways been extraordinary: peaking with the rich liturgical ruminations of Vatican II, which we are still unpacking, this century has seen more careful attention paid to worship than any other in church history.[12] Yet worship renewal has not, as many hoped, brought widespread and lasting church renewal. Part of the problem here is simply one of exaggerated and romanticized expectations. As the liturgical scholar Michael Aune notes, some have claimed that "initiation rites can cure juvenile delinquents or that communing with the earth will make right our relationship with the environment. Or, perhaps ritual activity is even more powerfully salvific than this, healing even all the ills that afflict modern life."[13] This is a lot to expect out of two hours once a week. It is a lot to expect not least, as Aune goes on to say, because "such testimonies and scholarly efforts" consider "ritual/izing" as if it were "independent of *any* sociocultural or historical context . . ."[14] Such exaggeration and abstraction, Aune argues, can in fact undermine worship's power and effectiveness. As Catherine Bell has written, "[M]any liturgies lose authority primarily from lack of modesty. They are trying too hard to be too much, to claim too much. [Worship] alone cannot do all the things [we] want it to do."[15] I devoutly believe liturgical, eucharistically centered worship has great power. But I think Aune and Bell are quite right to, as it were, call the bluff on exaggerated and dehistoricized, albeit glowing, accounts of worship and its potentialities. For the fact, as I have suggested, is that Christianity's privatization has domesticated the faith, and disconnected corporate worship from "real life."

The anthropologist Talal Asad has worked quite illuminatingly on this point. Asad observes that his fellow anthropologist Clifford Geertz expects ritual worship to induce, in Geertz's words, "a certain distinctive set of dispositions (tendencies, capacities, propensities, skills, habits, liabilities, proneness)." But Asad begs to differ. He says that in the modern world worship in fact does not produce or eventuate in such distinctive sets of dispositions. In my view, Asad overstates the failure of traditional ritual worship here: I think worship still does have formational impact on the lives of those who regularly worship. But I agree that worship's formational potency is seriously hindered and crippled in modernity. Why? "The reason, of course," says Asad, "is that it is not simply worship but social, political, and economic institutions in general, within which individual biographies are lived out," that form individuals into the kind of characters or persons they are. And it is not "mere symbols that implant true Christian dispositions, but power . . ."[16]

For Asad, "power" includes law, sanctions, rules, and expectations to which members of a polity or other social institution will submit themselves.[17] In short, Asad's "power" is discipline. He notes that in classical Latin, *disciplina* applied to war (strategies for defeating enemies), politics (good government of and for public life), and the domestic realm (the virtues and obligations family members upheld for the family's collective good). Such discipline was a communal, social matter: formation was not left, as it ostensibly is under the regime of advanced capitalism, to the atomistic individual. Likewise, says Asad, in the Bible discipline (the Greek *paideia*) was the "physical, intellectual, and moral cultivation of the person."[18] Here notice that such discipline included the physical; in other words, it was envisioned that the church had something to do with telling its members what they should do (or not do) with their bodies. This is a long way from the "mere belief" extolled by George Will. In modernity, Asad notes, discipline—inherently social, communal, and physical as well as spiritual—would "gradually abandon religious space, letting 'belief,' 'conscience,' and 'sensibility' take its place."[19]

What takes place with the domestication of faith by privatization is a kind of double disembodiment of Christianity. Disciples (note the linguistic tie of this word to *discipline*) are separated from the social body of the church, and their faith, as belief, is separated from their own physical bodies and the social, material world they inhabit. Corporate worship is subordinated to individual worship, made an adjunct or ancillary practice of the worship private persons undertake on their own. Such worship cannot help but be, to borrow from George Lindbeck's analysis of doctrine, a kind of experiential-expressivism.[20] This worship is the individual's expression of his or her own experience and privately tailored belief. Such worship and spirituality is, of course, eminently agreeable to capitalism's ethos, which favors the endless multiplication of individual choice.

And, in terms of classical Christianity, it puts things just exactly backwards or upside-down. At the root of the faith is the memory not that individuals find and choose the true God, but that God sought out and chose Israel and the church. None but modern believers can imagine that Christians are fundamentally Christians apart from the social, corporate body of the church. As the New Testament scholar Charles Talbert writes, "'Members' . . . is Paul's term for the parts of the body through which the life of the body is expressed (see 1 Cor. 12:12, 14–26; Rom. 6:13). Paul is saying then that individual Christians in their corporeal existence are the various body parts of the corporate personality of Christ through which the life of Christ is expressed."[21]

As a youngster growing up in the country, I sometimes practiced football by myself. I kicked and punted. I threw the ball through a swinging tire. But I never imagined these activities as constitutive of or more basic than an actual football game. That required ten other people on my team and, more than that, eleven other people on another team. Tossing and kicking the ball made me more able for the game, but the game itself—irreducibly a social event—was of prime importance and, in fact, the motivator and goal of my private practice. But a capitalistically disciplined Christianity views corporate worship as secondary and derivative of individual faith, as a warmup or recharging for private worship and conduct.

The Way Forward

But now am I not at loggerheads with myself? I have tried to look ahead to the future by first observing what is behind us, a Constantinian Christianity in which the church allied itself with the state and other surrounding social institutions. And I have posited an advanced capitalism that has privatized, individualized, and dematerialized faith, not least by removing its disciplinary capacities—capacities that are necessarily social and physical.

Am I then pushed into a kind of sentimental capitulation or nostalgic retrenchment, with Christianity and its ritual worship either way a feckless, vestigial presence in the world of our future?

The question becomes one of whether or not Christianity can have or be a social embodiment, a kind of culture or way of life with, among other things, genuine disciplinary power, without expecting the rest of the world, or at least a major part of it, to be itself Christian. And of course the answer of history is that it can be, because it has been. The postmodern world is, in many ways, like the pre-Constantinian world inhabited by the Christians of the first three centuries. Now as then, there are many religious options at hand; the church does not control governmental seats of power. We could even say that the masses are distracted by spectacles of violence and sensuality, that advanced capitalism has through mass media its own versions of the Roman gladiatorial games. There is much the church has to learn, and its twenty-first century future will in large part consist in this learning, from an early church that wrote and canonized its Scriptures, developed its forms of worship, and formulated most of its root doctrines in a position at the margins of Empire.

Yet on the other hand, the postmodern world is of course very different from the world of the first three centuries of the common era. Those were, after all, episodes in a *pre*-Christian era. It is another thing to confront and engage a *post*-Christian era. There can, there must, be a reappropriation of Christian tradition (and not just of its first three centuries), but it is necessarily a *re*-appropriation, not simply a rote imitation or repetition of the tradition as it was embodied centuries earlier. In God's providence, we are now witnessing marvelous demonstrations or at least hints toward such timely reappropriation: deeply Christian thinkers who are steeped in the tradition but also keenly aware of the unique challenges of postmodernity. I have in mind the work, largely convergent in my view, of postliberal and postconservative evangelical Protestants,[22] of the growing "school" of radical orthodoxy (represented by the likes of John Milbank and Catherine Pickstock),[23] and of an emerging group of what might be called post-Constantinian Roman Catholic radicals, including Michael Baxter and William Cavanaugh.[24]

One thing all these folk have in common is the understanding that Christianity, as a living tradition necessarily composed of and integrated by both convictions and practices, uniquely and finally tells the true story of the world. As Milbank puts it, "There is no independently available 'real world' against which we must test our Christian convictions, because these convictions are the most final, and at the same time, the most basic, *seeing* of what the world is." It was the profound and consequential modern error to suppose that

there is some neutral "reality" to which Christians bring their insights. But Christians, like everyone else, are scions of language, bound to structures in which reality is already "worked over." Like everyone else we assume that our constant revisions of our language are evidence that it is indeed *reality* we are dealing with, but either the *entire* Christian narrative tells us how things truly are, or it does not. If it does, we have no other access to how things truly are, nor any additional means of determining the question.[25]

It is my contention, and one on which I have learned a great deal from Milbank, that this all-encompassing Christian narrative is preeminently learned, rehearsed, and enacted in corporate worship. Of course, this contention is not new or original. In his work rooted in patristic sources, the Benedictine liturgical theologian Aidan Kavanagh has condensed this insight in a wonderful aphorism: In worship, the church "does the world as God means it to be done."[26] Modernity's and capitalism's discipline and domestication of the church made worship a retreat or escape from the "real world," the public world of politics and economics. But as Alexander Schmemann has so lucidly reminded us, *leitourgia* should not be restricted to a compartmentalized cultic activity. Originally it meant "an action by which a group of people became something corporately which they had not been as a mere collection of individuals—a whole greater than the sum of its parts. It meant also a function or 'ministry' of a man or a group on behalf of and in the interest of the whole community." So the *leitourgia* of ancient Israel "was the corporate work of a chosen few to prepare the world for the coming of the Messiah."[27] And so the Eucharist, the regular, corporate liturgy of the Christian people, should not and indeed cannot be separated from the rest of the world. Sunday liturgy is "not an escape from the world, rather it is the arrival at a vantage point from which we can see more deeply into the reality of the world."[28] Or, as Schmemann puts it more pointedly in another place, "The Eucharist is the sacrament of unity and the *moment of truth*: here we see the world in Christ, as it really is . . ."[29]

In the world after Constantine and in the thrall of advanced capitalism, then, ritual or liturgical worship offers the church tremendous resources and has a sturdy future. The liturgical renewal of the twentieth century is bearing fruit, showing us how the Christian faith finally cannot be privatized and individualized. That liturgy cannot be left in a vacuum and be true to itself, since it tells and enacts the story not just of our Sundays, but of all our Mondays through Saturdays, and not just of atomized individuals who have made Christ a hobby or special interest, but of the whole world and the entirety of history. The very content, logic, and trajectory of the Eucharist propel it out of the boundaries set for it by capitalism, and, indeed, push us toward its reconnection with the Christian discipline of our social and physical bodies.

We have seen the beginnings of a recovery of discipline in such phenomena as the Roman Catholic Rite of Initiation for Adults (RCIA). The RCIA and similar efforts arise from the dynamic memory of the ancient Christian catechumenate which, as Robert Jenson notes, "was born as liturgical rehearsal and interpretation, as moral correction and discipline, and as instruction in the identity of a particular God . . ."[30] I have no illusions that such a recovery will be simple or easy. But for reasons I have argued earlier, I think it utterly necessary. The *cultus* of Christianity can no longer accept capitalism's discipline of itself and its members, but must to a real degree reassert its own discipline.[31] Three brief comments on this renewed discipline.

First, we must help ourselves and other members of Christ's body recognize that no world is free of discipline. It is one of the illusions of modernity that individuals can and should be autonomous, that they can create themselves and be their own law unto themselves. But in fact humans are social creatures—we are constituted and formed socially. To grasp the actuality and potency of capitalism's ongoing discipline, imagine a specific church that presumed to tell its members where they will live, what kind of clothes they will wear, what sort of food they will eat, and expected them to routinely devote sixty to eighty hours every week to the church's work. Such a church would, in our climate, be denounced as "authoritarian" and worse. Yet, as good moderns, effectively disciplined by advanced capitalism, we rarely balk at the demands of the culture of the business corporation—which does indeed make all these demands on its employees. People who could barely conceive of moving to another location to be members of a given church repeatedly move at the behest of their company; the "corporate uniform" (suit and tie for men, dresses and hosiery for women) is unquestioned; managers know they are expected not to eat sack lunches at their desk or drive rusty cars to work; and in a time of downsizing, corporations expect more hours from their employees, even with stagnant pay. I note all this not to complain that corporations are totalitarian and reprehensible. Rather, I admire the commitment they elicit from their employees, and want us simply to acknowledge that people do not and cannot live in a world free of discipline. Any social body with a common good and purpose requires the commitment and discipline of its members. The transnational corporation never hesitates to make demands on its employees. But the church, mired in the categories of a more and more dormant Constantinianism, shies away from making any demands or setting any expectations on its members. As a pastor poignantly noted recently in *The Christian Century*, "It occurred to me . . . that the Zionsville Rotary Club was asking me to make a greater commitment of involvement—and promising swift retribution if I fell short—than I had ever dreamed of demanding of church members. And I was the leader of a community pledged to transform human history."[32] Church members—and prospective members of the church—simply will not take us seriously unless we take ourselves seriously enough to reclaim some degree of Christian discipline.

That is the first comment. The second is a reminder that Christian discipline is of and for the church. Standing in the ruins of Constantinism, some Christian leaders confuse matters by asserting, for example, that, "Our responsibility in the church is to insist that the laws of this Christian nation be consistent with God's Word."[33] The United States is not, and in a profound sense has never been, a Christian nation. Talk of America as a "Christian nation" rightly and understandably raises the hackles of the millions of Americans who are not professing Christians. Yes, it is the classical Christian conviction that the end of all human desires and interests, "the supreme and ultimate value of all that exists," is revealed through Israel and Jesus Christ.[34] But that classical conviction rests in an eschatological context, recognizing that the present age is a time between the time of the kingdom's inauguration in the life, work, death, and resurrection of Christ, and that kingdom's consummation and fulfillment yet to come. The church, then, is not about trying to coerce the rest of the world to be the church. Discipline, like judgment, begins at home, within "the household of God" (1 Pet. 4:17).

The third comment: Though Christian discipline is *church* discipline, it is not on that account purely about "private" matters. The church is a social and corporate body, in many important senses its own polity. Accordingly, its discipline cannot be confined to categories designed and allowed for it by advanced capitalism. A telling aspect of any *cultus* is its taboos, and one of the taboos of advanced capitalism is that what the individual does with his or her money is private business. In fact, the sociologist Robert Wuthnow has found that the persons church members are *least likely* to discuss their financial affairs with are other members of their own local church.[35] For the sake of its own *cultus*, for the right formation of its members, the church must violate this taboo. I doubt the most helpful and healthy form such a Christian discipline might take would be, in corporate worship, standing up and announcing our respective salaries. But I can imagine, for instance, that one requirement of church membership—not for inquirers or visitors—might be joining a small group within the body, where trust can be built, and where, among other things, Christians will discuss with one another what we do with our money.

Liturgy in the Age of the Image

This third comment points to what in some ways would be a small beginning. But of course any working pastor would remind us just how dramatic and demanding it would be perceived to be, in this culture. For that matter, disciplined as I am by modernity and capitalism, I gulp at its ramifications myself. But then the God that I, that we, worship is "the power at work within us [which] is able to accomplish abundantly far more than all we can ask or imagine" (Eph. 3:20), as we Anglicans are reminded at the end of the daily offices.

There is no shortage of vertiginous challenges as the church sheds the robe of Constantine, now tattered rags, and begins to break out of its privatized captivity. But I hope I have said enough to indicate how liturgical, ritual worship, ancient as it is, is an overflowing treasure chest of resources not just from the past, but for the future. Let me very briefly suggest just one more instance.

Even now, as many people increasingly turn away from the printed word and books, and turn to the power of the photographed and televised and digitized image, the eucharistic liturgy holds new and barely imagined surprises. Advanced capitalism has capitalized (pun quite literally true) on the power of the image.

Eucharistic, ritual worship, with its own set of potent images—the body in the bread, the blood in the cup, crucifixion, resurrection, eschatological wedding banquet, and on and on—is equipped to join the battle of images with the *cultus* of advanced capitalism.[36] As the British theologian David Ford writes, the eucharist is "probably the ritual most participated in and most discussed in human history. It is the principal act of worship of the majority of the billion and a half or so Christians in the world today and has been of some importance for most of the minority. . . . [F]rom the beginning of the church the eucharist has been intrinsic to its identity" and it "continues to generate endless streams of devotion, practical implications, theological interpretations, music, art, architecture, mystical experiences, conversions, philosophical speculations, political ideals and, through them all, controversies, travesties and betrayals."[37] Rejoined with corporate discipline, the eucharistic liturgy will surely generate controversy—and, yes, inevitable travesties and betrayals. But its generative powers are not exhausted.

Back at the Intersection

I began with an old man, on foot, crossing the street in front of my then-new, smartly idling Toyota Tercel. He carried the ancient practices of the Mass out of the church building into the street, beyond Sunday morning into a dreary Monday. Sometimes, driving again and now in a newer and faster car, I hurtle down another street at fifty-plus miles per hour, zooming by blurred miles of strip malls, half-listening to a frenetic succession of radio ads, my mind on e-mails to answer or the most recent crisis of one or another nation-state, then, topping a hill, I pass my own church building. And I cross myself.

The worship endures.

PART 3

Trespassing Secular Borders:
Politics and Economics

eleven

Calling the Religious Right to Its Better Self

Moods of fear and anger dominate the conservative evangelical subculture. Walk into any evangelical bookstore, listen to any evangelical radio station, and you will quickly learn that evangelicals consider their family and other values under hateful attack. In many ways they are correct. Even columnist Ellen Goodman, certainly not a partisan of the right, recognizes that parents are now expected to raise children in opposition to "dominant cultural messages." Yet the sheer intensity—and even comprehensiveness—of desperation within the conservative evangelical subculture is disturbing.

Evangelicals and the religious right, perhaps more than any other Americans (who were much more in sync with Ronald Reagan's economic than his social conservatism), had banked on the "Reagan revolution" to save and protect their way of life. That revolution, of course, was rudely interrupted by the Clinton Administration. And if—or when—the Republican party more strenuously attempts to prevent fundamentalist infiltration of its grassroots organizations, the religious right will probably become more desperate. The culture wars may escalate to such a pitch of divisiveness and exclusivity that we may long for the comparative "calm" of Pat Buchanan at the 1992 Republican National Convention.

The way to avoid such escalation is not, I think, to keep arguing politics. The religious right must be engaged *theologically,* at the motivating core of its mission and its vision of the world. Since it is theologically founded, the religious right's most disagreeable (sometimes deplorable) political stances are based on even more disagreeable theological errors.

But leaders and followers of the religious right are acting sincerely out of their religious convictions. They will listen to genuine, earnest theological argument. What they need to know is that there are alternative biblical and theological readings of the nation's cultural and political situation— readings that do not necessarily lead to the poisonous fear and anger that increasingly pollute the air they breathe. Instead of merely debating politics, we fellow Christians need to call the religious right to its roots, to its own better self. So I want here to sketch an alternative reading; not the only one, to be sure, but most certainly a biblical, evangelical, and catholic reading.

The religious right needs to be challenged to reconsider its doctrines of creation and redemption.

Its sense of crisis lends its conception of all political concerns an unrelentingly military air. Frank Peretti's novels of politico-spiritual warfare are easily among the most read books of the religious right in recent years. *This Present Darkness* and *Piercing the Darkness* have sold over three million copies between them. Peretti's human protagonists are fundamentalists who embody "traditional" family values and empower the spiritual protagonists—angels—by praying. Strengthened by prayer, the angels engage demons in the sort of combat that might be depicted with adequate violence only in a Steven Seagal movie. A sample: The angel "Guilo returned the blow, their swords locked for a moment, arm against arm, and then Guilo made good use of his foot to cave in the demon's face and send it tumbling out over the canyon."

This is life and destiny as ultimately agonistic. Good is pitted against evil and each struggles, with the same means (force and violence), to destroy the other. Yet, as anthropologist Paul Hiebert has argued, this *mythos* is more a species of Indo-European paganism than a Christian conception of reality. In the Christian story, God is a good and loving creator without counterpart. God creates, according to the first chapter of Genesis, by word that coaxes and draws out the essential goodness of the creation. (This in contrast to myths, like the Babylonian account of Marduk and Tiamat's epic battle, that see creation itself as an act of warfare.) And God redeems, according to the Gospel of John, by coming in the vulnerable person of a carpenter's son whose true glory is revealed only when he is naked and crucified.

Instead of desiring the defeat and vanquishment of a rebellious creation, I would argue that the God of Genesis and John desires its reconciliation. The Indo-European story sees powers exercised through force and raises a sword as its symbol; the Christian story sees power exercised through influential love and raises a cross as its symbol.

All this has palpable political outworkings. The religious right argues, as a friend who is a proponent recently put it to me, that "truth is impositional." As a more flagrant example, consider the California organization called Citizens for Excellence in Education, dedicated to restoring prayer to the schools and the creation-science version of Genesis to the classrooms. According to the *Wall Street Journal,* the group works to elect Christian governmental officials, believing with one of its affiliates that government should be "the police department with the Kingdom of God on earth," ready to "impose God's vengeance upon those who abandon God's laws of justice."

My suggestion is that there are strong theological reasons for arguing that truth (and goodness) in the Christian way of life is a matter of persuasion rather than imposition. To propose that it is impositional posits what theologian John Milbank has called an "ontology of violence," an ontology that comports poorly with the Christian doctrines of creation and redemption. Instead, as Milbank makes clear, the ontology of violence is the ontology of classical liberalism, the Hobbesian struggle of all against all. The question to the religious right then is ironic: Are you striving to be truer liberals than Christians?

The religious right also needs to be challenged to reconsider its doctrine of ecclesiology.

The religious right ends up trying to impose truth and goodness via legislation partly because it has such a weak ecclesiology. Thoroughgoing individualists (another sign of faithful liberalism?), proponents of the religious right work from a tradition that has recently given little thought to the communal dimensions of faith. Suddenly reawakened to the political realm around issues such as abortion and the eclipse of the traditional family, the religious right had stopped considering the church itself as a polity, as a "holy nation" (1 Pet. 2:9), as a "city built on a hill" (Matt. 5:14), as the social body claiming Christians' fundamental allegiance and altering their political status from "aliens" to "citizens with the saints" (Eph. 2:19).

Unable to see the church as its fundamental polity, and steeped in the mythology of Christian America, the religious right has implicitly (sometimes explicitly) seen America as the church, as God's social agency for proclaiming salvation on earth. Thus one prominent leader could bluntly claim, "The only way to have a genuine spiritual revival is to have legislative reform. We are now, socially, so removed from a Christian consensus, that if we were to have a revival it would be short-lived."

This correctly recognizes that Christians will never live faithful lives except communally, but it erroneously assumes there can be no such communal support unless it is provided (or at least propped up) by the government. And this again leads the religious right to an ironic question: You generally call for less government. Are you actually asking for more government in areas where it is theologically least appropriate? Is it not perhaps time for the church rather than the nation-state to be the church?

In this direction lies a much better response to the pluralization of America than the religious right has offered. Islam, Hinduism, Buddhism, and a host of "new religions" are growing in our country. Gallup says the fastest growing community of "moral conviction" is that of professing secularists, swelling from two percent of the population in 1962 to nearly eleven percent by the end of the eighties.

Without reconsidered doctrines of ecclesiology (and providence), the religious right can only respond to these developments with alarm and stepped-up attempts to impose a quasi-official pseudo-Christianity on the nation. An odd thing about all this is how little representatives of the religious right have noticed that current developments put them in a situation much more closely analogous to that of New Testament Christians than the Christendom for which they nostalgically long. Why have those who place such emphasis on the Bible not paid more attention to the abundant resources it offers to Christians living in a wildly diverse and contested world?

3. *Finally, and fittingly, the religious right needs to be challenged to reconsider its doctrine of eschatology.*

One way the religious right can be read is as the latest manifestation of the evangelical refusal to admit and accept the passing of Americanized Constantinianism—which basically means evangelicalism's own hegemony over the culture. The religious right tenaciously, if vaguely, holds to the memory of the evangelical religious, legislative, and educational domination of this country that did not erode until the late nineteenth century.

A few years ago, historian Douglas Frank provocatively suggested that American evangelicals in the late nineteenth and early twentieth centuries switched from a postmillennial to a premillennial eschatology because they lost control of the nation. Put oversimply, when things were under their reign, evangelicals easily assumed God was triumphing through their regnant institutions. When the Lord returned, he would be greeted by a materially triumphant church. But when things were no longer under their reign, evangelicals assumed the country was going to hell, yet ingeniously gained another sort of control by claiming to possess ultimately powerful knowledge—the exact timetable for the Lord's return, and the way to escape God's wrath while seeing justice done to those who resisted the true way.

Such an eschatology allows—if not encourages—the anger and fear now so pervasive among conservative evangelicals. It expects matters to grow worse and worse (read, more and more out of evangelical control), eventually pitting out in an absolute moral and social nadir just before Jesus returns. Whatever its strengths, this eschatology is terribly susceptible to an ugly and smug spirit of triumphalism. There is little about it that urges conservative evangelicals to beware their own sinful and self-deceptive construals of unfolding history.

An alternative eschatology might emphasize that we have been living in the "end times" since Jesus was crucified and resurrected (1 Cor. 10:11; Gal. 4:4). It might emphasize that Christians are not provided detailed knowledge—coded or otherwise—of when Christ will consummate his reign (Matt. 24). It might emphasize, against self-interested and self-deceptive inclinations, that believers will not only be judged but will be judged first of all (1 Pet. 4:17). And it might reread the book of Revelation from the vantage point it was originally written and read—namely that of a long-suffering religious minority rather than a hegemonic religious establishment. (Along such lines, see Wayne Meeks's treatment in his *Moral World of the First Christians*.)

I hope a major political and cultural effect of such a rereading of Christian doctrines would be a truer and fuller pluralism. The evangelical and catholic support cannot be for a pluralism that gives up on truth or pretends all religious cultures more or less equally lead to truth. It is, instead, for a pluralism that allows various religions to hold their admittedly conflicting construals of reality, and allows them roughly equal ground on which to make their cases, to attempt persuasion through the communal embodiments and the formalized arguments of what they believe to be the ultimate truths of human existence. From an evangelical and catholic standpoint, the irrefutable vindication or demonstrable proof of our faith can only occur eschatologically, for "now we see in a mirror, dimly, but then we will see face to face" (1 Cor. 13:12).

On the religious right's behalf, I must say this truer and fuller pluralism does not yet exist. On many campuses and in many media, conservative evangelicals (and Roman Catholics) are the last American "niggers," those still often treated with open and unchallenged disdain. I have no intention of comforting any bigots—whether they position themselves inside or outside the religious right. Yet I do want the religious right and conservative evangelicals to recognize that one of the *legitimate* reasons they are sometimes refused a hearing is their none-too-veiled agenda for reasserting a (white) evangelical moral and social hegemony. Then, I want to say, they are not only failing to be politically correct. They are failing to be theologically correct.

twelve

From Family Values to Family Virtues

The Family Values Debate

Since at least the summer of 1991, when Vice President Dan Quayle attacked a television character for her loose living, Americans have been heatedly involved in a debate over "family values." It has been a debate about profoundly important matters, usually conducted shallowly and histrionically. Sadly, though Christians have been among the main players in the debate, they have brought little real theological orientation or perspective to it. I brazenly propose, in what follows, to do exactly that—to ask what, if any, business Christians, exactly as Christians, have in fighting for family values. Brazen, but not entirely foolish, I will theologically appropriate the esteemed work of philosopher Alasdair MacIntyre. Christian convictions (for example, that Jesus' cross calls his followers to a cruciformly nonviolent way of life) will precede and adjust MacIntyre's terms and arguments. But MacIntyre's terms and arguments will help to crystallize and, I hope, point beyond limitations in the family values debate.

So equipped, and focusing on a specific aspect of the family values debate, I will be enabled to suggest that the view of human sexuality presupposed in the family values debate—the sexual person as a consumer—is profoundly in tension with a more decidedly Christian understanding of sexuality and family life.

The Historicity of "Family"

From at least as early as 1966, with the publication of his *Short History of Ethics*, Alasdair MacIntyre has emphasized the historical situatedness of ethics—and indeed, of all philosophy and ways of life.[1] Human beings, as historical creatures, simply cannot escape to timeless and placeless vantage points from which to view "reality" or "the way things are actually." MacIntyre has instead argued, compellingly and in detail, that particular persons and communities see and respond to the world as they do because they are situated in a tradition that significantly determines the shape of the world for them. He has accordingly rejected post-Enlightenment attempts to belittle and escape tradition, attempts to appeal instead to a universal, timeless, and placeless Reason. Without capitulating to any radical relativism (a persuasive tradition must, after all, account for physical objects, events, and other phenomena that really are "out there"), he has worked to revive respect for tradition, and to interpret tradition as something dynamic and flexible enough to negotiate the undeniable changes of history. Hence MacIntyre's famous definition of a *tradition* as a "historically extended, socially embodied argument."[2] It is "historically extended" in that the argument goes on over time and "socially embodied" in that it is carried on by a community dedicated to pursuing the good as understood by that tradition.

In stark contrast, the family values debate has been carried on with blithe indifference to historical particularities. It is arguable, in fact, that much of the popularity of the term is due to its vacuousness. "Family values" are something that almost everyone can rally around, because they can in the end be defined almost as anyone would like. In the speech that ignited the debate, Vice President Quayle apparently referred to the bourgeois, heterosexual nuclear family. He worried over the "breakdown of family structure" due to "a welfare ethos that impedes individual efforts to move ahead in society." He protested against women bearing children outside marriage and quipped that "a welfare check is not a husband."[3] Quayle's references to welfare and illegitimate births were understood as thinly veiled code words for black, and especially ghetto, families.

But beyond this reference and apparent indication that true families are not on welfare, the vice president did not specify what he meant by "family values." MacIntyre would drive us to push the definition, and in so doing to pay attention to social and historical contexts. For instance, does it exemplify family values to build hardness into boys by compelling them to disturb a hornets' nest, be repeatedly stung, and suffer punishment if they cry? The Sioux believed so.[4] Does it exemplify family values to suppress a child's willfulness through fierce beatings, exhibition of corpses, and tales of castration and abandonment? The Puritans were so convinced.[5]

The debate subsequent to Quayle's speech has continued with indifference to the family values of any actual traditions, with the implicit pretense that family values are absolutely objective and obvious to anyone, anywhere, at any time. Christian proponents of family values have been especially apt to refer to the "traditional family," but without any deep MacIntyrean sense that a "traditional family" must belong to one or another specifiable tradition. Thus many of these Christians have easily elided "the traditional family" into "the natural family."

When we examine what clues we can about the "traditional family" called for by such Christian proponents of family values as James Dobson, Pat Robertson, and James Robison, it seems that they long for the bourgeois traditional family: the nuclear family, with home as an emotional haven from the heartless realities of commerce and politics, providing all religious and moral "values" for its members—values that are by definition "private" and "personal."[6] In so doing, they exalt a "traditional family" that is hardly two centuries old, a kind of family decisively shaped by the advent of capitalism and industrialization. It was these historical developments that separated nuclear families from their extended families, severely divided the world into public and private spheres, and pushed Christianity (and any other religion) out of the public sphere into the cozier but much less significant private sphere.

This says enough to suggest that Christians, with only a bit of theological reflection, ought to have some suspicions about this particular "traditional family." After all, how can we fit the confession that Israel's and Jesus' God is the Lord of the entire universe with the bourgeois relegation of God to the status of (private) household idol? It simply will not do to assume, as many eager Christian proponents of family values have, that this "traditional family" is identical with "the biblical family." It will not do, at least, if we actually pay attention to the shape and substance of biblical households. The ancient Hebrews, for instance, did not even conceive of what we call the nuclear unit apart from the extended family of kin and even servants. The average North American household of today consists of two to five people. The average Hebrew household, on the other hand, numbered fifty to one hundred inhabitants. Jacob's family, we are told in the Book of Genesis (46:26) consisted of sixty-six people. What we call the nuclear family the Israelites saw seamlessly woven into the multigenerational extended family. Every family centered on a patriarch. Each son, with his wife, children, and (in some cases) servants, lived in a separate shelter. So a Hebrew family or household would in effect have been a small village of several adjacent buildings. What's more, these households would sometimes induct and include as members of the family aliens or sojourners who had permanently taken shelter with them.[7] The same sorts of points could be made regarding the other defining traits of the bourgeois traditional family. Hebrew culture made no sharp separation between public and private life and certainly regarded Yahweh as something much more than a household god.

Likewise, the Roman society of the New Testament period made no sharp separation between public and private life. Household relationships that bourgeois moderns consider private carried important social and political baggage in the Roman world. No doubt the home was a place of comfort and rest for family members, especially the paterfamilias, or male head. But streams of commerce and politics flowed daily through the home. There the paterfamilias paid court to clients. Clients were those he sponsored in public life, such as poets and philosophers dependent on patrons for a livelihood. So the paterfamilias's social and political obligations did not end when he crossed the threshold into his home. If anything, they began there. These facts rehearsed, we do well to remember that the early church was based in the households of Rome. The Christians of the New Testament worshiped together in their homes, and challenged the undue claim of Caesar in homes. On all counts, they regarded the home as something more significant, more challenging, and more exciting than a privatized, sentimentalized haven.[8]

Now none of this suggests that we could (or should want to) simply graft the Hebrew or New Testament family tradition onto our current, late modern setting. Among other things, both of these families were harshly patriarchical, even by the terms of those "traditionalists" who would today argue for a modified and milder patriarchicalism.[9] But again, MacIntyre has reminded us that traditions are not static and changeless. Standing in the Christian tradition, we are called to formation by the profound theological convictions originally embodied—however partially or imperfectly at points—in the convictions and practices of Israel and the New Testament church. Consequently a MacIntyrean tack on "family values" would urge us to problematize the family values debate by first determining *whose* or which tradition's family values are being promoted.[10] It would then pay more attention to the Christian family tradition exactly as a tradition—"a historically extended, socially embodied argument." We would then have to devote more focus to the social embodiment of the Christian argument, namely the church, and much less to the isolated nuclear family (or the "American family," whatever that is).

yes!

Though I do not have luxury here to make the case in detail, I would hold that Christians should in fact understand the church as their first, or primary, family—the social allegiance most determinative of their identity and aspirations in life. N. T. Wright nicely encapsulates the theological basis of this case when he notes that, for the earliest Christians, "from baptism onwards, one's basic family consisted of one's fellow-Christians. The fact of widespread persecution, regarded by both pagans and Christians as the normal state of affairs within a century of the beginnings of Christianity, is powerful evidence of the sort of the thing Christianity was, and was perceived to be. It was a new family, a third 'race,' neither Jew nor Gentile but 'in Christ.'"[11]

The Family Values Platform as Hanging Gallows

It seems to me that a Christian focus on the church as First Family—or the primary community and *polis* of those baptized in the name of Father, Son, and Holy Spirit—is congruent with MacIntyre's insistence that we are shaped and formed by particular communities, specific living, and active traditions. In the now famous closing passage of *After Virtue,* MacIntyre called for the "construction of local forms of community within which civility and the intellectual and moral life can be sustained through the new dark ages that are already upon us. . . . We are waiting not for a Godot, but for another—doubtless very different—St. Benedict."[12] What I am here suggesting is that Christians already have (or are possessed by) such a community: the community called church.

So from a Christian theological standpoint, we must first of all and most determinatively ask what "family values" mean for the church. The vacuous, exceedingly fuzzy, sentimental family values of the 1990s debate do not help here because they do not locate a community whose tradition and embodiment of family they purport to represent. As I have noted with reference to Dan Quayle, when "family values" have been specified at all, they have been specified mainly in negative and oppositional terms—for example, by denouncing homosexuals or employing racist code words—and so their major effect has been to batter the already precarious civility of the American public square. Significantly, for Christians, not only do such family values fail in helping us to behave civilly (to love our neighbors and even our enemies), but they take any self-critical eyes off ourselves. Focusing debate about family values on supposed ghetto behavior and the immorality glorified in the popular media neatly lets affluent American Christians off the hook.

In truth, we inhabit and too often live in accordance with a culture a good deal more corrupt than graphic entertainment or ghetto crime alone can indicate. It is a culture almost entirely defined by what MacIntyre calls the "bureaucratic manager," seeing people as means rather than ends, and obsessed with maximal profits as the real "bottom line."[13] So it is a culture in which family (and friendships) are viewed from the managerial vantage point of "productivity" and therefore are "invested" in until they no longer serve productivity, then are "terminated." It is a culture in which elite economists can seriously propose solving the adoption shortage by quoting baby prices like soybean futures, and where a day-care franchise can unironically call itself Precious Commodities. In the prophetic words of a post-World War II retailing analyst, we have made "consumption our way of life" and converted "the buying and use of goods into rituals" from which we seek "spiritual satisfaction."[14] In short, if we are actually going to be capable of such Christian family practices as fidelity and commitment, we need to be a good deal more radical and self-critical than sentimentalized family values will make us.

The family values sloganeering, so far, then, has foreclosed debate at just the point where it should begin for Christians. We need to ask hard questions about exactly what kind of people—what kind of families—we want to be, and whether those goals are promoted or retarded not just by our popular entertainment but by our economics as well. Family values as they are usually sketched concede the game at the start to an advanced capitalist way of life. Yet it is capitalism and industrialization that isolated and insulated the nuclear family. "Family values" as we have known them in the 1990s assume this isolation but hope to make it palatable by rendering it magnificent. The family is now not only atomized, broken off from any comprehensive institution that might give it content and purpose, but is made the very foundation of all order and morality. So Dan Quayle contended that "the single most critical threat" to society is "the dissolution of the family."[15] And the vice president's speech to the 1992 Republican National Convention was titled "The Family Comes First."[16]

How strange it is to take a family that is now a pale shadow of its former self—a postindustrial family no longer serving primary educational, economically productive, or welfare functions, one reduced to the private promotion of affection—how strange to take this family and place on it the weight of the entire society. The household that once served major social and economic purpose is now a "haven" from the "real world." It is a retreat for the wage earners and a nest for children who await true personhood in the form of maturity and independence. All it can provide is affection and intimacy, which tend to be cheapened and sentimentalized because they are not seen to have a tie to the truly significant wider world. This is affection and intimacy powerless to affect reality, affection and intimacy that quickly erode into the triviality of "warm fuzzies."

Family values, then, work against a more Christian conception of the family as a quite public and political good, family based in and defined by the *polis* of the church. And they most directly threaten to kill the family by conceding and even promoting its privatization. So doing, family values elevate the family to a platform without realizing that the platform is a hanging gallows. Family needs purpose beyond itself and its mere sentimentality to survive and prosper. As sociologist Robert Nisbet writes,

> To suppose that the present family, or any other group, can perpetually vitalize itself through some indwelling affectional tie, in the absence of concrete, perceived functions, is like supposing that the comradely ties of mutual aid which have grown up incidentally in a military unit will outlast a condition in which war is plainly and irrevocably banished. . . .
>
> The family is a major problem in our culture simply because we are attempting to make it perform psychological and symbolic functions with a structure that has become fragile and an institutional importance that is almost totally unrelated to the economic and political realities of our society.[17]

The Trouble with Values

We are brought at last to what may be the preeminent irony of the family values debate. Though they were later touted by the likes of Bill Clinton, family values were originally presented and promoted by ostensible conservatives. But in fact the terms of the debate have been set on thoroughly liberal grounds. I refer here to the classical liberalism undergirded or championed by such Enlightenment luminaries as Immanuel Kant, John Locke, and Adam Smith. This is the liberalism that defines (and now, at least in some ways, stunts) most contemporary political argument. As MacIntyre observes, "It is of the first importance to remember that the project of founding a form of social order in which individuals could emancipate themselves from the contingency and particularity of tradition . . . was and is not only, *and not principally,* a project of philosophers. It was and is the project of modern liberal, individualistic society."[18]

It was classical liberalism, after all, that enshrined the privatization of family (and faith). It also enshrined the concomitant distinction of *fact* and *value. Fact* was understood, and still is widely understood, to be that which is public, universal, and self-evident to "reason." *Value,* on the other hand, was and is thought to be private, particular, and chosen by the individual.

Thus the surest sign that Quayle and company are involved in internecine liberal warfare is their very language. They battle for family *values*. MacIntyre, of course, would call us to a quite different language— the language of family *virtues*. Classical virtues, as opposed to modern and liberal values, are not preferences that the autonomous individual creates or validates, but are instead excellences or skills that precede the individual and remain objectively praiseworthy even if a particular (vicious) individual would never choose them. To accept the privatization of family, to strive for family values ráther than the contentful family virtues of a particular tradition, to designate said "values" with little more than sentimental commonplaces—all this is to champion family with an unmistakable liberal pedigree. And despite liberalism's purported neutrality, the consequences of such a view for our political and common life are considerable. As Michael Sandel comments in another context, "As long as it is assumed that man is by nature a being who chooses his ends [the liberal view inherent to "values" language] rather than a being, as the ancients conceived him, who discovers his ends, then his fundamental preference must necessarily be for conditions of choice. . . ."[19]

In short, we are unavoidably mired in liberal emotivism, the view that any morality or faith or philosophy is simply the private preference of the one who professes it. And as MacIntyre notes, emotivism entails that "the choice of any one particular evaluative stance or commitment can be no more rational than any other."[20] Thus "family *values*" ironically casts matters in terms that cannot consider any type of family (or nonfamily, or antifamily) any better than another. So-called conservatives who stand on this ground are consequently poised, not even on sinking sand, but on thin air. Such proponents of "family values" are accused of being coercive, of imposing their favored picture of family on everyone else. And indeed the emotivist terms of their argument and attempted persuasion can finally allow for nothing but coercion and imposition. Emotivism, in MacIntyre's words, "entails the obliteration of any genuine distinction between manipulative and non-manipulative social relations."[21] My values—even my family values—are simply and finally only that: what I prefer or value above all other options. You, on the other hand, have your own values or preferences, determined by yourself. With no effective appeal to anything other than individually self-determined preferences, I can only "win" you to my values by trickery (manipulation) or sheer force.

So it is that the terms, conceptualities, and aims of the family values debate serve to disarm the family of what little defense it has left in a liberal, capitalistic, consumer society. After all, no one can really "choose" a mother, a father, or a particular child. Yet in liberal eyes family (like faith) can be only, at best, akin to a hobby. Blood is supposed to be thicker than water, but in the terms of liberal and family values, devotion to one's family means nothing more substantial than a personal preference for blood over water.

Consumer Sexuality

In short, those Christians who argue for family values cannot help being drawn into forms of expression—and ways of life—that are radically at odds with their own professed aspirations. Perhaps this point will make more concrete sense, and gain more credibility, if we dwell at some length on a single aspect of the family values debate. I have in mind the contentious subject of sex.

Many Christian proponents of family values believe that sexuality is best constrained and channeled, and that the best place for genital sexual expression is within the bonds of marriage. Sexual fidelity is, in fact, one of the primary family "values" they are fighting for. Yet the very same champions, buying into the inherently liberal, emotivist, consumeristic conceptuality that undergirds values language, publish books and magazine articles insisting that sex is really more pleasurable if you save it until after you are married. Evangelical Christian marriage seminars, for example, offer T-shirts with the legend, "I'm having a wonderful affair—with my wife." Such attitudes make the most prominent apologia for Christian marital fidelity the argument that monogamy is an aphrodisiac superior to free love. In other words: choose the "value" of fidelity for the sake of better sex.

MacIntyre's contextualized, historicized account of ethics helps us to ask what view of human sexuality is at work here. Rather than simply and grossly assuming that human sexuality is a given, an instinct identical in all times and places, we can ask what account of sexuality and marriage lies behind the propensity of (even) some Christians to make fidelity an aphrodisiac, and thus a commodity more appealing to the sovereign consumer. Accordingly, I argue that what lies behind it is the tradition of romantic love, a tradition that is part of the bourgeois package of family values but one that Christians more mindful of their own tradition would do well to challenge.[22]

The Myth of Romantic Love

It may not be hyperbolic to say that romantic love is one of the master stories or traditions of liberal, advanced capitalistic society. Think of it this way: As historian Eamon Duffy shows in a richly detailed account, fifteenth-century English folk could hardly make it through a waking hour of the day without encountering living manifestations of the Christian tradition. Church bells rang. Processions recalling Christ's sacrifice paraded by homes. Duffy writes,

> With the liturgy, birth, copulation, and death, journeying and homecoming, guilt and forgiveness, the blessing of homely things and the call to pass beyond them were all located, tested, and sanctioned. In the liturgy and the sacramental celebrations that were its central moments, medieval people found the key to the meaning and purpose of their lives.[23]

Now compare how easy it is to pass through an hour of the Western, late-twentieth-century day without any reminders of the Christian tradition, but how difficult it would be to avoid fragments of the tradition of romantic love. Popular, jazz, and country radio stations are saturated with it, heralding it in song around the clock. Escaping it would mean never turning on the television, watching a movie, or overhearing office gossip. It's apparent on billboards and in magazines and newspapers and, as I've observed, barely less prominent in Christian literature and media.

Inherent to the ethos of romantic love is the notion that it is "natural" and universally inevitable. People fall in love as surely as the earth orbits the sun and heavy objects roll down hills. No doubt much of the uncritical acceptance of romantic love among Christians is due to the perception that it is natural, rather than a contestable tradition. It has been second nature to most moderns to think of emotions (like romantic love) as somehow deeper, truer, less contrived than thoughts or behavior. But emotions have histories and social origins too. They are, after all, more than mere sensations—else how do we distinguish between abject fear and cheerful excitement? In either case, heartbeat speeds up, stomach tightens, lungs draw air more rapidly. What sorts of things will frighten or happily excite someone? Who should feel fear (or excitement), and when? How is fear (or excitement) expressed—is it hidden, demurely shown, displayed in weeping or laughter? Emotions are interpretations of objects and circumstances, and as such they are always culturally formed and informed. "Feelings," anthropologist Michelle Rosaldo has well said, "are not substances to be discovered in our blood but social practices organized by stories we both enact and tell." Feelings, like selves in general, are shaped by culture and may be understood as the "creation of particular sorts of polities" or embodied traditions.[24] The emotional life, it turns out, is no less political and traditional than the thought life.

Accordingly, women and men everywhere may be sexually attracted, have intercourse, and often produce offspring. But romantic love is far more complicated than that. How is sexual attraction experienced? Is it considered to be mere animal magnetism (as in paganism); is it simultaneously alluring and a disgusting temptation (as in antiphysical accounts); or is it, among other possibilities, part and parcel of "falling in love"? Is attraction to be resisted, indulged, or somehow channeled? Where may it lead, what potential does it present—is it apt to suggest a one-night stand or marriage, possible and eventual satisfaction or unending though sometimes delicious frustration? This is the level at which cultural and political traditions must come into play.

The Roots of Romantic Love

Once we recognize as much, we may not be in a position simply to shake off the spell of romantic love. It is far too potent magic for that. But at least we are in a position to assess its narrative in Christian terms and begin concocting an antidote. Then we are poised to remember that it is only since the Middle Ages that romantic love has been prized as an ideal, the *sine qua non* for marriage and the fully vital human life. Marriage in history has more typically been arranged between families than chosen merely by a man and a woman "in love." In fact, in most of Western history the sweeping intensity, confusion, and absorption of what we have come to know as romantic love was considered a misfortune. Friendship was the higher love.

The roots of romantic love lie in heresy. Denis de Rougemont traces it back to the Cathari, who emerged in twelfth-century Germany.[25] True to their name (which means "pure ones"), the Cathari were obsessed with evil and believed its origins were found in physical matter. Accordingly, they prohibited sexual intercourse even within marriage. Certain of the Cathari's themes were picked up by twelfth-century court bands. From there they made their way into written verse romances, and finally into modern romantic literature. Perhaps the tidiest way to lay out the narrative tradition of romantic love is to recount the story of Tristan and Iseult, memorialized in so many medieval poems and songs.

Tristan and Iseult, Carolyn and Scott

In the tale Tristan, an orphan, becomes the adopted son of King Mark (in some accounts he is the nephew of the king). Early on he proves to be a fine warrior. With this attribute in mind, the king sends Tristan to fetch the king's bride-to-be, Iseult, from Ireland to Mark's realm of Cornwall. Returning from Ireland, Tristan and Iseult drink the love potion intended for her and King Mark. They fall in love and succumb to temptation. Yet both attempt to remain loyal to the king, so Iseult is delivered to Mark. Tristan and Iseult's duplicitous sexual adventures continue in the castle, until the couple flees to the forest of Morrois, to live for three years in the hardship of poverty. Then the couple repents, and Iseult returns to Mark. But Tristan and Iseult soon plot reunion. Before they are reunited and manage to manifest their love in its fullness, both die.

Once the core narrative is exposed, even in such sketchy detail, several enduring dynamics of supposedly natural romantic love rise into view. True love is something that falls on people, like a spell. The couple on which it falls is special, admirable at least from outside the social circles where their love wreaks havoc, and yet the couple is tragically ill-fated. To the limited extent that romantic love can be realized, it is realized fitfully and fleetingly, clandestinely, in poverty, and in opposition to society. Quintessential love is understood as unsatisfied yearning, as desire exquisitely deprived. It cannot end in consummation or steady, unfolding fulfillment, but only in death. According to the myth of romantic love, true love is too good for this sordid world.

In an illuminating chapter of his *Ethics,* James McClendon demonstrates how these themes of the narrative of romantic love remain prominent in massively popular tales like Erich Segal's *Love Story* and in sturdier, more sophisticated work like the novels of John Updike.[26] For my purposes and more abbreviated space, I turn to a true life story.

The spring and summer 1988 odyssey of Carolyn MacLean and Scott Swanson serves my purposes because Carolyn and Scott were students at Wheaton College, that midwestern bastion of Protestant evangelicalism, and as such an institution devoted to the intentional cultivation of the Christian story and its attendant traits of character. So it is all the more striking that Carolyn and Scott, seniors about to graduate from the college, fell in love and then disappeared one April day. Both came from wealthy families, and Carolyn's BMW was found abandoned in a Chicago alley. A harried, highly publicized four-month search ensued. Then, late in July, Carolyn and Scott turned up in San Diego. It seems their intended marriage was opposed by their families. In addition, Scott's education was partly financed by his participation in ROTC, and in a few months military service would separate him from Carolyn.

What could this couple, this Christian couple, do? They knew the romantic script well. As a *Chicago Tribune* headline later reported, "Missing Wheaton couple did it all for love."[27] Scott and Carolyn eloped and ran off because, Carolyn said, "We loved each other so much that we wanted to give up everything for each other." They left behind the encumbrances of wealth, lived in a cut-rate apartment, and waited tables in restaurants to experience "unadorned love." Their safe return was a relief to police, friends, and family but also the occasion for anger at all the unnecessary worry and expense Tristan and Iseult—I mean, Scott and Carolyn—had put them through. In response, Scott averred that their extraordinary relationship simply wasn't understood: "We feel like we're on a different level than a lot of people . . . Carolyn's my life, and me to her, her to me. I would die for her and she would die for me."

The couple admitted that they modeled the entire episode on *A Severe Mercy,* Sheldon Vanauken's intensely romantic account of his love affair and marriage, in which he and his wife rejected any interference with their love, including material goods or children. Vanauken creates an admittedly moving account of his and lover Jean's rapture, replete with starlit nights on a sailboat, and then her wrenching, untimely death. But Scott and Carolyn apparently missed the ultimate point of the book. After Jean's death, and counseled by C. S. Lewis, Vanauken comes to see that his and Jean's attachment was too exclusive, too all-encompassing, and finally just plainly and destructively selfish. The book's title comes from Lewis's penetrating insight that Sheldon's forced, agonizing separation from Jean might be perceived as "a severe mercy" rescuing the pair from the poisonous effects of extreme romantic love.

The Fallout of a Tradition

But perhaps I should not be too hard on Carolyn's and Scott's reading of the book. In the end, Vanauken (and Lewis too) remained a committed if chastened romantic. Though with the help of such brilliant guides as Lewis (and his friend Charles Williams), Christians might well appropriate aspects of romantic love, I suspect our environment is now so completely corrupted by this myth that whatever remains redeemable of it lies only on the other side of more radical, thoroughgoing critique than Lewis ever suggested.

For what the narrative of romantic love tells us is that we are powerless to "make" and sustain real love. Remember, according to this tradition true love can never last. We simply fall into it and are swept into the arms of that special person destined just for us. (The feeble Christianization of this romantic plotline is the supposition that God has somewhere out there that one person exactly right for each of us to find and marry. Hence the widespread and heightened anxiety that "I might be making a mistake," for well you might if there is only a single person genuinely fit for you in a world of several billion. This is searching for a unique needle in a haystack full of needles.) Even at its most sentimentalized, when the tale of romantic love ends with the couple living "happily ever after," the marrow of the fairytale is never about actually living happily ever after; romantic love cannot even provide us with a description of "ever after." It is all about a goal, a goal that can never be achieved but is by definition best dreamed about and pined after.

I think of a friend who tells about warding off her husband's lovemaking advances so that she might rather read, in bed beside him, her latest romance novel. That's romantic love in its essence. It is first and finally gnostic, antiphysical, drawn more to fantasies than any actual, particular body near to hand. A pernicious irony of the narrative of romantic love is that, for all its supposed adoration of the love object, romantic love is not really about loving a particular person—it is about being in love with love.

Romantic love is based on inconstancy, on feelings unanchored in reality. That is why so many popular romantic love songs protest of illicit affairs, "How can this be wrong when it feels so right?" Of course, many of those who have succumbed wholeheartedly to this myth realize, at least when they're not in the throes of love's latest spell, that they said exactly the same thing to the earlier lover they're now betraying. So it is that romantic love leaves us prey to both sensuality and cynicism. And in that regard it's worth noting how well the narrative of romantic love supports the ethos of advanced capitalism, which demands that the ideal consumer be perpetually frustrated and never really contented. It's not for nothing that the story still flourishes in a day far removed from the courtly world of Tristan and Iseult.

The now faintly quaint custom of dating, after all, is a preeminently capitalistic practice, a sign of just how far the market has transgressed beyond any proper boundaries. In theory a young man or woman dates in order to grow in the knowledge and ability to make a more informed marital choice. Yet we have little or no sociological evidence that dating, after almost a century of its practice, reliably results in happier, longer-lasting marriages. What is clear is that dating's inexorable consumerist logic has been extended to encompass premarital cohabitation. If romanticized sexual compatibility is so important to the success of a marriage, and if it is more found or "fallen into" than made, it only makes sense to experiment before taking any vows. No sensible consumer would buy a car without test-driving it, or a stereo without first listening to it. So how dare choose a mate without first living with him or her? I say all this by way of suggesting that challenging the myth of romantic love is a matter not merely of confronting Grace Livingston Hill or Danielle Steel; it's a matter of going toe-to-toe with Wall Street and Madison Avenue. And there's something that may be more interesting than falling in and out of love *ad nauseam*.

McClendon properly reorients Christians for just such a fight when he writes, "While the romantic myth moves from love to death, the Christian master story moves (through death) to newfound life—in the body."[28] In the shadow of Christ's death and the light of his resurrection, the Christian master story recasts the story of love so that it does not *end* at the wedding and the commencement of "ever after," but instead *begins* there. As Michael Ignatieff puts it, the Christian marriage ceremony, with its vows to love in sickness or health, until death, replaces the romantic tale of falling in love with the "arduous drama of staying in love."[29] Romantics make love in private, at best oblivious to the welfare of the surrounding community. Christians make love in public, realizing that Christian love is much more than mere sexual passion, and trusting that they can build an enduring, open, and generous love only through participation in the surrounding community called church.

I suspect that we might best de-idolize romantic love by giving more attention to friendship in the context of *koinōnia,* or churchly community. I have in mind Aristotle's highest form of friendship—the friendship of those devoted to a common cause. Christians are those people caught up in an adventure involving nothing less than the destiny of the world. As such, we hardly need the comparatively puny and petty adventure of romantic love. Christians do not get married because monogamy is an aphrodisiac; they get married because this is the key way they participate as sexual beings in an adventure far surpassing the potentials of any aphrodisiac, the adventure of witnessing to and building up God's kingdom on earth.

The important question for Christians, then, after five, ten, fifty years of marriage, is not, "Am I still in love with my spouse?" The better question is, "Are we stronger, deeper, continuing Christian friends?" That is to say, are we supporting and challenging each other in the faith, in service to one another, to our children, to our church, to our neighbors? In the words of Diogenes Allen, when Christian marriage is friendship rather than romance, "We do not fight dragons or villains, as in 'love stories,' but fight with ourselves, as more and more of our self and our partner is revealed with time and through the ups and downs of life. We face an inward struggle with what we are [and, I would add, a political struggle with what the world wants us to be]. What is won is oneself and the other. Married people *become* people who love each other."[30] In short, the sex lives of Christians can improve. But they can improve only once we learn how to make love after we have fallen out of love.

The Noncommodified Christian Family

We have now theologically viewed the family values debate with a MacIntyrean lens and devoted considerable attention to what is literally the "sexiest" aspect of that debate. My conclusion is that if there is any hope for living such Christian family virtues as fidelity and commitment, it will be only in a community that can stand in some considerable tension with the liberal, advanced capitalistic way of life. Believing this would mean taking seriously a number of Christian convictions that can only appear odd in the veiled liberal terms of the family values debate. We do not, for instance, hear much in that debate about certain statements of Jesus, such as, "I have come to set a man against his father, and a daughter against her mother . . . and one's foes will be members of one's own household" (Matt. 10:34–36) or St. Paul's, "So then, he who marries . . . does well; and he who refrains from marriage will do better" (1 Cor. 7:38). We do not hear much about the biblical, and ancient Christian, conviction that the church is the Christian's first and primary family, that through baptism we are grafted into a community of adopted siblings who are our truest sisters and brothers because they do the will of the God of Israel and Jesus the Nazarene (Mark 3:31–35; Gal. 4:1–7).

Christians, in the end, can do much better than fight for family values. We can strive better to discern and live out distinctively Christian family virtues, and through this way of life demonstrate that there is an alternative to the liberal capitalistic way of life. Only such an imaginative and costly embodiment can provoke and encourage other (that is, non-Christian) families. Only such a flesh-and-blood embodiment can free people to dream and hope for a better way of living together. If Christians live out Christian family, if we even to a degree make the church our first family, then at least others will know that family can be other than—and more than—a feckless haven, a commodity, or a personal hobby.

thirteen

The Theology of Consumption and the Consumption of Theology

Toward a Christian Response to Consumerism

Every person under the sun must eat to live. In that sense we are all blame-less and—as at a feast lovingly prepared by a grandmother—glorious con-sumers. There is nothing wrong, and much that is right, about consuming to live. Hence I have heard a rabbi speak winningly from his tradition of "consecrated consumption." What worries some people about consump-tion (and I confess at the outset to be one of these ambivalent creatures, fat but troubled in paradise) is that the affluent, technologically advanced West seems more and more focused not on consuming to live but on liv-ing to consume. The problem with consumption, and the consumer capi-talism that has pushed it to feverish historical extremes, is that it has become so all-consuming.

Even Americans—we citizens of what Harvard historian of marketing Richard Tedlow cites as the premier "nation of consumers"—recognize problems with the extremes to which we have taken consumption as a way of life.[1] The trash buckets for recycled garbage, nonexistent ten years ago but now standing sentry outside every suburban home in my neighborhood, bear testimony to one of the most obvious problems. We are sensitized to the ecological damage fostered by the centralized, technology-intensive, intentionally wasteful ("planned obsolescence") society fostered by consumer capitalism. Perhaps the environmentalists sometimes go too far, but however overstated their warnings may be, there is no denying the murky brown clouds of smog hanging over Los Angeles or the swimming beaches shut down on Lake Michigan as tides of sewage roll ashore.

A hardly less obvious, or problematic, feature of consumer capitalism is the inescapable barrage of advertising, coaching and coaxing multitudinous desires innocent and not-so-innocent. One observer estimates that the average American is exposed to sixteen thousand commercial messages, symbols, and reminders every single day.[2] So inundated, we are hardly aware how pervasive and even invasive these images and messages are.

Their force struck me in 1996 while, in the course of researching the subject of consumption, I spent three days at a Christian community bereft of televisions and radios and removed from billboard-besieged highways. When I arrived back at Chicago's O'Hare Airport, the Abercrombie & Fitch and Calvin Klein posters in the terminal were the same ads I passed three days before with hardly a second thought, except to notice a pretty face here or a shapely figure there. Half a week out and the ads seemed decidedly hollow, ridiculously mannered, artificial, even unnatural. And driving away from the airport down I-294, I was greeted—no, *assaulted,* as it seemed to senses gentled by a brief respite—by a gauntlet of towering billboards. One of the first on the route was a garish yellow and red pitch for a nightclub called Bare Assets, teasing, "Do you like to watch?" I muttered under my breath, "This is not the way things are supposed to be."

But consumer capitalism is much more pervasive, and much less obvious, than smog or billboards. Look harder, and you can see it at work all around: shaping attitudes, bending behaviors, grinding and refracting an endless series of lenses through which to see and experience the world in a particular way.

Tracking the sly beast, I flew to New Hampshire to visit Lendol Calder, a Christian and historian concerned enough with consumerism that he devoted his dissertation study to the subject.[3] When, I asked him, did you first begin to notice the depth and width of consumerism in our culture? He recalled a Christian camp in college composed of persons from several nations. A get-acquainted exercise involved dividing campers up by their nationalities and assigning them to come up with a song representing their culture that all could agree on and sing to the rest of the assembly. Most groups had agreed on a song (nearly all were indigenous folk songs), practiced it, and were ready in ten to twenty minutes. But not the Americans. They debated over twenty minutes, then an hour. Some wanted a rock song but could achieve no consensus. Others suggested a series of country songs, only to have them roundly rejected. At last they settled—on Coca-Cola's "I'd Like to Teach the World to Sing." The jingle ringing in his ears, Lendol realized that commercial culture was what finally and ultimately bound these Americans—these American *Christians*—together.

This is what I am after. Not just consumerism in its most undisguised, hackneyed manifestations, but as an ethos, a character-cultivating way of life that seduces and insinuates and acclimates. This, too often, is consumption that militates against all sorts of Christian virtues, such as patience and contentedness and self-denial, but almost always with a velvet glove rather than an iron fist. It speaks in tones sweet and sexy rather than dictatorial, and it conquers by promises rather than by threats.

Consumerism envelops us, as surely as the air we breathe—but not as naturally as the air. Consumerism (and the capitalism that created and sustained it) is not a force of nature. It has a history. Of course it cannot, and should not, be replaced overnight. It did not appear overnight, but over the course of centuries. Yet the fact that it cannot be changed wholesale and immediately is no excuse—at least not for Christians—for failing to engage it critically, understanding it as best we can for what it is, and resisting its ill effects in nooks and crannies, bits and pieces, as vigorously as we can. That unplanned obsolescent, Karl Marx, was right about this much: people can make history, change the course of cultures, even if not within circumstances of their own choosing. Consumer capitalism, both for good and for ill, is a pervasive and foundational reality of our day, yet people can respond to it in significant ways and potentially change its course.

Christianity before Capitalism

With the fall of Soviet communism and the political successes of Thatcherism and Reaganism in the 1980s, capitalism appears to need no justification. To argue for or against it today, from almost anywhere in the world, seems to make about as much sense as arguing for or against the force of gravity or the wind in your face. Capitalism is natural, a kind of cosmic given. It seems as inevitable and ineradicable a feature of the social landscape as the Rockies are of the geographical landscape.

But unlike the Rockies, which have stood beyond justification for millions of years, capitalism has been naturalized only over the last three or four centuries. In fact, several essential characteristics of capitalism, especially of the advanced or consumption-oriented variety we now know, were either unimaginable or positively condemned throughout most of Christian history. We do not question the legitimacy of making money with money. But the church through the Middle Ages, Martin Luther included, proscribed the charging of interest and would have regarded speculation of the sort we now routinely engage in with our stocks and bonds as nothing more than profligate gambling. We suffer no crisis of conscience, nor even a second thought, about consuming goods or experiences solely for relaxation and amusement. Yet Puritans and Christians of many other stripes understood consumption principally for pleasure as outright sinful indulgence.

We presume the obvious rightness, so long as it is done legally, of making a profit, indeed of maximizing that profit. It did not so easily make sense to the church fathers. At the end of the first century, the author of the *Didache* exhorted, "Never turn away the needy; share all your possessions with your brother, and do not claim that anything is your own. If you and he are joint participators in things immortal, how much more so in things that are mortal?" In the second century the *Shepherd of Hermas* counseled directly against investment and the accumulation of profit, observing that Christians are aliens to this world and have no call to amass worldly wealth. "Instead of fields, then, buy souls that are in trouble. . . . Look after widows and orphans and do not neglect them. Spend your riches and all your establishments you have received from God on this kind of field and houses!"[4] Much later, in Boston in 1635, a Puritan merchant was charged by the elders of his church with defaming God's name. He was hauled before the general court of the commonwealth and convicted of greed because he had sold his wares at a six percent profit, two percent above the maximum allowed.[5]

One more example should suffice to drive home the point that capitalism and consumerism have a history and at one time needed justification. Max Weber reminds us that modern capitalist employers depend on increased "piece-rates," or more pay for more production, and that such a thing was not at all second nature to a traditional or precapitalistic way of life. Again and again, he says, incipiently capitalistic employers found that raising piece-rates did not automatically raise production.

A man, for instance, who at the rate of 1 mark per acre mowed 2 ½ acres [of hay] per day and earned 2 ½ marks, when the rate was raised to 1.25 marks per acre mowed, not 3 acres, as he might easily have done, thus earning 3.75 marks, but only 2 acres, so that he could still earn the 2 ½ marks to which he was accustomed. The opportunity of earning more was less attractive than that of working less.[6]

Weber continues that it was not just that working less was more attractive than earning more. There simply was no conception of an economy that might rise limitlessly, of progress and career tracks and salary increases. The traditional man or woman saw no sense in making more than necessary to meet his or her customary needs. As Weber puts it, "A man does not 'by nature' wish to earn more and more money, but simply to live as he is accustomed to live and to earn as much as is necessary for that purpose. Wherever modern capitalism has begun its work of increasing the productivity of human labour by increasing its intensity, it has encountered the immensely stubborn resistance of this leading trait of pre-capitalistic labour."[7]

Given the inescapably Christian history of the West and the West's prodigy, including consumer capitalism, it is a matter of concern (and not just to Christians) to rehearse how it is that capitalism came to be justified and finally, as it is now, go beyond justification. That is to say that there once had to be a working theology of consumption. Pervasively Christian polities and people did not, in fact could not, suddenly one day simply assume the rightness and goodness of profit-making, of taking interest on loans, of consumption for pleasure, of the accumulation of resources exceeding immediate needs. Through centuries they honestly and reverently grappled to interpret and shape their material lives in the light of God. They theologized, and only so did they legitimize, what we now call capitalism and consumerism.

Of course the fact that capitalism no longer needs justification is an indication that it no longer needs theology. Economists rarely consult theologians; quite a number of them actually consider the market outside theological and moral inquiry. So do the rest of us most of the time. As Ronald Reagan remarked when he defended the mania of the 1980s for getting and growing personal wealth, "That is not materialism. That is Americanism."[8] In Oedipal fashion, consumption has consumed theology. Thus, if there is any worry about where we stand and where we are going, Christians at least must understand both the theology of consumption and the consumption of theology.

The Beatification of the Merchant

As we begin to consider what I am calling a theology of consumption, it is only fair to observe that at no point did any theologian set out to consciously construct such a theology, let alone to justify such abuses of consumptive economies as price gouging, addictive shopping, or ecological damage. Most of their theologizing, if not all, was done without economic matters directly in mind, so that in sketching a "theology of consumption" we are talking about indirect and often even undesired effects. That said, the place to begin is the Reformation, and as you might expect, the leading guide is the venerable Max Weber and his *Protestant Ethic and the Spirit of Capitalism.*

As Weber and many others note, the mercantile way of life was not held in high esteem prior to the Reformation. If America's business is business and the businessperson is our saint, we stand as a historical anomaly. For good and for ill, it is Luther and Calvin who laid the groundwork for the respectability and later the beatification of the merchant. In the church before Luther, the exemplars of faith were found in the monastic system. The laity lived by a comparatively relaxed ethic. The religious answered to the higher and more demanding ethic of the evangelical counsels, which included vows of poverty and celibacy. Luther, himself formerly an Augustinian monk, challenged this system head-on. He asserted that God called the individual to a particular way of life within and among the world, and so that calling had to be fulfilled within and among the world. He could paint the monastic life as selfish and indulgent compared to the lives of believers who, by working out their calling in the world, served their neighbors.[9]

To understand how this concept and practice of calling took on a deeper and more urgent significance, however, we must turn to Calvin and his followers. As Weber demonstrates for purposes of understanding its economic effects, Calvinism made the doctrine of individual predestination key. Calvinists emphasized the absolute transcendence and sovereignty of God. This God's ways are incomprehensible, mysterious, and incontrovertible. And this is the God who, at the dawn of time, predestined every individual who would exist to everlasting blessedness or everlasting damnation. So, in Weber's words, the meaning of our individual destiny is "hidden in dark mystery which it would be both impossible to pierce and presumptuous to question." Weber believes this doctrine, in its terrible and "magnificent consistency," must have had enormous psychological consequences for those who were enthralled by it. "That was a feeling of the unprecedented inner loneliness of the single individual. In what was for the man of the age of the Reformation the most important thing in his life, his eternal salvation, he was forced to follow his path alone to meet a destiny which had been decreed for him from eternity. No one could help him."[10] No church, no priest, no sacraments, no ritual of confession. The Calvinist relied on unmediated grace; consequently the "Calvinist's intercourse with God was carried on in deep spiritual isolation." Weber offers the example of John Bunyan's pilgrim setting off in his quest for his own salvation. The pilgrim's wife and children cling to him, but he stops his ears to their cries and trudges off alone.[11]

There must have been a great deal of psychological and spiritual pressure here. The afterlife is paramount, and yet God's electing ways are profoundly obscure. In addition, the individual cannot rely for reassurance on the church or any other social system. So how do I know if I am elect? How can I be sure I am in a state of grace? This is excruciating, like waiting on medical tests for cancer and knowing that even once the results come back the physician cannot effectively mediate them for me, and they will be almost impossible to decipher.

Later Protestants would deal pastorally with this pressure in a variety of ways, including, as we will see, direction to a powerful inner feeling and sense of union with the Holy Spirit. But not the earlier Calvinists. With their utterly sovereign and transcendent God, these pastors would not imagine the human vessel in any way containing or supplementing or commingling with the divine energy. But they could and did imagine the divine energy acting on, directing, and controlling the alien human vessel. You could not enter into union with the Holy Spirit, but you might be a "tool" of the Holy Spirit. So individual Calvinists were urged to be conscious of their worldly conduct, the living of their Protestant calling, trusting that their conduct worked for the glory of God because the power of God worked on and guided them from the outside. These Calvinists certainly did not create their salvation, but by fulfilling their callings they attained conviction of their salvation.[12]

It is important to note that the Calvinists fulfilled their calling in the entirety of their lives, not just in any one part or specifically "religious" sphere of life. Before the Reformation a believer, if I can put it this way, was most holy or drew nearest to God through demanding, ascetic prayer or contemplation. With their doctrine of calling and their abolition of monastic orders, Protestants universalized or declericalized asceticism. For the Catholic laity, ascetic acts had been separated from each other or from life generally. In repentance, you might undertake the occasional fast, and you would make confession to a priest monthly or on some other occasional basis. Your asceticism or religious devotion happened at particular times and in particular places, such as the confessional booth. For Protestant laity, on the other hand, asceticism or religious devotion was undertaken in one's calling, and one's calling was nothing less (if a bit more) than one's daily work—everything one did from sunup to sundown. Asceticism had been carefully planned, rationalized and accounted for prior to Protestantism, but only for life in the monastery. Protestantism, and early Calvinism preeminently, wove asceticism into a systematic, carefully calculated program for organizing and shaping the whole lives of an entire

people. From this flows the rationalization of time and admiration of indus-
triousness so necessary for capitalism to thrive.[13]

Thus did the Protestant Ethic enable the spirit of capitalism. Strictly
speaking, it is perhaps more correct to call this a theology of production
than a theology of consumption. For as Weber is at pains to remind us, the
Protestant Ethic was not originally consumer-oriented, let alone hedonis-
tic. In fact it featured a "strict avoidance of all spontaneous enjoyment of
life."[14] Yet I think it fair to say that the early Protestant Ethic at least laid
the groundwork for a theology of consumption by rationalizing and sub-
mitting all of life to the criterion of efficiency, by rendering the making of
money honorable, by isolating or individualizing the believer, and by so
doing turning the believer's attention inward, toward introspection. I make
no global judgment on the Protestant Ethic, and in fact certainly appreciate aspects of it. But as historian Jackson Lears comments, "The consequences were ironic and unintended. The Protestant Ethic provided the
psychological justification for the organizational spirit of rational capitalism; a drive toward systematic control of the inner self eventuated in a
drive toward systematic mastery of the outer world."[15] This "systematic
mastery" is the overly zealous exploitation of the earth now routinely
lamented for its ecological effects.

The ecological was not the only ironic consequence. As John Wesley
worried, the Protestant Ethic must "necessarily produce both industry and
frugality, and these cannot but produce riches. But as riches increase, so
will pride, anger, and love of the world in all of its branches." On the one
hand, he said, "we must exhort all Christians to gain all they can, and to
save all they can; that is, in effect, to grow rich." Yet on the other hand,
"wherever riches have increased, the essence of religion has decreased in
the same proportion."[16] We have here a hint that the line between a theology of production and a theology of consumption quickly and easily blurs.
Determining where the theology of production ends and the theology of
consumption begins is probably as difficult as determining where the snake's
tail begins. I am satisfied to argue that we step into the region of the tail as
soon as the Protestant Ethic moves out of strict Calvinism and into other,
later forms of Protestantism. Pietism would lay more emphasis on enjoyment of salvation in this life than on the ascetic struggle for certainty about
the afterlife. With Puritanism, it would introduce the idea that success in
one's labors was a reassuring sign of God's election. Methodism would put
more emphasis than Calvinism on emotion and teach that certainty of salvation rested on an intense feeling at a conversation that could be pin-
pointed to an exact moment. Baptists would play up the role of individual
conscience and so further tendencies to introspection.[17] With these developments the snake's head is in the tent. And the tail, it seems, is sure to
follow.

The Theology of Consumption

To track the progress of head to tail, we need to switch sociological guides. In 1987 the British sociologist Colin Campbell published in a Weberian vein his *Romantic Ethic and the Spirit of Modern Consumption*. To show how Christian theology and ways of life laid the groundwork for the later Romantic preoccupation with self and the self's pleasures, Campbell focuses on those extremely influential later Calvinists, the Puritans. Earlier Calvinist churches and movements were territorial and Constantinian, closely allied with regional or national authorities and self-admittedly consisting of merely nominal as well as true believers, of the tares mixed with the wheat. The Puritans, of course, wanted to establish a pure church, composed only of genuine believers. To demonstrate one's authentic belief, a confession of faith was necessary but not sufficient. Nor were good works guaranteed to filter out hypocrites. Thus, Campbell writes,

> the Puritans were necessarily drawn to place an ever-greater importance upon signs of saving grace as the crucial ingredient in any test of suitability for membership in the church of Christ. . . . What this meant in practice was that the test adopted was one in which the confession of faith included the declaration of the experience of the work of grace, that is, of how the individual became convinced that he had experienced such an event.[18]

So it is that "an intensely personal, subjective experience" is used to gauge the authenticity of faith. "It is not the individual's knowledge or conduct which is under scrutiny so much as the nature and quality of his inner state of being. The queries raised were typically about such issues as the depth and genuineness of his 'humiliation' or conviction of sin, the authenticity of his grief for his sinfulness, the pervasiveness of doubt, and the continuing bouts of despair."[19] As the historian William Haller put it, Puritans "were taught to follow by intense introspection the working of the law of predestination within their own souls." The "theatre" of the most intense drama imaginable was inside "the human breast."[20] Consequently it comes to pass that a melancholy bearing, self-debasement, and fascination with one's own death were considered outward signs of inward godliness. True faith was associated with a certain "profound emotional sensibility." And "a link was forged between displays of feeling and assumptions about the fundamental spiritual state of an individual which was to long outlive the decline of Calvinism and to influence profoundly the eighteenth-century movements of sensibility."[21]

In short, Campbell argues that Romanticism is in part Puritanism secularized. The eighteenth century saw increases in technology and affluence that lengthened life expectancy and prompted more optimistic attitudes about life and the world. The Enlightenment took hold, and religion was forced to let go, or at least relax its grip. But with secularization, the religiously created emotional sensibility of godly melancholy did not pass away; it was instead transformed. Even as old beliefs in sin, hell, and eternal damnation paled, "there was a reluctance to abandon the subjective states with which they had been associated," since these "religiously generated emotions had become a source of pleasure in themselves." As Campbell observes, "Once convictions become conventions . . . the possibility of emotional self-indulgence is a real one."[22] In describing intense emotion as enjoyable, Campbell is talking about something like our relishing the frights of a horror movie so long as we know there really is no lunatic with a butcher knife behind us, or delighting in an amusement park ride so long as we know that the roller coaster is not going to fly off the track. We pay money to savor the tears we weep, on cushioned theater seats, at a Shakespearean tragedy. So have our feelings become "a source of pleasure in themselves" and, as we will see, the primary consumer "object" of late modernity.

Campbell persuasively argues that the gradual move from conviction to convention, from intense faith to secularization, accounts for the transformation of Calvinist sensibilities into sentimentalist sensibilities. Both sensibilities value similar emotions, but the sentimentalist artificially stimulates emotion for the pleasure it gives. The seventeenth-century terror of death gives way to "a typical eighteenth-century liking for pensive sadness. . . . Death, having lost some of its power to sting, becomes romanticized." As Campbell acutely observes, "One way of looking at this change is to regard the Puritans as having developed a 'taste' for the strong meat of powerful religious emotion, and when their convictions waned, seeking alternative fare with which to satisfy their appetite." Those who inherited the Puritans' mentality "had become addicted to the stimulation of powerful emotions, and were now seeking substitutes for the original."[23]

So it was that gradually and subtly, between 1660 and 1760, the middle classes reinterpreted Protestantism sentimentally rather than Calvinistically. As literary critic Hoxie Neale Fairchild remarks, the influences of the Enlightenment decay the Calvinist's beliefs and leave the Calvinist's descendants with, "in a blurred and softened form, the emotions which his creed had both reflected and fostered. The God above him becomes more shadowy than the God within him, until at last he is left with the basic attitude of sentimentalism—a sense of inward virtue and freedom which must find corroboration in the nature of the universe."[24] This is what Campbell calls the "Other Protestant Ethic." Weber's Protestant Ethic stresses "rationality, instrumentality, industry and achievement."[25] The Other Protestant Ethic stresses fervent feeling, sentimentality, luxurious introspection, and an abiding emphasis on self-fulfillment.

As historian Jackson Lears comments, for those shaped by the Other Protestant Ethic, "a state of constant, feverish, spiritual yearning was the sine qua non of salvation." People were exquisitely attuned to intense emotion and so primed to stimulate it and repeatedly play infinite variations on it. This was the dynamic of deprivation at the heart of expanding consumption: purchase brought momentary satisfaction, followed by dissatisfaction and renewed longing."[26]

This Other Protestant Ethic had a great influence on both evangelical and liberal Protestantism, as well as secular cultures. We do well to remember that Western civilization did not go to bed one night full of faith and wake up the next morning absolutely secular. Even today, of course, faith is not finally vanquished; neither is it unmarked by secularization. In the actual, messy world, Christians—quite apart from their ancestors' sobriety and wariness of hedonism—still had a thing or two to teach the world about consumption. Consider the example of revivalism.

Revivalism and Christian Architects of Consumerism

By underscoring the importance of making a decision for Christ, Charles Finney and other revivalists helped along the sanctification of choice. Revivalism encouraged rapturous feelings and a liquid self, open time and time again to the changes of and the choice for conversion and reconversion. This became translated into a propensity toward "conversion" to new products, a variety of brands and fresh experiences. As Jackson Lears writes, "By popularizing a pattern of self-transformation that would prove easily adaptable to advertisers' rhetorical strategies, evangelical revivalists . . . played a powerful if unwitting part in creating a congenial cultural climate for the rise of national advertising."[27]

In fact, peddlers were fixtures on the fringes of revival meetings, where they hawked counsel and medicines promising transformation of the buyers' lives. Modern advertising grew directly out of the patent medicine trade. Advertising testimonials drew directly on the before-and-after pattern of evangelical testimonies. The difference, as Lears notes, was that "in the patent medicine literature, soul-sickness took bodily form and required physical intervention. Suffering was caused not by sin but by constipation, catarrh, bilious liver, seminal losses, or the ubiquitous 'tired feeling.'" Not unlike a witness at a revival meeting, a Mr. Karl Barton in 1875 confessed that his life before his first bottle of Dr. Chase's nerve pills was a mess. "It was a pretty hard matter for me to call attention to anything in particular. It was a general, debilitated, languid, played-out feeling, and while not painful, depressing."[28] In the ads the nerve pills were, of course, his salvation and road to a new, born-again life.

Other examples might be added to that of revivalism. In fact, Christians were, in a remarkable number of cases, architects of twentieth-century consumer culture. Many influential advertising managers and copywriters, for instance, were the offspring of ministers. But some famous individuals stand out, such as Coca-Cola magnate Asa G. Candler and department-store impresario John Wanamaker.[29]

Candler bought the formula for Coke from its pharmacist-inventor in 1891. Brother to a Methodist bishop and a devout Methodist himself (Emory University's Candler School of Theology bears the family name), Asa, according to his son, made his faith "the central purpose" of his life.

Candler believed Coca-Cola cured his chronic headaches and promoted it with something like evangelistic zeal. "If people knew the good qualities of Coca-Cola as I know them," he said, "it would be necessary for us to lock the doors of our factories and have a guard with a shotgun" to control demand. In such spirit, he liked to conclude sales meetings with a group singing of "Onward Christian Soldiers."

Coca-Cola was one of the earliest commodities to be massively advertised. In 1912, the Advertising Club of America declared it the best-advertised product in the United States. Economic historian Richard Tedlow believes that Candler's breadth of marketing vision grew out of his involvement in national and international missions.

John Wanamaker, founder of Wanamaker department stores, was a lifelong, intensely faithful Presbyterian. He was an inveterate Bible reader and a close friend and supporter of Dwight L. Moody. He was also heavily involved in the Sunday-school movement and refused the sale of wine and liquor in his stores "on principle."

At the same time, Wanamaker, more than any other merchant of his time, brought French fashion and merchandising to America. He had the country's biggest furniture showrooms and was pleased that he could translate "luxuries into commodities or into necessities" more rapidly than any other merchant.

From the 1910s until his death in 1922, Wanamaker was also a main player in the commodification of the Christian holy days of Christmas and Easter. At Christmas time, Wanamaker turned the grand court of his Philadelphia store into a veritable cathedral, replete with stained glass, stars and angelic statuary. The effect was so churchlike that gentlemen, upon entering, instinctively doffed their hats. The store was also sacredly decked out at Easter, when Wanamaker displayed giant paintings of *Christ before Pilate* and *Christ on Calvary.*

This brief look at revivalism and such men as Candler and Wanamaker shows that, following historian R. Laurence Moore, Protestantism in clear if sometimes strange ways "was excellent preparation for the pleasures of . . . modern consumer hedonism." It sanctified choice. It brought Christianity lock, stock, barrel, and Bible into the marketplace and redefined faith in terms of the marketplace. It refined close observation and exquisite stimulation of feelings, and "since the Protestant imagination was free to venture forth on its own without the intervention and control of priests, it luxuriated in novelty."[30]

Making Consumers

Such examples indicate that Christians, acting out of particular Christian understandings and motivations, played an important role in the creation and growth of consumerism. If our Christian predecessors, using Christian means, helped create it, then likewise we might use Christian means to correct, modify, and offset its ill effects. That said, it would of course be a gross distortion to act as if Protestantism alone invented and sustained consumer capitalism. It is crucial to note other historical factors essential to the birth and growth of consumerism.

In terms of the push and pull of the everyday economy, historians are agreed that production-oriented capitalism moved on to become consumption-oriented capitalism because it was so successful. We need to recall that until the twentieth century most American homes were sites not only of consumption but also of production. Even as late as 1850, six of ten people worked on farms. They made most of their own tools, built their homes and barns, constructed their furniture, wove and sewed their clothes, grew crops and raised animals, chopped wood, and made candles to provide heat and light. One nineteenth-century Massachusetts farmer, for instance, produced so much of what he needed at home that he never spent more than ten dollars a year.[31]

The Industrial Revolution changed all that, very quickly. As the factory system and mass production became dominant over the space of decades, it displaced home production by drawing and forcing millions into wage labor, by driving out cottage industry, and by cheaply producing a host of commodities formerly made at home. From 1859 to 1899 the value of manufactured goods in the United States shot from $1.9 billion to $13 billion annually. Factories grew from 140,000 to 512,000.[32]

Suddenly this economic system could produce many, many more goods than the existing population, with its set habits and means, could afford and consume. For instance, when James Buchanan Duke procured just two Bonsack cigarette machines, he could immediately produce 240,000 cigarettes a day—more than the entire U.S. market smoked. When Henry P.

Crowell of Quaker Oats built an automated mill in 1882, most Americans ate meat and potatoes, not cereal, for breakfast. Such overproduction was the rule, not the exception, throughout the economy. From flour manufacturers to stovemakers, there was a widespread and acute recognition that the amount of goods available had far surpassed the number of buyers for those goods. There was, in short, a huge gap between production and consumption. How to close it? Industrial production's momentum was on the rise, so cutting production was not feasible. Manufacturers decided instead to pump up consumption, to in effect invert neoclassical economics and increase demand to meet supply.[33]

However, manufacturers realized consumption was a way of life that had to be taught and learned. People had to move away from habits of strict thriftiness toward habits of ready spending. To be adequate consumers, they had to depart from a dependence on traditional skills, on production by family and artisans, on local merchants. In turn they had to convert to a trust and reliance on a multitude of products and services manufactured and promoted from far away, by complete strangers.

By trial and error, manufacturers arrived at methods for just such training and rehabilitation. They instituted money-back guarantees and credit buying. They introduced brand names and mascots to give their mass-produced goods an appealing "personality." They introduced mail order and, as in the case of Sears, coached and reassured semiliterate customers to order by post ("Tell us what you want in your own way, written in any language, no matter whether good or poor writing, and the goods will promptly be sent to you").[34] And, of course, they advertised.

Advertising and the Cultivation of Consumers

As we have seen, many other factors were important in the rise of consumerism, but since advertising is the most insistent and undisguised face of advanced consumption, it merits special attention.

Until the late nineteenth century, advertising had been mainly informational. Ad pages in eighteenth-century newspapers looked like the classifieds in today's papers. There were no pictures, and rather like news items, the ads simply did such things as announce when a shipment of rice would arrive from the Carolinas. But faced with a mass market and the crisis of overproduction, manufacturers by the late nineteenth century initiated an advertising revolution. New advertising departed the realm of information, incorporating images and a host of persuasive tactics. It was, and remains, a primary tool in teaching people how to be consumers.

Colgate, for instance, used advertising to teach people who had never heard of toothpaste that they should brush their teeth daily. King Gillette, the inventor of the disposable razor, coaxed men to shave daily and to do it themselves instead of seeing a barber. His ads included shaving lessons ("Note the angle stroke"). Eastman Kodak used ads to tutor the masses in making the portable camera their "family historian." Food manufacturers such as Shredded Wheat published cookbooks training housewives to cook with exact measures of (branded) products. Newly empowered by preservatives and far-flung distribution networks, Domino Gold Syrup sought in 1919 to explicitly "educate" people that syrup was not only for wintertime pancakes. Said the sales manager, "Our belief is that the entire year is syrup season and the people must be educated to believe this is a fact."[35]

The effectiveness of advertising in selling any specific product remains debatable. What cannot be doubted is that early advertising successfully introduced an expansive array of products and services, playing a key role in the replacement of traditional home production by store-bought commodities. Furthermore, advertising and related media have served and still serve as important shapers of an ethos in which the good life is attained through the constant acquisition and consumption of new products and new experiences.

Indeed, advertisers soon recognized that they must not simply cater to preexisting needs but create new needs. As Crowell of Quaker Oats noted, "[My aim in advertising] was to do educational and constructive work so as to awaken an interest in and create a demand for cereals where none existed." And as *The Thompson Red Book on Advertising* put it more generally in 1901, "Advertising aims to teach people that they have wants, which they did not recognize before, and where such wants can be best supplied." The nonadvertisers at whom ads were targeted intuitively realized what advertising was about early on. Said one newspaper reader in 1897, not so long ago people "skipped [ads] unless some want compelled us to read, while now we read to find out what we really want."[36]

Advertisers did not act alone in the training of consumers. Government began in the early twentieth century to solidify and boost the newly emerged strength of business corporations, capping this alliance with Herbert Hoover's expansion of the Department of Commerce in the 1920s.[37] Schools quite self-consciously cooperated with corporations in molding young consumers. One 1952 Whirlpool short subject, for instance, featured three teenage girls around a kitchen table, at work on a report about the emancipation of women. Did emancipation mean winning the vote or assuming property and other legal rights? No, the girls decide, as the host rises from the table to attend a shiny washing machine. Real emancipation came with release from the drudgery of chores, from washing machines and dryers that liberated women from clotheslines and "dark basements."

Business Screen magazine gave clear instruction for the film's use in its review: "Some good clean selling takes place during this half-hour. . . . The film will have special appeal to women's groups of all kinds and to home economics classes from teenage on up."[38]

In short, consumers were made, not born.

What Consumption Is

Into the nineteenth century, then, advertising and consumption were oriented to raw information and basic needs. It was only in the late nineteenth century, with the maturation of consumer capitalism, that a shift was made toward the cultivation of unbounded desire. We must appreciate this to realize that late modern consumption, or consumption as we now know it, is not fundamentally about materialism or the consumption of physical goods. Affluence and consumer-oriented capitalism have moved us well beyond the undeniable efficiencies and benefits of refrigerators and indoor plumbing. Instead, in a fun-house world of ever-proliferating wants and exquisitely unsatisfied desire, consumption has become, most profoundly, the consumption of novelty. As Colin Campbell puts it, individuals consume for the "pleasure which they derive from the self-illusory experiences that they construct out of the images or associations attached to products."[39]

Sex appeal, for instance, sells everything from candy bars to toothpaste. (Recently a cancer detection ad on the back of a Christian magazine headlined, "Before you read this, take your clothes off," then in fine print counseled how to do bodily self-examinations.) Cigarette and alcohol ads do not even depict their product being consumed, but instead prime us to associate them with robust cowboys and spectacular mountain vistas. By 1989 the American Association of Advertising Agencies explicitly stated that consumer perceptions "are a fundamental part of manufacturing the product—as much as size, shape, color, flavor, design, or raw materials."[40]

As early as 1909 an advertising manager for Winton Motor Cars complained, "When a man buys an automobile he purchases a specific entity, made of so much iron, steel, brass, copper, leather, wood, and horsehair, put together in a specific form and manner. . . . Why attract his attention to the entity by something that is foreign thereto? Has the car itself not sufficient merit to attain that attention? Why suggest 'atmosphere,' which is something he cannot buy?"[41]

By 1925 "atmosphere" no longer seemed beyond the reach of the market. In that year advertising copywriter John Starr Hewitt wrote, "No one has ever in his life bought a mere piece of merchandise—per se. What he buys is the satisfaction of a physical need or the gratification of some dream about his life."[42] In the same year Earnest Elmo Calkins, the cofounder of the Calkins and Holden ad agency, observed, "I have spent much of my life trying to teach the business man that beauty has a dollars and cents value, because I feel that only thus will it be produced in any quantity in a commercial age." Calkins recognized that "modernism offered the opportunity of expressing the inexpressible, of suggesting not so much the motor car as speed, not so much a gown as style, not so much a compact as beauty."[43] All, of course, with a dollars and cents value attached.

Thus, for modern consumers, speed, style, beauty, sex, love, spirituality have all become categories of ideals to be evoked and sampled at will by selecting from a vast array of products, services, and commodified experiences. Colin Campbell considers contemporary tourism a prime example. Tourism as an industry and a commodity depends for its survival on an insatiable yearning for "ever-new objects to gaze at." The same can be said for shopping, spectator sports, concert-going, movie-going, and other quintessential "consumer" activities. "Modern consumers will desire a novel rather than a familiar product because this enables them to believe that its acquisition and use will supply experiences they have not encountered to date in reality."[44]

Moreover, as the many now blissfully lost in cyberspace will attest, reality can be more inconvenient and less purely pleasurable than virtual reality. Virtual camping is camping without mosquitoes and smoky clothes and two days of caked-on perspiration. Virtual war is war with some glory and thrill of conquest, but no stench of rotting corpses and no real risk of one's getting killed.

In 1627 Francis Bacon's *New Atlantis* dreamed of a utopia in which technology could adjust growing seasons and create synthetic fruit tastier and better looking than natural fruit.[45] In our culture the New Atlantis has, after a fashion, come into being, and its plenty includes cosmeticized fruit, artificial sweeteners, nonalcoholic beer, and fat-free junk food.

Such matters remind us, as Campbell writes, that "actual consumption . . . is . . . likely to be a literally disillusioning experience, since real products cannot possibly supply the same quality of perfected pleasure as that which attends imaginatively enjoyed experiences."[46] So we modern consumers are perpetually dissatisfied. Fulfillment and lasting satisfaction are forever just out of reach. And if we cannot escape completely to cyberspace, we reach for and grab again and again the product or commodified experience that provides temporary pleasure. We are profoundly schooled and thousands of times daily reinforced—remember, the average American is exposed to more than sixteen thousand sales messages daily—into an insatiability that is, as the theologian Miroslav Volf remarks, "unique to modernity."[47] Insatiability itself is as old as humanity, or at least the fall of humanity. Unique to modern capitalism and consumerism are the idealization and constant encouragement of insatiability—the deification of dissatisfaction.

So it is that consumption has devoured classical Christian theology, and with it much of classical Christian practice. From the theology of production we moved to a theology of consumption. But consumption all too easily becomes an end in itself. Economics and the consumerism it serves are, as the economist Robert Nelson candidly admits, "our modern theology." Modernity is that age that has believed in the future against the past, in limitless progress that would eliminate not just the practical but the moral and spiritual problems of humanity. Many of the major concerns and practices of classical Christianity were accordingly redefined along economic lines. Material scarcity and the resulting conflict over precious resources were seen as the sources of human sinfulness. So economic progress and the building of consumer societies have "represented the route of salvation to a new heaven on earth." Economic efficiency has replaced the providence of God. Christian missionaries traveled to spread the gospel; economic theology has missionaries such as the Peace Corps and international development agencies delivering the good news of "economic progress, rational knowledge, and human redemption." Christianity understood history's supreme revelatory moment to be the coming of Christ. Economic theology considers it to be the discoveries of modern science and technology. Twentieth-century religious wars are no longer fought between Roman Catholics and various Protestants but "among men often inspired by Marxist, fascist, capitalist, and still other messages of economic salvation."[48]

The Importance of Character

"Whoever has the power to project a vision of the good life and make it prevail," writes historian William Leach, "has the most decisive power of all. In its sheer quest to produce and sell goods cheaply in constantly growing volume and at higher profit levels, American business, after 1890, acquired such power and has kept it ever since."[49] Since consumer capitalism—today not just in America but around the world—so effectively promotes its version of the good life, and since consumers are made rather than born, a Christian response demands a consideration of character.

That is, every culture or way of life requires a certain kind of person— a "character" with fitting attitudes, skills, and motivations—to sustain and advance the good life as that culture knows it. Thus Sparta was concerned to shape its citizens in the character of the warrior, Aristotle hoped for a polity that would make aristocrats, and twentieth-century America charged its public schools with the task of instilling the American way of life in their students.

In the postwar boom days of 1955, retailing analyst Victor Lebow echoed his advertising predecessors, declaring,

> Our enormously productive economy . . . demands that we make consumption our way of life, that we convert the buying and use of goods into rituals, that we seek our spiritual satisfaction, our ego satisfaction, in consumption. . . . We need things consumed, burned up, worn out, replaced, and discarded at an ever increasing rate.[50]

Can there be any doubt that we now live in the world Lebow prophesied and desired? That shopping has become one of our signal rituals is facetiously but tellingly betrayed in such slogans as "I shop, therefore I am," and "They came, they saw, they did a little shopping," scrawled on the Berlin Wall shortly after East Germans were allowed to pass freely into West Germany. Planned obsolescence, installment buying, and credit cards—all creations of this century—were key means to making consumption a way of life.

Our language is one significant indication that consumption is a way of life. We are encouraged to see and interpret more and more of our activities in terms of consumption. People who go to movies are no longer "audiences" but "consumers;" people who go to school are no longer "students" but "educational consumers." Those who visit the physician are no longer "patients," those who go to church are no longer "worshipers," those who go to libraries and bookstores are no longer "readers," those who go to restaurants are no longer "diners." All are as frequently, and in many respects more fundamentally, designated "consumers." Social scientist Daniel Miller comments,

> As is often the case in such shifts in the language of legitimation, this represents a movement in ideology with specific political implications. Increasingly in market-driven politics, all action is being termed consumption choice. No account is made of the relative access to resources that make choices illusory or real. . . . There need be no concern with the imperatives behind consumption, the moralities, the experiential aspects of consumption or its responsibilities, since all these are discounted by the economists' notion of individual rationalities that simply secure self-interested needs through choice.[51]

The church must examine and challenge consumerism at exactly this point. What sort of people would consumer capitalism have us be? What are the key character traits of the consumer par excellence? And how do these stack up against the standards and aims of Christian character?

The Character of the Consumer

As we have observed, the consumer is schooled in insatiability. He or she is never to be satisfied, at least not for long. The consumer is taught that persons consist basically of unmet needs that can be requited by commodified goods and experiences. Accordingly, the consumer should think first and foremost of himself or herself and meeting his or her felt needs. The consumer is taught to value above all else freedom, defined as a vast array of choices.

One of the most striking ways we are trained and reinforced in the consumptive way of life is exactly through a flood of ever-proliferating choices. In 1976 the average American supermarket carried nine thousand products; today it stocks thirty thousand. The typical produce section in 1975 had sixty-five items; today it stocks 285. The median household with cable now picks up more than thirty TV stations. During the 1980s a new periodical appeared for every day of every year.[52]

Is this all bad? Certainly not. As a movie lover, I can tell you that the typical video store stocking five thousand videos is more likely than another stocking one thousand to carry first-rate foreign films. Most of us can affirm much about the undergirding philosophy of freedom as noncoercive choice, and surely the diversity of commodities and commodified experiences can (although not necessarily) foster increasing openness to people and cultures different from our own. Yet we are so trained and reinforced in understanding freedom as choice that we fail to question if many of our choices are actually significant. Is quality of life really improved by having four rather than two brands of catsup to choose from? Is rock troubadour Bruce Springsteen too far from the mark when he complains of TV that there are "fifty-seven channels and nothing on"?

No less important, we have become obtuse in noticing a whole array of significant possibilities that are eliminated when consumer choice rules all. As Alan Ehrenhalt relates in marvelous detail in his book *The Lost City*, the worship of choice and the spread of the market mentality have without doubt weakened communities. These developments have dissolved locally owned banks, newspapers, grocery stores, and restaurants. As late as the 1950s, "the very act of shopping was embedded in the web of long-term relationships between customer and merchant, relationships that were more important than the price of a particular item at a particular time. The sense of permanence that bound politicians to organizations, or corporations to communities, reached down to the most mundane transactions of neighborhood commercial life."[53]

This is a way of life that we can no longer choose, even should we want, for it has been practically obliterated. Instead, as Ehrenhalt eloquently concludes:

> Too many of the things we do in our lives, large and small, have come to resemble channel surfing, marked by a numbing and seemingly endless progression from one option to the next, all without the benefit of a chart, logistical or moral, because there are simply too many choices and no one to help sort them out. We have nothing to insulate ourselves against the perpetual temptation to try one more choice, rather than to live with what is on the screen in front of us. [54]

The Character of the Christian

Classical Christianity, as we have earlier observed, was wary of insatiability. There was, in fact, only one acceptable sort of insatiability: the unquenchable desire for relationship with the God of Israel and Jesus Christ. In the psalmist's words, "As a deer longs for flowing streams, so my soul longs for you, O God" (Ps. 42:1). Augustine would surely consider our consumer compulsions a symptom of disordered desire, of the sort of desire that should be directed only to God instead of to God's creatures. This is theologically a serious matter indeed, since such disordered desire can verge on, if not become outright, idolatry.

Additionally, though Christianity offers a tremendously fulfilling way of life for the individual, it does not teach or promise fulfillment construed in the individualistic terms. The church ultimately hopes and yearns for the fulfillment of all creation through the rightful worship of God and fulfillment of God's kingdom. Thus the initial petition of the Lord's Prayer implores (in the first-person plural), "Our Father, who art in heaven, hallowed be thy name; thy kingdom come, thy will be done, on earth as it is in heaven." Likewise Paul sees the church as a formative community whose members are variously gifted by the Holy Spirit "for the common good" (1 Cor. 12:7). The Christian hope to overcome evil and death is not, according to the New Testament, for the escape of the individual soul to heaven (or of individual pleasure fulfilled in a consumeristic heaven on earth) but for the creation of a new heaven and earth and, at that occasion, the corporate resurrection of all the blessed.

Finally, it bears mentioning that the consumer way of life fosters a number of virtues at loggerheads with many Christian virtues. Can we simultaneously seek and to some degree realize both instant gratification and patience? What about instant gratification and self-control? Is gentleness cultivated in an ethos that must become ever more coarse and gross to excite overloaded, jaded consumers, or joy cultivated by an economic system that deifies dissatisfaction? Since these virtues are at the heart of Christian character, they deserve more extensive consideration. We can explore these matters in more detail by turning to a related, cardinal Christian virtue that the other virtues are all rooted in: fidelity.

Fidelity and the Consumer Way of Life

Among other things, the Christian practice of marriage is an exercise in the virtue of fidelity. Christians aspire to be enduringly faithful to one particular God, not to a succession or collection of gods, and in this manner a Christian marries and commits himself or herself exclusively to a particular mate—"till death do us part." Yet the consumer marries because marriage will serve his or her interests as he or she understands them at the moment. Commitment in the Christian way of life is an ideal and a goal; commitment in the consumer way of life is an instrumental and typically temporary good. Like any careful contract, marriage in the consumer ethos should continually be open to reevaluation. If at any point it fails to promote the self-actualization of one spouse or the other, the option of ending the partnership must be available. In the Christian way of life, lifetime monogamy makes sense. In the consumer way of life, serial polygamy (a succession of mates over a lifetime) is a much more sensible practice. A high increase in divorce rates signals many things, but one of them surely is that consumption is our way of life.

Another sign of our commitment to consumption is the profound societal confusion and ambivalence about children. On the one hand, we idealize children as innocents and perhaps sentimentalize them more than any other society in history. On the other hand, as the sociologist David Popenoe bluntly says, "American communities are strikingly unfit for children." Children want and need social stability, yet our communities are "transient, anonymous, diverse and increasingly unfriendly to children."[55] Children need communities in which they are physically secure, yet even those of us in comparatively safe suburbs can hardly allow our younger children to walk to school by themselves. Children need communities that are accessible to them, yet there are few self-contained neighborhoods, so that most activities require automobile, and thus adult, transportation.

The fact is that under the sway of the consumer ethos we have shifted from child-centered to adult-centered families, fostering higher divorce rates and constructing communities that often subordinate the needs of the young to the needs (and felt needs) of grownups. Frankly, consumption as a way of life renders it difficult to justify having children, since children represent the commitment of a lifetime. In the wonderfully apt phrase of novelist Michael Dorris, children "hold us hostage to the future." They limit a parent's mobility, dictate through their needs the spending of much parental money, and create "agendas" a parent otherwise would never have imagined, let alone chosen. Attempting to stay true to consumption as a way of life, we soberly build daycare centers that label children Precious Commodities, fixate on the monetary costs of rearing a child from diapers through college, and seriously wonder whether or not we should "force" our faith and morality on our children.

Beginning the Resistance

I hope it is abundantly clear by now that consumerism is an ethos or way of life that envelops and in many ways defines our world. There are aspects of consumer capitalism that Christians can certainly appreciate and defend, but it is so dominant and unquestioned in our setting that I have emphasized characteristics and tendencies that bring it into tension with the faith. Consumer capitalism grew over centuries; it will not change overnight. People of faith living amid overweening consumerism have a responsibility to resist where they can, to cultivate the good life as it is understood in the Christian tradition. So we are impelled both theologically and strategically to devote attention to the peculiarly and explicitly Christian formation of character, to building a Christian way of life or, if you will, culture.

To get a sense of how Christians can undertake such a resistance, I visited believers who represent three socioeconomic classes: the affluent (Malcolm Street), the middle class (Lendol and Kathy Knight Calder), and the voluntary poverty of intentional Christian communities (the Bruderhof). The financial means and lifestyles of some of these folk are closer to my own than others, but I found that I could learn something from each about vital Christian responses to the challenge of consumerism.

Intentionally Vulnerable

Malcolm Street grew up in the wealth of a Texas oil family. At least in financial terms, he has always been well off. Yet he is anything but a comfortable or complacent man. During our three days together, he repeatedly prodded me to ask him the hard questions, to push the line of faithful logic past the point of his own comfort. Congruently, his reading is engaged and critical. Browsing through Christian magazines in his apartment, I found margins laden with scribbled comments ("Enlightened social policy won't get it. Only Lordship will.") and grades ("B+," "A+," "A++") assigned to articles in the table of contents. With such glimpses of Street, I was not surprised to learn that his vigorous confrontation of consumerism and the temptations of wealth grew out of determined questioning and examination.

During the fifties, while studying finance in college, he had a summer job at a bank in Fort Worth. Upon graduation he was given a full-time position, and by the time he was in his late twenties Street was an upper-level officer. It was then that he had a conversion that brought to life the Methodism in which he had been reared.

He noticed that several of the older, economically successful men and women he counseled financially were deflated, sometimes despairing, wondering (in the words of the old Peggy Lee song), "Is that all there is?" Street says, "All their lives they had focused on climbing the ladder, only to find when they got to the top that it was leaning against the wrong building."

The young banker then began a process of reexamination. Intense and willingly self-critical as I have noted, Street reacted to the prologue of 1 Corinthians 13 by deciding he had a "calloused heart." He realized, among other things, that it was too easy for the affluent to be disconnected from the pains and needs of "ordinary" folk. "If the public school goes downhill, we send our kids to a private one. If the neighborhood gets violent, we move behind the walls of a peaceful one. If we don't get satisfactory medical care, we switch doctors."

Now fifty-three, Malcolm Street has in the intervening decades repeatedly exposed himself to the neediest of the needy, with mission trips to such places as Haiti, Liberia, and Honduras. He devotes thirty percent of his time to service on the boards of Christian organizations. He believes that money has a purpose—"to make friends for God"—which in practice means that business is about "maximizing human benefit, not profit." Profits, he says, "are essential if services are to be proportional to human needs, but they are not the ultimate 'bottom line.'" In keeping with that perspective, he has over the last thirteen years built and operated "assisted living" apartments for the frail elderly. Determined to make himself vulnerable to the needs of those who are not as insulated as he, Street lives on the premises of a Fort Worth complex called the Courtyards, where he leads a weekly Bible study for residents and meets monthly with male residents for breakfast.

Street's way of life demonstrates that a kind of intentional vulnerability can help revivify sensibilities and empathies dulled by satiating overconsumption. A degree of affluence not only insulates us from a keen awareness of our limits and mortality but, through indulgence, can coarsen the senses of sight, sound, taste, smell, and touch so that we require increasingly gross stimuli to experience pleasure. To help others and to reawaken our truest senses, we can regularly draw close to those suffering from want, sickness, or loneliness. Street has also learned from spiritual director Henri Nouwen the importance of periodic spiritual retreats. To withdraw for a weekend of vulnerability to silence, away from television, radio and bookshelves, is to force a reconnection with things deeper than the inundating ephemera of mass consumer culture.

Finally, Street emphasizes that generosity is a crucial, life-enriching habit for wealthy Christians. "Giving proportionately to your ability is a way to force yourself out of the insulation of affluence, beyond your comfort zone. For the upper-income Christian, a ten percent tithe is just the threshold of your capacity to give 'to the least of these.'"

Hearing the Water Speak

Until their recent move to a college in Illinois, Lendol and Kathy Knight Calder lived near New London, New Hampshire, where Lendol taught history at Colby-Sawyer College. I visited them at their New Hampshire home, nestled in the White Mountains and a five-minute walk from a breathtakingly beautiful mountain lake.

Kathy and Lendol, who met in a college InterVarsity chapter, have had their sensitivity to consumerism heightened by Lendol's doctoral dissertation on that subject. Their modest New Hampshire home, also occupied by their two small children, was filled with wall-hung quilts and furniture passed down from family members.

They worry that consumer culture tends to mediate all "reality." People in a mass consumer society watch television and movies created, promoted, and distributed by other people, they listen to prerecorded music rather than make their own, and they buy birthday cards instead of writing a poem. Consumer reality, then, is secondhand and often sanitized—you can, for instance, "play" basketball by watching Michael Jordan without ever straining a muscle or touching a ball. Lendol is struck that most of his CSC students could look out their dorm windows at mountains that they might hike, ski, and climb, but instead spent their time watching television and listening to CDs. Likewise, on a splendid spring day in New Hampshire, "in the safest place in the world," he says, residents of his town exercised on a treadmill inside a gymnasium.

In contrast, the Calders try to take full advantage of their natural surroundings. Lendol runs, bikes and, when in New Hampshire, climbs mountains. He and Kathy take frequent walks with their children. They encourage the kids to appreciate and participate in the wonder of creation. (One afternoon we walked to the lake, still and serene as a mirror, and three-year-old daughter Abigail proclaimed that the lake was not talking or laughing today. Lendol explained that they have discussed how different parts of creation "speak" to God.)

Kathy and Lendol agree that consumer culture reigns partly because it so thoroughly defines time for most people. In response, they try to pay more attention to natural and liturgical rhythms. As Episcopalians, they prize the church year on this count, believing it provides a significant alternative to consumer holidays and the values they promote. In Kathy's words, the weeks leading up to Christmas are in the church year a time for penitence, not "stuffing your face." During Advent the Calders eat more simply, so that they might truly feast at Christmas.

Such appreciative celebration is reinforced by the cultivation of gratitude. Consumer culture would have us feel constantly unsatisfied. In response, Kathy practices gratitude as a kind of spiritual discipline. In difficult times, such as when she is tempted to feel dissatisfied, she sometimes lists simple, basic things she has enjoyed that day but easily taken for granted. "Thank you for the roof over my head," she prays. "Thank you for the good, warm bed I slept in last night. Thank you for the cup of tea I had at breakfast. Thank you for my husband." As the list lengthens, she finds herself less desperately in need of a new dress or book.

Like Malcolm Street, the Calders emphasize the importance of generosity. While the consumer mentality focuses on the immediate and ceaseless gratification of our own desires, Lendol and Kathy have found gift-giving an excellent and enjoyable way to resist that constant inward pull. They present gifts not just on birthdays, but to friends on special occasions or to those who welcome them into their homes overnight.

In all this I was perhaps most impressed that the Calders' down-to-earth attempts to resist and reshape consumer culture were undergirded by a profound sense that they (and other like-minded Christians) are in this struggle for the long haul. Lendol suggests one of the best analogues to resistance of consumer culture is the challenge of Eastern European Christians and intellectuals to communism. They did not, in the apparently "small" and mundane actions of their lives, set out to overthrow communism. In fact, many have since said they expected to live the rest of their days under the sway of communism and recognized that they were a part of a system they considered the Big Lie. Yet they stood against it when and where they could, and one thing eventually led to another.

Likewise, we Western Christians cannot escape consumer culture. We are part of it and in many ways (again, not all for ill) molded by it. The Christians of the East remind us that even small exercises in resistance are significant. They open our imaginations, and who knows where that will take us, or our children, or our children's children?

VCRs and Song

The Bruderhof is a collection of eight communities in the Eastern United States and in England, most made up of three hundred to four hundred men, women, and children, and descended from the Anabaptist tradition of the Hutterian Brethren. Members hand over all personal wealth (including automobiles and inheritances) upon entering and make major life decisions, such as where to live, with the assistance of the "hof." I visited the Woodcrest and Pleasant View communities in upstate New York.

What most forcefully struck this outsider is that the Bruderhof is a kind of family monasticism. Marriage is vigorously encouraged, and since members do not practice birth control, most families have six to eight children. Children are prized as children but also as exemplars of true Christian spirituality—Bruderhofers take very seriously Matthew 18:3, "Unless you change and become like children, you will never enter the kingdom of heaven."

The Bruderhof is certainly a radical response to consumer capitalism; this only underlines how profoundly pervasive and penetrating that system is. The Bruderhofers in no way think it can be completely avoided, nor that all aspects of it should be. They operate thriving businesses, providing furniture and play equipment for preschools. On visiting their operations at Woodcrest, I found twenty-some men and women seated at computers, the women wearing telephone headsets over their characteristic Bruderhof headscarves, all taking orders from around the country. I overheard two computer specialists discussing how they might find an out-of-print book via the Internet and talked with the Bruderhof equivalent of a business manager (they do not go for titles) about what he called a looming "paradigm shift" in preschool furniture.

Still, the Bruderhof's communitarian way of life enables members to be much more judicious in their appropriation of consumeristic technologies and lifestyle than is the typical North American Christian. When I asked elder Christoph Arnold for an example of a consumer technology that the Bruderhof tried and then quit, he thought only briefly before he replied, "VCRs. We had VCRs for a while, but then we noticed the children weren't singing. They weren't playing and running and making up songs. They wanted to put in a tape and sit in front of the TV. So we locked up the VCRs. Now the children are singing again."

In such ways the Bruderhof exemplifies the importance of a culture that encourages and supports practices alternative to a pervasive and powerful consumerism. Although most Christians may not be prepared to relinquish the degree of autonomy necessary to be a Bruderhofer (I confess I am not), we can take steps toward openness and accountability that may loosen the uncontested stranglehold of consumeristic attitudes.

After all, focusing on consumption only or primarily as an issue for individuals plays right into the consumption ethos (which, as we have seen, was partly created by an overly individualized and introspective Christianity). For instance, one of the most popular and enduring responses to Christian worries over materialism has been the counsel that the Christian may hold any amount of possessions so long as he or she has the right attitude—an inner detachment—toward those possessions. There is surely much value in this approach, but we have at the same time left the assessment of *genuine* inner detachment up to the isolated, individual Christian. (Ask yourself how much you actually know, in some detail, about any other believer's salary or tithing.) Thus any authority the faith has in regard to our economic behavior is entirely privatized.

As Robert Wuthnow indicates (and Bruderhofers would surely agree), in practice this amounts to complete capitulation to consumerism. Attitude and behavior are of course not so easily separable. Nor are we wise to think that we can accurately assess our attitudes in solitude, apart from the counsel and discernment of others. With such powerful social forces as the market and the media constantly exhorting us to excesses of consumption, it is ludicrous to think the most viable and faithful response is to face these forces as an isolated individual or family.

Yet the taboo on discussing what we do with our money is so strong that according to Wuthnow's data, churchgoers are less likely than the general population to discuss their finances with someone else—and less likely yet to discuss finances with a fellow Christian![56] Consumerism will continue to exercise undue influence over Christians until we desecrate this unholy taboo and stop regarding our economic lives as an entirely private matter, finding ways to open our wallets and checkbooks in front of trusted Christians. In this and in so many other ways, we need what Wuthnow calls a "critical and *collective* resistance."[57]

The Bruderhof, by its radical embodiment of faith, hopes to call other Christians to just such a critical and collective resistance—however different it may look from their own.

Whither Stewardship?

Malcolm Street, the Calders, and the Bruderhof are all fine examples of Christian stewardship, of spending time, money, and the resources of the earth for the service of God. Yet, though *stewardship* has been used since the 1970s to encapsulate the dominant Christian response to issues of materialism and environmental crises, I have not mentioned the term until now.

There is a reason for this. In the last two decades the concept has come in for considerable (and often effective) criticism from many angles. A number of Christian environmentalists, among others, have urged the church to dispense with the term altogether. I agree that in our current setting, without careful attention, *stewardship* can be too easily co-opted and subverted by the consumer ethos. But stewardship has a genuine and dignified Christian pedigree. I do not think it can be dismissed without loss, but it would be better complemented and corrected with another venerable biblical concept—that of priesthood.

Priestly Stewardship

Priesthood is a biblical notion of such centrality that it might be said biblical narrative operates by a kind of priestly logic. That is to say that priesthood most fundamentally has to do with Israel being chosen by God to declare and exemplify the will of God to creation, and in turn to represent the needs and praise of all creation to God. This is expressed most concisely in Exodus 19:6, when Yahweh tells Moses that he is Creator and owner of the whole earth, but Israel "shall be for me a priestly kingdom and a holy nation."

This priestly logic is such that Israel's status as "a light unto the nations" is necessary for Yahweh to be revealed to the nations. Without Israel's engagement with God, and the telling of the story of that engagement, this God simply will not be known by the nations. Priestly logic also entails that Israel's witness cannot be interpreted individualistically. Jewish political scientist Gordon Lafer observes:

> The institutions of solidarity that mark off Jews' commitments to one another from their more minimal obligations to outsiders are not designed to be applied as universal law governing relations among all people, but rather to be reiterated within each particular nation. This, then, is the universalist mission of Judaism: not to be "a light unto all individuals," not to establish an international system of justice, but rather to teach specific nations how to live *as* a nation.[58]

The church is expected to live by this same priestly logic, so that in 1 Peter 2:9 it is designated "a chosen race, a royal priesthood, a holy nation." Just as Israel must tell and embody its story to make known its God, so must the church tell and embody Israel's story and the story of Jesus Christ. Thus theologian George Lindbeck asserts that the church is called to an ecclesiology "more Jewish than anything else." And against individualistic conceptions of this representative and mediatorial priesthood, Lindbeck writes, "It is above all by the character of its communal life that [the church] witnesses, that it proclaims the gospel and serves the world."[59]

Complementing stewardship with priesthood is helpful in confronting consumerism because it helps Christians retain the classical and uniquely God-centered basis of our stewardship.[60] *Stewardship* today can have a decidedly managerial tone to it and in fact is often employed in purely secular fashion. Yet Christians are stewards not simply or primarily for a corporation or for humanity, but for God. And though Christian stewardship has its individual component, it is most fundamentally a corporate or communal stewardship.[61] Luther's priesthood of all believers, understood as he intended it, means that we mediate God's care to other Christians and to all humanity. Priestly stewardship can remind us that the fundamental Christian witness is not that of the isolated individual but that of the church.

Priesthood can protect stewardship from another destructive vulnerability. Since the 1980s, stewardship has met with increasing opposition from environmentalists.[62] Some fear that stewardship promotes anthropocentrism and the assumption that the world and its resources are at our human disposal, to use or abuse as we like. The concept, they suggest, can reinforce human detachment from the world and so strengthen the sense that "nature" is nonrational and even "dead" matter, fit merely for human manipulation.[63]

Here priesthood provides a marvelous complement. Priesthood indicates that all of creation, human and nonhuman alike, exists ultimately for and to the praise of God. A host of Old Testament texts demonstrate that the nonhuman creation does not exist solely for human benefit. Significantly, God in Genesis 1 pronounces the rest of creation "good" *before* humanity is created.[64] The psalmist as well as the prophets Isaiah, Jeremiah, and Ezekiel speak of mountains, trees, sun, and moon praising and otherwise responding to God.[65] Unlike an office complex or gymnasium, which have no value if people do not inhabit them, creation can glorify and bring God delight apart from human presence. Flora and fauna exist first and foremost not for human use or enjoyment but for God's pleasure.

A priestly stewardship is quick to admit and encourage as much, since it emphasizes that the right end and ordering of all creation is doxological. Human and nonhuman creation alike exist ultimately for the praise of God. Priestly stewardship interprets all creation as the sign and means of God's love, wisdom, and power. Yet it does understand humanity to have a special role within God's creation, and that is the role of priest. In the Jewish and Christian conception, Orthodox theologian Alexander Schmemann observed, woman and man are called to stand "in the center of the world and [unify] it in the act of blessing God, of both receiving the world from

God and offering it to God" in thanksgiving.[66] Something of this conception seems to be at work in Paul's writing of Romans 8. Here the nonhuman creation is seen to groan, as in childbirth, both in pain and anticipation, for the redemption of the world. C. E. B. Cranfield comments that

> the non-human creation is frustrated because it has not been able properly
> to fulfill the purpose of its existence, God having appointed that without man
> it should not be made perfect. We may think of the whole magnificent the-
> atre of the universe together with all its splendid properties and all the cho-
> rus of sub-human life, created to glorify God but unable to do so fully, so long
> as man the chief actor in the drama of God's praise fails to contribute his
> rational part.[67]

So faithful humanity articulates the praise of all creation; it pronounces
the resounding and thankful "yes" grateful creatures would utter to their
Maker, Sustainer, and Redeemer.

Exactly on the point of redemption, priesthood offers another, and final,
complement to stewardship. Stewardship language can obscure and neglect the great hope of redemption. It can imply that "nature," or the nonhuman creation as we know it, is basically in fine shape. All humans need
do is tend it as it is and otherwise stay out of the way of its "natural" tendencies. But "nature" is not synonymous with unfallen creation. All of creation, even innocent "nature," is awry and in need of redemption.[68] Moreover, creation suffered its fall before it reached maturity and fullness.
Christians hope for a redemption that is much more than a return to the
Garden of Eden. Fulfilled, consummated creation will be grander and richer
by far than the unsullied but also unripened creation of Eden. The venerable Irenaeus poetically anticipated grapevines that would grow each vine
with ten thousand twigs, each shoot with ten thousand branches, each
cluster with ten thousand grapes, and each grape yielding 225 gallons of
wine! Demonstrating that the tradition of what I am calling priestly stewardship goes back to the early days of the church, he wrote, "And when
any of the saints shall take hold of one of the clusters, another cluster shall
call out, 'I am a better cluster; take me, and bless the Lord through me.'"[69]

Thus, acting as priestly stewards to preserve and enhance the other parts
of creation given into our care, we look not only back to Genesis but also
ahead to the coming kingdom of God in Christ. Then lion will lie with lamb,
and no child will want for food, and every act of consumption will be an
act of praise.

fourteen

The Transnational Corporation

More Church Than the Church

Once in a while Christians exhort one another to be better, more loyal Christians by pointing to the zeal and dedication of the adherents of another faith. The Moonies, for example, might be disdained in general, but more than once I have heard Christians marvel at the sacrifices and commitment of members of the Unification Church, and wish it for their own. For that matter, how many pastors of evangelism dream about church members who might speak of their faith half as boldly as the Mormons and Jehovah's Witnesses who routinely go door-to-door in the neighborhoods of strangers?

It is in this time-honored spirit of exhortation that I offer a different rival faith for our consideration and, indeed, our emulation. This rival faith, this church, is in fact much more widely spread than Mormonism or the Moonies, and more profoundly respected by followers of all religious faiths—especially Christianity. It is altogether more powerful, in terms of financial resources and governmental influence, than any other sect. It demands the comprehensive commitment of its members' lives more effectively than any mainline or evangelical Protestant denomination, and even more effectively than the Roman Catholic Church. And it scatters its message globally with stunning efficiency. The church I now present for our consideration is the transnational corporation.

I know the transnational corporation is not traditionally thought of as a church. But then perhaps that is part of its genius. "Religion" and "church" do not always have the most exciting connotations. Why burden your adherents—or potential converts—if you can actually induct them into a compelling way of life without such bothersome and dull labels as "religious" or "churchy"? There are many ways in which the transnational corporation operates potently as a church. Here I will suggest only five.

1. Dedication to Global Mission

Years ago, corporations began to develop "mission statements." In doing so, they borrowed directly from the Christian church. They, too, saw themselves with a mission. And like the church, large corporations have increasingly seen their mission in global terms. The full blooming of transnational corporations, especially in the last two decades, is little short of spectacular, and the result of intentional planning and enormous expenditures of energy and money.

Of course, the fundamental, underlying mission of any corporation is to make as much profit for its shareholders as possible—the stock market has come to expect a twenty to forty percent annual increase in the price of shares. To that end, corporate, global spending on advertising now rivals military spending: In 1994, $778 billion was invested worldwide on weapons, but nearly $500 billion on advertising. Put another way, transnational corporations spend half as much on advertising as all the world's nations spend on education. By this and other means, transnational corporations have grown tremendously. Out of the world's one hundred largest economies, fifty are now corporations. Mitsubishi's total annual sales are greater than the gross domestic product of Indonesia, the world's fourth most populous country. Wal-Mart's internal economy is larger than that of 161 of the world's countries, including Israel, Poland, and Greece.

Corporations don't get this big by confining themselves and their mission to a single country. And so the transnationals have seen themselves as citizens of the world. While U.S. churches still routinely hang flags in their sanctuaries, and often confuse the church and its work with "Christian America," transnational corporations carefully cultivate a global identity, awareness, and presence. Ted Turner's CNN outlaws any internal use of the word "foreign"—it is, after all, an international network. In 1996, Coca-

Cola stopped dividing its markets between the categories of "domestic" and "foreign." It reorganized and redesignated sales by regions, such as North America and Southeast Asia. (True enough to reality: by 1996, four out of every five bottles of Coke were sold outside the United States.) The head of General Electric has called his charge "a boundaryless company" that "will recognize no distinctions between 'domestic' and 'foreign' operations."

With increasing deregulation, and with trade agreements such as NAFTA and GATT, the transnational corporations have more and more understood themselves in distinction from the nation-state and its purview. This came home in an amusing, but not entirely trivial, fashion at the 1992 Olympics. Then basketball players Michael Jordan and Charles Barkley, premier endorsers of Nike products, balked at wearing a warm-up suit with Reebok's logo emblazoned on it. They "think they're here representing Nike instead of the United States," a *New York Times* columnist groused. Other journalists said the '92 Olympics became not so much the United States vs. Russia, or the United Kingdom vs. China, as "Nike vs. Reebok."

I won't belabor the point, but merely observe that the church is a "citizenship" (Eph. 2:19) of people made brothers and sisters by virtue of their baptism into the body of Christ. Yet, after centuries of Christian siblings killing each other in the name of their host nation-states, we seem to cling much more vigorously to distinctions between "domestic" and "foreign" than do transnational corporations.

2. Discipline and Commitment of Employees

It has taken centuries, but we are only now beginning to see how profoundly disastrous was the church's acceptance of the modern strict division between the "body" and the "spirit," and the "private" and the "public." Liberal, capitalistic modernity placed Christianity, along with other "religions," in the "private" realm and assigned it responsibility over the "spirit." Corporations, though, as straightforwardly economic entities, have considerable "public" relevance and power, and can discipline their employee's bodies (as well as their spirits).

To grasp how deeply this division has affected the church and its mission, imagine a specific church that presumed to tell its members where they will live, what kind of clothes they will wear, what sort of food they will eat, and expected them to regularly devote sixty to eighty hours every week to the church's work. Such a church would, in our climate, of course be denounced as "cultic," "authoritarian," and worse. Yet, as good moderns, we rarely balk at the demands of corporate culture. People who could barely conceive of moving to another location to be members of a given church repeatedly move at the behest of their company; the "corporate uniform" (suit and tie for men, dresses and hosiery for women) is unquestioned; managers know they are expected not to eat sack lunches at their desk or drive rusty cars to work; and in a day of downsizing, corporations expect more hours from their employees, even with stagnant pay.

I aim here not to complain that corporations are totalitarian and reprehensible. Rather, I admire the commitment they elicit from their employees, and the effectiveness of discipline in their ranks. Any social body with a common good or purpose requires commitment and discipline of its members. But while the contemporary Christian church shies away from challenging or somehow "offending" its members, the transnational corporation never hesitates to make demands on its employees.

Some time ago I spoke with a business consultant. He remarked on the emergence of workers who were called "transpatriates." No longer, he said, were employees of transnational corporations that worked outside their countries of origin simply expatriates. It was understood that they would not settle in a new country, but move, and move often, from one country to another, in service of their corporations' missions. So, the consultant said, transpatriates developed community with other transpatriates working for their company. They looked to one another for support and friendship. Separated by countries and sometimes continents, they flew to a common location and gathered on holidays and vacations.

How like the church truest to itself, I thought: strangers and sojourners spread across the face of the earth, ready to be at "home" anywhere on their mission, looking to others on the same mission as their primary support and community.

3. Sense of Itself as a Social or "Corporate" Body

In 1886, the U.S. Supreme Court ruled that a corporation is legally a person, entitled to the legal rights and protections the Constitution provides any flesh-and-blood human being. Corporations now enjoy theoretical immortality—they can survive the lifespan of any of their employees, executives, or shareholders. Just like any individual person, they can amass property and other financial resources, make contributions to political candidates, exercise the free speech provisions of the First Amendment, and hire lawyers to protect their interests.

Thus corporations, though at any one time functioning by the energies of hundreds or thousands of individuals, have a vital sense of social solidarity. The corporation is bigger, deeper, in some sense more real than any of its employees, managers, or stockholders; it is more than the sum of its individual parts. Certain members (such as chief executive officers) can sometimes represent the whole, but they are never more important than the whole—in fact, the parts are defined by the whole.

But consider again the Christian church's unhappy modern assignment to the realm of the "private." Just as the modern, privatized church can barely imagine disciplining its members, it assumes its members' faith is fundamentally private and individual—prior to and more determinative than the church's corporate faith. The modern church cannot see itself as a corporate (bodily) whole more than the sum of its parts.

With this incapacity, the modern church is far from the self-understanding of the church through most of its history. The New Testament church spoke of itself as the body of Christ. Paul famously compared individual members of the church to the parts of a physical body: what good is a foot apart from the rest of the body, an eye or an ear severed from the corporate whole with and for which it sees or hears? The New Testament scholar Charles Talbert reminds us that just as the name "Israel" could stand for both an individual (Jacob) and the nation descended from that individual, Paul can use "Christ" to designate both the individual Jesus and the church. For Paul, "individual Christians in their corporeal existence are the various body parts of the corporate personality of Christ through which the life of Christ is expressed."

Exactly because faith has been privatized, the church is fragmented into individual and uncoordinated parts, crippled in its pursuit of a common good and mission. Here again, the transnational corporation surpasses the church in being understood, inhabited, and embodied as a singular social "person."

4. Rock-Solid Confidence in Its Eschaton

In 1989 an official at the U.S. Department of State named Francis Fukayama wrote what quickly became a widely celebrated essay. He called it "The End of History?" but the question mark was purely rhetorical. There was little doubt in Fukayama's mind that the end of history had indeed arrived. The Soviet Union had collapsed, the Berlin Wall had fallen, Eastern European countries were at last open to the free market. It was the capitalist system that, in Fukayama's view, "satisfies the most basic human longings." And now that it appeared to have triumphed over its most serious opponents, it was only a matter of time before consumer-based democracy would assert itself the world over and shower its consummate blessings on all peoples.

It is of course impossible to miss Fukayama's theological language. He essentially declared that the eschaton, the end of time, had arrived. In the ten years since his heralding, the capitalistic faith—and it is very much a religious faith at work when people locate that which they think "satisfies the most basic human longings"—has been chastened. But only chastened. Transnational corporations, exploding at phenomenal rates, spread the gospel that the whole world can now enjoy the technology, affluence, and consumer bliss already enjoyed by the majority in North America and Western Europe. Given limited natural resources and the fouling of our ecological nest, that faith strikes some of us as incredible and utopian, but it is a faith held no less robustly for such objections. The point is that adherents of this modern faith in unending economic progress, exemplified in practice by transnational corporations, believe that the kingdom has come and that the world awaits only its consummation.

Again, I can only, if backhandedly, admire the transnational corporation's faith in its own eschatology. Such institutions really believe, as the economist Robert Nelson put it, that economic progress and the building of consumer societies "represented the route of salvation to a new heaven on earth." The astounding energy, discipline, and mustering of resources transnational corporations devote to their mission witness to their confidence in their eschatology. What would happen if the church held with equal confidence its conviction that the end of history came not in the ascent of capitalism, but in Jesus of Nazareth?

5. Comprehensiveness of Vision and Practice

Concordant with its robust eschatology, its global reach, and its claiming of its adherents' whole lives (spirits and bodies), the transnational corporation possesses a comprehensive vision. That is to say that it wants to interpret and engage all of reality on the terms and through the language of its faith. It is one thing to recognize the market as the best means now known for the exchange of material goods, and another to commodify and recast all of life in light of the market. Unstinting in its economic faith, the transnational corporation does the latter. As author Edward Luttwak notes, global capitalism "not only conquers markets and economic relationships, but also extends the reach of the market into every sphere of human activity." Thus Christian worshipers become "church-shoppers" and students become "educational consumers." Hospitals and other medical institutions are converted into profit-maximizing corporations and "patients," most now with patchier medical care than they received before, become "health care consumers." Forests are interpreted as "available board feet," and living communities seen only as labor and consumer pools. So successful has the evangelism of transnational corporations been that body parts are commodified and sold ($10,000 for a kidney in Egypt, $4,000 for a cornea in India). In 1980, the U.S. Supreme Court agreed with the corporate argument that life forms are simply chemical products that can be patented and sold like any other "manufacture;" in 1988 the U.S. Patent and Trademark Office issued the first patent on a living animal, a genetically altered mouse.

The Christian church possesses (or is possessed by) a story and language every bit as comprehensive as that of the transnational corporation. After all, it confesses of Jesus Christ that "all things have been created through him and for him" (Col. 1:16). But it has been more reticent in employing its language, in living by its vision, than the vanguard institution of global capitalism.

Here, as in other ways, the transnational corporation seems more church than the church.

fifteen

The Not-So-Naked New Public Square

Uncivil as the times may be, America is not without a public square, a place where its citizens may meet, mingle, and sometimes attempt to sort out their differences. It's just that America has a new public square.

You don't have to tell me that downtowns are eroded. In my suburb, downtown stores regularly struggle for their lives. Not a year passes without another stalwart draining and dwindling out of business. The old courthouse is vacated, its vital public activities transferred to a new building on the outskirts of town. Our new courthouse stands just down the road from a local version of the new public square: a shopping mall.

Shopping malls have quite consciously been built and presented as public squares, commons, or downtowns. Many reflect this intention in their names, such as (to cite a few I have known) Yorktown, Crossroads Mall, Stratford Square, and Town Square. Mall architecture incorporates—albeit in an artificial, thermostatically regulated fashion—many of the fixtures of older downtown areas. Walkways laid out in squares and rectangles, urging circuitous wandering. Fountains shoot. Trees and lesser greenery soften and enliven the scene. Benches invite rest, lingering, and the possibility of conversation. Amphitheaters await performances and audiences.

In addition, malls no longer simply sell products in myriad stores. They have expanded to include chapels, dentists, optometrists, medical clinics, counseling centers, ice rinks, miniature golf courses, food courts, child care, banking services, postal services, and branch offices of local, state, and federal governments. Some (such as the famous Mall of America, which sports its own zip code) include full-scale amusement parks. Others (such as Canada's West Edmonton Mall) contain zoos.

In short, you can now pass an evening or a Saturday afternoon in a shopping mall just as such times were once passed downtown on the square. You can meet friends for a meal, window-shop, take in a movie, toss pennies in the fountain, listen to a few songs from a local band. Just as you might once have done downtown, you can arrive early and, before meeting friends, visit the dentist and mail a birthday package. All the while you will pass knots of teenagers gathered outside soda shops. And you might anticipate returning to the mall the next morning, for prayer, worship, and the singing of hymns.

Some folk in Silver Spring, Maryland, want to build a megamall in their Washington suburb. Said a member of the task force charged with promoting the venture, "The central forces used to be schools or the church. That is not the case anymore. A mall, if properly managed and structured in terms of its services, can meet those needs from another perspective." So the mall is the new public square. But what is this other "perspective" it operates from? And how does this new public square compare to the old?

In truth, the shopping mall is a rather ambivalent public square. Once again, its architecture is telling. The older downtown and public square was thoroughly accessible. It might be reached from any direction and by several means of transportation—car, bus, train, or foot. It was open to the sky, unbounded by walls. It was centrally located, so citizens often passed through it even on their way to other business or concerns.

The shopping mall, on the other hand, is more like a medieval feudal village. You are welcomed, but reticently and with the implication that the aims and ways of the lords who own the property must be honored during your stay. Thus malls are found in the outskirts of suburbs, removed from train and bus stations, impossible to access by foot for all except those who enjoy strolling on the shoulders of Interstates or six-lane freeways. Malls are surrounded, moat-like, by huge parking lots that distance them from any nearby establishments or neighborhoods. They are flanked on every side by the imposing guard towers of Penney's, Sears, Montgomery Ward's, Von Maur's, Marshall Field, and other merchandising giants that serve as "anchor" stores. The overall effect is one of the public square not so much as "commons" or crossroads as fortress.

Once you are inside the mall, the "public" spirit is not just circumspect, but circumscribed. As much as mall owners and operators want people to frequent their space, and to consider malls as warm and open as town squares, they are quick to remember when necessary that malls are private property. Only the states of California, Oregon, Massachusetts, Colorado, and Washington have recognized some limited right of expression in "private" shopping malls. Many malls, entirely within their constitutional rights as now interpreted by the courts, forbid regular religious services.

The technically private status of the new public square also allows its arbiters to control access. If a newsworthy event happens in a downtown park, journalists and photographers can simply walk into the park and go to work. If the same event transpires in a shopping mall, the same journalists and photographers must seek permission to enter and do their work—and they may or may not get it. Similarly, last August the Mall of America instituted a Friday and Saturday night ban on all teenagers under age sixteen entering the mall without an adult chaperone.

The legally private nature of shopping malls also gives mall police latitude for "enforcement" not at all enjoyed by city or county police. It is not widely known or appreciated that malls are monitored, via remote camera, quite closely and sometimes invasively. Parking lot cameras, for instance, have reportedly been used to window-peep on teenaged couples making out in their cars. And mall gendarmes can be forthrightly arbitrary about who they will keep off the premises. Mall cops at a St. Louis mall informed one group of kids that they were not allowed to wear baseball caps backwards. At a Washington, D.C., mall in 1992, a club of computer hackers was interrupted and frisked in the food court. When one hacker objected that the searches violated due process, the mall police replied that they were within their rights because the mall was private property, allowing them to do "whatever we want—and you'll play by the rules or we'll arrest you."

All this may indicate that we should not be content with the shopping mall as the new public square. The old public square included the jostling forces of church, government, culture, and commerce. Whatever its shortcomings, it allowed each a voice, some power to challenge the dominance of any other. But the new public square is a fortress of commerce, the walls of which religion, government, and culture may enter only if and so long as they serve the ends of commerce. Faith may be expressed only so long as it does not offend shoppers. Free speech is allowable only if it does not lead to conflict that may steer customers away from a favorite mall. Journalists, teenagers, homeless people, and other potential nuisances that might spoil the atmosphere may be prohibited from the premises. Malls are also highly controlled spaces in other, less dramatic ways. They pipe in soothing music to relax inhibitions, and bask customers in unvaried artificial light that prevents the sun from ever going down and ending a shopping day.

Thus the shopping mall is the implacable symbol and embodiment of the more pervasive, abstract, and attitudinal American public square as it now actually stands. That public square, in the words of essayist Wendell Berry, "exists to protect the 'right' of profit," and will "inevitably gravitate toward protection of the 'rights' of those who profit most. Our present public economy is really a political system that safeguards the private exploitation of the public wealth and health."

Americans are, of course, notorious for the shortness of their memories. And here is one of the instances where our willful ignorance of history most painfully hurts us. This is a time of growing "conservatism," but of an odd, lopsidedly present-oriented conservatism. It is a conservatism that has little respect for institutions predating World War II and—as the reckless debt-building of the Reagan eighties demonstrated—little real concern for the burdens or treasures we may leave to posterity. We may be thankful that this conservatism has attuned the nation to the perils of big government. But true conservatives of the not-so-distant past (such as G. K. Chesterton, William Jennings Bryan, the southern agrarians, Robert Nisbet, and Christopher Lasch) were wary not just of big government but of *any* monolith—including big business.

Besides cutting itself off from its own tradition, today's conservatism obscures history and the realization of how much commerce owes to what Berry calls "the public wealth and health." For instance, the railroads that opened the West and provided American businessmen a massive market distribution system were built with public resources. The corporation, with its legal status as a "person" and attendant rights and privileges, is a creation of modern law and government. And the Department of Commerce, as fashioned by Herbert Hoover, offered business such invaluable tools and services as demographic surveys that were mined for abundant market information.

All this suggests that American Christians might be a good deal more critical and cautious in their dealings with the new public square than many have been up to this point. Paying ironic if unconscious homage, megachurches have already mimicked the architecture of corporate office buildings and, like the malls, put up their own food courts.

More deliberately, a Minnesota coalition of Christians, Jews, Buddhists, Hindus, Muslims, and others have established the Mall Area Religious Council to establish a "spiritual presence" at the Mall of America. According to its Web page, the Council planned to open The Meaning Store at the mall in 1997. "It will be a store where 'meaning in life' is made available in a spiritual manner." Patrons may use the store's Reflection Center for meditation and worship, glean "reliable information about local and world religious traditions," or shop for "books, music, [and] artifacts of world religions."

For all the good intentions behind it, The Meaning Store crowns mall culture's victory. It reduces Christianity, Judaism, and other faith to name brands, objects of comparison shopping. They are simply differently packaged containers of "meaning in life," now made available for today's purchase and, should it be desired, tomorrow's disposal.

So The Meaning Store is the perfect religious symbol of the trivialization of real choices in the new public square's endless promotion of pseudo-choice. It is true that the malls, with their rows on rows of stores, apparently overflow with choice. But mall stores carry a small, least-common-denominator stock that can cater only to the taste of the masses—not to those who would genuinely be different in their clothing, jewelry, reading, or music listening. More significantly, mall culture inhibits community; it denies and destroys smaller ways of life, such as folk songs and art, or strains of apples and brews of beer peculiar to a region. As Wendell Berry puts it, mall culture will not allow us to conform to local ways and conditions, but forces on us "a rootless and placeless monoculture of commercial expectations and products."

In like manner, The Meaning Store presumes faiths are, finally, not that different from one another. By confining Christianity (among others) to "meaning in life," and commodifying it, the Store endorses an attitude of spiritual seeking as shopping and makes the "customer" sovereign. Seriously obscured, if not lost, is any sense that the seeker's desires might be misguided and in need of conversion, a transformation wrought by a Sovereign other than the self. And so buried, too, is the glorious hope that the seeker might make the really important and significant choice, the choice to petition the God "who by the power at work within us is able to accomplish far more than all we can ask or imagine" (Eph. 3:20) and embark on an adventure bigger than any mortal individual's meager dreams and puny plans.

Such, I fear, are the deeper ramifications and trajectories of the new public square. Richard John Neuhaus worried that the old public square was naked, denuded of vital religious trappings. The new public square is not naked, but dressed in armor. We ought to start looking for the chinks.

PART 4

**Trespassing Secular Borders:
Popular Culture**

sixteen

The Sin of Winnie-the-Pooh

A noted Western philosopher, introduced to the world in 1926, was one day sitting on a log when he heard a buzzing sound. He was puzzled and fell to pondering. As his leading chronicler remembers the event, the philosopher reasoned along the following lines:

"'If there's a buzzing-noise, somebody's making a buzzing-noise, and the only reason for making a buzzing-noise that *I* know of is because you're a bee.'

"Then he thought another long time, and said: 'And the only reason for being a bee that I know of is making honey.'

"And then he got up and said: 'And the only reason for making honey is so *I* can eat it.'"

Now, even though this philosopher carries the strange title of Winnie-the-Pooh, and even though his work is mostly appreciated by children, this bit of reflection deserves our serious attention. After all, it resembles the way the American church is more and more thinking about God and discipleship.

This incident shows Pooh to be a pragmatic individualist. He cannot imagine the bees possessing an existence and purpose apart from his own use and interest. The Pooh is the quintessential consumer, entirely practical and entirely self-centered: The only reason for being a bee is to make honey, and the "only reason for making honey is so *I* can eat it."

Thus reasoning, the Pooh has a range of other possibilities blocked from his vision. He cannot see, for instance, the wider ecological purpose of bees, how they weave into a fabric of flora and fauna not only by providing honey, but also by such crafts as pollinating flowers. Another thing Pooh cannot see is a theological purpose for bees: that in the wonder of their existence, they speak and spell the glory of a Creator God.

Pooh-speak

The Pooh, in short, is a bear of very little vision. And that is part of what makes these ingenious stories so amusing. What is not so amusing is that our language for God and life—our serious, Christian adult language—has become every bit as restricted as the Pooh's playful, areligious, childlike language. More and more, we American Christians are limiting ourselves to a kind of Pooh-speak for talking about God and discipleship. We are forgetting the language and grammar of Scripture. Increasingly, our only tongue is the language of pragmatic individualism and the grammar of consumerism.

The most obvious examples appear in the pervasive prosperity gospel and in the trend to "market" the church. Across all denominational lines, churches are promising health and wealth as shamelessly as once only extreme Pentecostals did. A suburban Lutheran church near San Francisco, for instance, recently advertised a "money back guarantee." Donate to the church for ninety days, and, if you aren't blessed, you can have your money returned.

American Christians largely envision the church as a spiritual supermarket. We choose churches on the basis of whether or not they "meet my needs." We move to a new community and describe our search for a place of worship as "church shopping." Recently I talked with a professor at an elite evangelical college. He brought up some problems at his church, then sighed, "Ah well, most churches only have a shelf life of about three years anyway."

All this is Pooh-speak, pure and simple.

There is less and less a sense that finding (and being found by) a church is something entirely different from choosing a new car. We seem increasingly blind to the limits imposed on us by consumeristic language.

Is Holiness Good for You?

Writing and editing in the evangelical world for over fifteen years, I have seen our language increasingly forced away from the language of the Bible and toward the language of religious consumerism. That is not to say that the language of pragmatic individualism does not have great power and even some benefits. Many Christians, for example, now insist their faith has something to do with everyday life. Also, we are now more inclined to dismiss theologies that assume God can only be glorified if we deplore ourselves or say that if we are having fun God must be dismayed.

But if we are only comfortable speaking as pragmatic consumers, we will ignore or distort entire vistas of the biblical terrain. This was brought keenly home to me recently when two authors independently submitted book manuscripts on the same topic—the holiness of God.

Both manuscripts worked directly, explicitly, and consistently from the biblical text. Both were well written and, on their own terms, interesting. I saw value in both and moved to the editorial task of conceiving how the authors might draw in the widest possible readership.

I needed, in other words, to start translating their manuscripts into a "marketable" language.

But here was a translating headache. The authors had begun with God; I would have to push them to begin with the individual human. They had addressed needs theologically perceived, fitting humanity onto God's agenda; I would push them to write about felt needs, fitting God onto the individual human's agenda. At the heart of what these authors had to say, in fact, was the conviction that humanity is in deep trouble exactly because it tries to use God to its own ends. So if I pushed these authors to speak in the idiom of pragmatic individualism, I would push them to say exactly the opposite of what they wanted to say!

In short, the holiness of God is not easy to conceive in Pooh-speak. More than that, if it is forced into Pooh-speak, it will no longer resemble any biblical sense of the holiness of God. God's holiness is not for my use or self-interest, though the language of consumerism would have me imagine it must be. It is the other way around. Apart from God I am lost, without direction and purpose, unable to know my true worth—the worth of a creature among creatures wrought and redeemed by a transcendent God.

Snared in the net of Pooh-speak, I live with a grossly stunted imagination. This stuntedness would have been well understood by the Puritan Richard Baxter, who wrote, "If you will glorify God in your lives, you must be chiefly intent upon the public good, and the spreading of the gospel through the world." The alternative, according to Baxter, was a "private, narrow soul . . . always taken up about itself, or imprisoned in a corner, in the dark." Such a soul "sees not how things go in the world: its desires, and prayers and endeavours go no further than they can see or travel."

If I can imagine a good that is bigger and grander than myself, a purpose beyond what will satisfy merely me, then, in Baxter's words, I can be a "larger soul" who "beholds all the earth, and desires to know how it goes with the cause and servants of the Lord." Thus, Baxter recognized, those who understand the holiness of God "pray for the 'hallowing of God's name,' and the 'coming of his kingdom,' and the 'doing of his will throughout the earth, as it is in heaven,' before they come to their own necessities."

Sabbath and Sex

Holiness is not the only biblical concern that drops from sight when we confine ourselves to Pooh-speak. Consider the Sabbath.

Recently I spent a weekend with a group of ministers. In one discussion, they emphasized the need for Sabbath rest in our frenetic society. The leader extolled the value of rest and restful exercise *because* it refreshed him and made him sharper at his ministry. The Sabbath, in other words, was useful since it facilitated his ministry.

Biblically, though, the point of the Sabbath is exactly its uselessness, its sheer impracticality for us and our work. It is a regular reminder that God alone is God; the universe and its maintenance does not depend on me or my ministry.

Another example is the Christian confusion over sexual ethics. We tell our young people they should reserve sexual intercourse for marriage. But then we justify our position in terms of consumer choices. We tell them that abstinence before marriage is the least harmful and most healthy alternative. We warn them about AIDS and venereal diseases. We talk about how the really "good sex" is had between two people without previous partners.

The problem is that this approach, presented by itself, encourages each teenager to think only about himself or herself. And if they think of themselves only as individuals, they can always find exceptions to the rule. Most people who have sex outside marriage never get AIDS; individuals who have had sex partners before their spouse may still have wonderful sex on their marital bed. What is "good for them" may not seem so obvious.

But what if we turn to a language and imagination more like Baxter's than Pooh's—a vision "chiefly intent on the public good"? Then it is not difficult to see how it is good to keep sex connected to marriage. Any worthy society will want to promote the birth and healthy upbringing of children, for only so can it insure its future. And children can be healthy only if their parents are capable of the commitment and fidelity that build family stability. As the political philosopher Michael Walzer recognizes, "From the point of view of society as a whole, private affairs are marginal and parasitic upon marriages and families."

Yet people who see sex individualistically, mainly as a means of recreation or self-fulfillment, are sensitive only to their own needs and gratification. Commitment and fidelity are beyond them.

A Zero-Sum War

In short, Pooh-speak disposes me to think first, and often only, of myself and my benefits. At its extreme, it reduces life to a contest of self-interests in a zero-sum economy: For me to gain, someone else must lose.

Enslaved to the language of individualism, we do not see our profound and unavoidable connections to others. Philip Slater writes, "The notion that people begin as separate individuals, who then march out and connect themselves to others, is one of the most dazzling bits of self-mystification in the history of the species." We are now so individualistic and pragmatic that we can fight against tax raises to improve schools for the next generation without ever feeling stingy or selfish.

Biblical language, Baxter's language, opens up other possibilities. It disposes me to see my connection to others and to see us benefiting together under God. Thus Paul, in 1 Corinthians 12, sees individual Christians as members of a community, each with gifts used to build up all. The kingdom of God is a limitless rather than a zero-sum economy. It is more like life as family than as war: The new child does not steal parental love from big sister, but instead creates more love to go around.

Biblical language, then, calls us into a new and wider world. "If anyone is in Christ, there is a new creation: everything old has passed away; see, everything has become new!" (2 Cor. 5:17). Incorporated into Christ, the individual can now see *everything* in a transformed way, connected under God, created and redeemed in Christ.

Such a vision is what Augustine had in mind in the rhapsodic final book of *The City of God*. There, looking ahead to the consummation, "God will be the source of every satisfaction, more than any heart can rightly crave, more than life and health, food and wealth, glory and honor, peace and every good—so that God, as St. Paul said, 'may be all in all.' . . . And in this gift of vision, this response of love, this paean of praise, all alike will share, as all will share in everlasting life."

That, to understate the matter, is not a pragmatic individualist speaking.

Called to Be Multilingual

The insidiousness of consumer language is that it confuses the kingdom with the kingdom's benefits. It mistakes certain effects of the gospel for the gospel itself. Someone who repents and follows Jesus can expect direction in life, an easing of guilt and anxiety, moral growth, and many other benefits. "But," as John Howard Yoder writes, "all of this is not the gospel. This is just the bonus, the wrapping paper thrown in when you buy the meat, the 'everything' which will be added, without our taking thought for it, if we seek first the kingdom of God and His righteousness."

For Christians, Pooh-speak cannot be our first tongue. Instead, we need a sharper and reinvigorated sense of how the people of God are called to be multilingual. We may need to know the language of pragmatic individualism (or, at other times, the language of existentialism or Marxism or the New Age). But our primary language, our first tongue in every time and place, must be the language of Scripture.

While the Assyrian army besieges Jerusalem (2 Kings 18–19), its negotiator Rabshakeh taunts the people of Judah in their own language. He stands just outside Jerusalem's wall and mocks Yahweh, comparing the Lord God to failed deities of other nations. Rabshakeh uses the language of Judah, but only to pervert it, to show Assyrian kings more powerful than Israel's Creator and Redeemer. Similarly, when we dress Pooh-speak in the language of the Bible, we twist the biblical language.

More important than the conversation at the wall, however, is the conversation going on behind the wall. Judah's King Hezekiah prays to Yahweh in the language of Judah, rightly recognizing the Lord as the maker of heaven and earth and the sole God over all the kingdoms (19:15). As Old Testament scholar Walter Brueggemann comments, "The conversation on the wall is crucial, because the Assyrians are real dialogue partners who must be taken seriously. They will not go away. But unless there is another conversation behind the wall in another language about another agenda, Judah on the wall will only submit to and echo imperial perceptions of reality."

Likewise, we must retain a facility in consumerism as a second language because it is the language of our society. It will not go away—at least not for a good, long time. In fact, I fear it may become so dominant that the "truth" and "reality" it presents will be more true and real to Christians than the truth and reality of Scripture. For example, some in the church already accept the idea that the "bottom line" reliably determines what we should be and do; or that theological designations such as the "Trinity" and the "kingdom of God" are supposedly more abstract and less "practical" than psychological formulations such as "dysfunctionality" and "self-esteem."

The conversation at the wall must always go on. But our hope lies behind the wall, where we must renew our first language. Pooh-speak is fun. Pooh-speak can be grand. Pooh-speak is sometimes useful. It just isn't the gospel.

seven t e e n

The Saxophonist
Who Would Be a Saint

Acknowledgment

By the time of his passing in 1967, just two months short of his forty-first birthday, the tenor (and sometime soprano) saxophonist John Coltrane had established himself as one of the very finest artists and composers in the history of jazz. With those accolades, I am restraining myself.

Before his death, some admirers pondered the possible significance that John Coltrane's initials were identical to those of Jesus Christ—blasphemous foolishness that shocked and dismayed a man who was by all accounts profoundly religious and genuinely humble. After his death, a church in San Francisco declared Coltrane its patron saint and retooled its liturgy around one of his chief achievements, the four-part suite *A Love Supreme*. Critics and historians, if not compelled to resort to such literally religious terms to comprehend Coltrane's greatness, nonetheless gravitate toward metaphorically religious language. Trane has quite soberly been declared a "jazz messiah" and, in Hegelian epochal terms, "the end of jazz history."

Indeed, to date Coltrane is arguably the last great innovator in jazz—a music that, rooted as it is in spontaneity and slaves' hope for a tomorrow brighter than yesterday or today, is innovative by definition. Coltrane's lifework ended in free jazz, an untethered form that ignored steady rhythm and encouraged instrumentalists to improvise together, all playing at once. His lifework began, professionally, in the bebop era towered over by alto saxophonist Charlie Parker. Partly because Parker so dominated the alto, Coltrane made the heavier, more insistent tenor saxophone his signature instrument.

If ever a musician mastered an instrument, John Coltrane mastered the tenor. As classical pianist Zita Carno wrote in 1959, in what remains one of the best technical studies of Coltrane's art, his range was a full three octaves up from the lowest note on the horn. Carno marveled at Coltrane's "equality of strength in all registers," his sound ringing as clear, full, and unforced in the highest notes as it boomed and scudded at the very bottom. "His playing is very clean and he almost never misses a note." A note? The man almost never missed a "split" note—several tones played on top of one another. His "harmonic conception," Carno added, was extremely advanced. He achieved an immediately recognizable sound tone, sometimes denounced as metallic, but undeniably bold and markedly free of vibrato. Many saxophonists produce a reedy, sometimes sibilant and boozy sound. You might say they play their mouthpieces. Coltrane filled the entire horn.

And then there was the speed. Bebop, of course, required it—when Parisians first heard Charlie Parker, they could not believe he had only two hands. Later, with Miles Davis, Coltrane was a pioneer in modal jazz, which shuffles and roller-coasts up and down the notes in unusual scales. Coltrane often blitzed modes at a frantic bebop pace. He learned circular breathing (a technique of breathing in through the nose while exhaling from the mouth, thereby eliminating pauses) and could furiously unfurl long ribbons of notes so rapidly that they almost blurred into one. Thus critic Ira Gitler famously dubbed Coltrane's approach in one period "sheets of sound" and said the gushing bursts of his outpourings seemed almost "superhuman."

Coltrane studied piano, bass guitar, and harp theory, privately played the flute and bagpipes, and strove to assimilate all these instruments' capabilities into his saxophone. He was born into the blues and later immersed himself in Western classical music (especially Stravinsky and Bartok), Latin music, African and Indian music, drawing reverently, deeply on them all. He built up an astounding stamina that allowed him routinely to solo for twenty or thirty minutes and left him capable of three-hour sets.

But what is all this by way of acknowledging the greatness of John Coltrane? In the end, I can only resort to my own much feebler grasp of the instrument we call language. Coltrane's music brims and overflows with the genius of an enormous heart and soul. I cannot begin to name a favorite piece, or even a single favorite album. I would hate to live without his elegant, stately ballads (especially those recorded with singer Johnny Hartman); without the breathtaking courage and confidence of his attacks on the songs of *Blue Train;* without the aching mournfulness of "Alabama"; without the polyrhythmically beating African heart of *The Africa/Brass Sessions* or the swirling Indian intricacies of "My Favorite Things"; without Trane contrasting Miles Davis's mood or Eric Dolphy backing Trane's; without the driving prayers of *A Love Supreme* or the serene petition of "Dear Lord."

You know how sometimes when you dream, you fly? I am insomniac. The world looks different at night. There is no better time for solitary thinking. Or for dreaming—awake or asleep. Often I put the headphones on and listen to Trane in the night. I drift into that hypnagogic state between utter relaxation and the sweet oblivion of sleep. And with Coltrane pushing and pulling, blowing as if his life depended on it (as indeed in his estimate it did), I rise. I float, then soar. I glide. Roll. Dip. Dive. Shoot straight up, farther and farther, past wispy clouds into the fire of the sun. Then I plunge straight down, gain velocity, hurtle into beauty. But all without fear, with trust and acceptance, for I have wings: Coltrane wings. All I can ever do, all I would ever want to do, is hang on—or, no, no . . . let go. Let go with that endlessly fascinating and insinuating sound.

Resolution

It's no surprise that an artist as gifted and prolific as Coltrane (in 1965 alone he recorded eleven albums) has attracted jazz critics and commentators in abundance. Especially notable in its eloquence and placement of Trane in the big picture of his influence on music is Eric Nisenson's *Ascension* (St. Martin's, 1993, still in print with Da Capo, 1995). Until 1998, two biographies of Coltrane had been published. Now we have what is surely the definitive biography: Lewis Porter's *John Coltrane: His Life and Music* (University of Michigan Press, 1998).

Porter is an associate professor of music and jazz historian at Rutgers University. He has approached his task with extraordinary care and dedication. Porter worked on musical analysis and discographical research of Coltrane for fourteen years before beginning this book. He tells us he has read hundreds of articles on Coltrane in English, French, Italian, and German. Concerned for inaccuracies in the earlier biographies, he not only conducted several fresh interviews, but reinterviewed living persons cited in those biographies and transcribed anew tapes of original interviews. He went to the trouble of tracing a Coltrane family genealogy back to the 1830s. He compiled an extensive chronology of Coltrane's life, replete with tour and show dates.

Accordingly, his book stands out for its meticulous detailing. It is now the baseline for establishing key Coltranian dates and events. No less, it stands out for its extensive and technical musical analysis of Coltrane's work (there are eighteen pages, for example, devoted to *A Love Supreme*). For readers like me, who have mastered no musical instrument other than the stereo, most of these passages will be obscure. But they should be a treasure trove for trained musicians and students. No self-respecting conservatory library should be without this book.

That said, Porter's book is not especially well-constructed or imaginative. Without the reader's own love of Coltrane, he does not really come alive. Chapter eighteen attempts to give some sense of "The Man: 'A Quiet, Shy Guy,'" but it consists of nothing more than quoted anecdotes strung together under the headings "Personality," "Sense of Humor," "Health Regimen," "Practicing," "Astrology," "Philosophy and Religion," and "Race and Politics." As for imagination, suffice it to say that the opening sentence of the book reads: "John William Coltrane, one of the great musical artists of the twentieth century, was born on September 23, 1926, in Hamlet, North Carolina."

Still, with the help of Porter and other more venturesome Coltrane writers such as Nisenson and Leroi Jones, we can get some idea of what formed the soul capable of producing such astonishing music. Coltrane's early years were those of a middle-class black family in the 1920s and '30s. Both his grandfathers were respected African Methodist Episcopal Zion pastors. His father earned a decent living for the family as a tailor, but when John was in his early teens his father died of stomach cancer.

On this point Porter allows himself one of his very few probing biographical speculations. He notes that the young Coltrane around this time took up the alto sax, then the clarinet. Trane practiced obsessively from the beginning "as if practicing would bring his father back, or maybe help him forget his father—as if, by succeeding in music, he could restore stability and control to his life." This seems eminently sensible and is corroborated by a high-school friend of Coltrane's, who told Porter, "For a while, I don't think he had anything but that horn."

As I have noted, Coltrane soon switched horns, to the tenor. Directly after high school, he and his mother moved to Philadelphia, which in the 1940s was a leading center of bebop. He was drafted into the navy in the waning months of World War II and, stationed in Hawaii, played in navy bands. Returning to Philly in 1946, he studied saxophone at the Granoff Studios, completing a four-year degree program with two classical music lessons per week. Meanwhile, he launched in earnest his professional career as a musician.

Coltrane was not a musical prodigy. He did not begin, Porter comments, with "obvious exceptional talent." Musician Benny Golson, also in Philadelphia during the 1940s, said, "Nobody had an *idea* that he would become the international icon that he turned out to be. Nobody!" So Coltrane would labor for a decade before he began to be recognized as a great jazz artist. At times he was reduced to "walking the bar" in showy bands. (In such bands tenor saxophonists especially were known for their theatrics, kicking over drinks and tearing off their shirts. This, to put it mildly, was not Coltrane's style.) At one point he nearly gave up music, applying for a job at the post office. His ascent, darkly, was significantly slowed by alcohol and drug abuse.

Trane was a lifelong lover of sweets (especially sweet potato pie) and hated dentists. He may have drunk heavily partly to dull toothaches. The alcohol did him little good, but he nearly destroyed himself with heroin. Remember that Charlie Parker had unwittingly become a musician's role model of heroin use. As Porter observes, for "virtually every young player" who began in the late 1940s and early 1950s, there was pressure to try heroin. Though Parker eventually made public disclaimers that heroin did not improve his playing, younger jazz musicians desperately wanted to be like Bird.

Trane took up the drug by 1948 and, like Miles Davis, Stan Getz, Dexter Gordon, Chet Baker, and others, he got hooked. His playing, if he showed up, was unreliable. Clad in days-old, slept-in clothes, he dozed off on the bandstand and, Davis complained, sometimes picked his nose. He was an artist of recognized talent, playing with some of the greats, but his addiction was such a hindrance that Dizzy Gillespie nearly fired him, and Davis once did.

The key year in Coltrane's life was 1957. Supported by his first wife, Naima, and friends, that spring he shut himself away for days and kicked the habit. It was, in every sense of the word, a conversion. As Coltrane wrote in the liner notes for *A Love Supreme* (1964). "During the year 1957, I experienced, by the grace of God, a spiritual awakening that was to lead me to a richer, fuller, more productive life. At that time, in gratitude, I humbly asked to be given the means and privilege to make others happy through music."

A practical Aristotelian, Coltrane became convinced that "you can improve as a player by improving as a person." Coltrane's was no trivial resolution. He believed music's capacities for enhancing this world were far from exhausted; indeed, his convictions concerning the power of music call to mind the mad dreams of other artists who entered a territory where inspiration and lunacy intermingle.

Music, he believed, could help bring social transformation and perhaps even end wars. He told an interviewer, "My goal is to live the truly religious life and express it in my music. If you live it, when you play there's no problem because the music is just part of the whole thing. . . . I think music can make the world better and, if I'm qualified, I want to do it." He searched for pitches and scales that would elicit specific "emotional meaning." He said, "I would like to discover a method so that if I want it to rain, it will start right away to rain. If one of my friends is ill, I'd like to play a certain song and he will be cured; when he'd be broke, I bring out a different song and immediately he'd receive all the money he needed." He told drummer Elvin Jones he suspected a particular combination of notes could make matter disintegrate. From the 1957 conversion on, he sought ceaselessly to reproduce a magical droning sound he heard in his mind.

Coltrane, an utterly serious man, was a priest with a horn. In the early 1960s he told Naima that from then on, ninety percent of his playing would be prayer. "That's what music is to me," he said later, "it's just another way of saying this is a big, beautiful universe we live in, that's been given to us and here's an example of just how magnificent and encompassing it is."

Pursuance

Someone with such ambitious aims might be expected to pursue his craft with dedication. I said earlier that Coltrane practiced obsessively from the start. He was repeatedly heard playing in the backyard at three and four A.M. Neighbors of his boyhood home complained that he kept them awake; a pastor gave him the church key so he could practice there anytime and leave the neighbors at peace.

By the time he became a professional musician, Coltrane was easily playing more than eight hours a day. When he studied at Granoff, in Philadelphia, he arrived before the doors opened, then stayed until evening. Back at his apartment he would practice into the night—just fingerings, no blowing, so as not to disturb the neighbors.

Throughout his adult life he was inseparable from his saxophone. He left it strapped around his neck at the dinner table; Naima often removed the horn when he fell asleep with it on. At gigs, after he finished a solo, he frequently wandered off the bandstand and practiced in the men's room until his next part was due. He also played there during intermissions. He taped his performances so he could run them back, listening, adjusting, improving, relentlessly searching.

He spent hours experimenting with different mouthpieces and reeds. Porter, ever reliable for technical details, notes that sound varies from player to player because of individual air cavities and sinus passages. Mouthpieces and reeds allow some adjustment to these anatomical idiosyncrasies. Coltrane arrived a full hour before gigs and recording sessions to determine the right mouthpiece and reed for the occasion. Despite his disdain for dentistry, he had his top teeth filed into a slight curve to match the arc of the saxophone mouthpiece.

Coltrane had a gift, most definitely. But he really stood out for his passion, his headlong, nothing-held-back pursuance of accomplishing everything humanly possible with his call and his chosen instrument. That is why, after the late bloomer came into his own around age thirty, the *Philadelphia Tribune* could fittingly headline: "Philly Jazz Artist Wailing Throughout the Entire Universe." The jazz critic Ralph Gleason once remarked to Miles Davis that his fusion jazz was so complicated he really needed five tenor players. In response, Gleason recalled, "[Miles] shot those eyes at me and growled, 'I *had* five tenor players once.' I knew what he meant."

Psalm

Let me get one thing perfectly clear: The mature John Coltrane was no classically orthodox Christian. Little has been written, with profundity, about his faith. Porter flatfootedly relays a passel of anecdotes. John Fraim gives attention to Trane's spirituality in *Spirit Catcher: The Life and Art of John Coltrane* (Greathouse Company, 1996), but not at all critically or probingly. Nisenson is the best I have read on this count, but his comprehension of religion is vastly exceeded by his grasp of jazz. Spiritually speaking, this Johnson awaits his Boswell.

But again, many details are available. I have said that Coltrane's roots were Christian. Both grandfathers were pastors; he reported that his mother was "very religious." The boy Coltrane every Sunday sat in a small brick church in High Point, North Carolina, hearing his maternal grandfather preach. In his teen years he went to church on Tuesday nights, rehearsing with a community band conducted by the Reverend Warren Steele.

I do not know of his liturgical habits in adulthood, first in Philadelphia and later in New York City. It appears that he never entirely lost faith, though, and in any event, his 1957 conversion to a better life was self-interpreted in largely Christian terms of "grace" and gratitude to "the Father." Many of his mature compositions bore Christian names and themes, and one, "The Father and the Son and the Holy Ghost," was ostensibly Trinitarian.

But Coltrane clearly rejected the exclusivity of Christ. In the liner notes to the album containing that Trinitarian title (*Meditations,* 1966), Trane tells Nat Hentoff, "I believe in all religions." There "certainly is meaning to life," but Coltrane wanted to get no more specific about it than to affirm a "force for unity." He once told an interviewer that in his late teens he "started to wonder about things" and "started breaking away. I was growing up, so I questioned a lot of what I found in [Christian] religion." In his early twenties he confronted Islam, which "took me to something I'd never thought about—you know, another religion? . . . I was disappointed when I found how many religions there were."

Disappointed or disturbed initially, Coltrane eventually adopted a kind of sixties perennialism, exemplified by his professed belief in "all religions" and the elaboration, "I've always felt that even though a man was not a Christian, he still had to know the truth in some way." He read eclectically, in the positivism of A. J. Ayer, in Indian Buddhism, in Gandhi, Western and Eastern astrology. He enthusiastically inquired of one interviewer's birth date and, after the reply, exposited, "For the Orientals, that was the year of the serpents, that's very good for you! I also have my moon in conjunction with Mars in Taurus, in direct opposition with Saturn, the deadly planet, in Scorpio, the sign of death! Also I have my ascendant and my Venus in the sign of Virgo; three bad aspects of my birth chart. I won't live to be very old!"

Coltrane's sense of foreboding turned out to be true. But it may have predated his trust in astrology: his father and other close relatives had died early of stomach cancer. He would succumb to a liver cancer that may have metastasized from the stomach. Just months before the diagnosis and his too-soon death, Coltrane was asked at a Japanese press conference, "What would you like to be ten years from now?" It is indicative of the seriousness of his searching, ever intense if sometimes scattershot, that he responded, "I would like to be a saint."

I'm not ready to rebuild the Christian liturgy around John Coltrane. But I do know that some of the most remarkable and, yes, holy sounds I will ever hear came from his saxophones. His playing was prayerful—sometimes petitionary, sometimes praising, sometimes interceding, sometimes lamenting, but always striving as best he knew how toward the throbbing, vital core of the universe. With his saxophone like a kind of miner's lamp, Coltrane explored the darkest caverns of human pain and yearning; with it embodying church bells and slave spirituals and heavenly harp sounds, he draws us beyond the narcissism that so often preoccupies us with our comparatively puny and increasingly solipsistic selves.

Describing the motivation for *Meditation* to Hentoff, Coltrane (probably unconsciously) alluded to 1 Corinthians 13. "There are always new sounds to imagine, new feelings to get at. And always, there is the need to keep purifying these feelings and sounds so that we can really see what we've discovered in its pure state. So that we can see more and more clearly what we are. In that way, we can give those who listen to us the essence, the best of what we are. But to do that at each stage, we have to keep cleaning the mirror."

He wanted to see through the glass less darkly. And with that horn, by God, he gave it his all.

eighteen

That Glorious Mongrel

How Jazz Can Correct the Heresy of White Christianity

The argument I want to make here can be simply stated: Jazz can make us—especially the "us" of white, middle- and upper-class, relatively comfortable American believers—better Christians. Put more pointedly and specifically, jazz can correct what James Cone, I am afraid with all too much justification, has called "the heresy of white Christianity."[1] But the argument, if simply stated, cannot be so simply made, and must begin with a series of disclaimers.

The first disclaimer is that I am no trained musician or musicologist. The Yogi Berra of jazz, the art form's champion aphorist, is Eddie Condon. And the bandleader had a couple of lines that would accurately apply to me. Condon remarked of a second-rate vocalist, "He once tried to carry a tune across the street and broke both legs." He complained of a shoddy instrumentalist, "He made the clarinet talk and it usually said 'please put me back in my case.'" Not least of all, I could truthfully confess what Condon said of himself: "The boppers flat their fifths. I drink mine."[2] My qualifications for discussing jazz, then, are those of the amateur—and hopefully an amateur in the strongest sense of the word, as someone who passionately loves the music and has found his life repeatedly enriched by it. And enriched not just by the music per se, but also by the history and the ongoing culture of jazz. So my remarks will center on that history and culture, with allusion to the music, which of course speaks for itself better than any commentary can.

The second disclaimer states a rather obvious truth. I am white, which is to say Anglo-American, while jazz is in its origin and at the marrow of its continuing practice a predominantly African-American music. Jazz circles are perennially marked by debates about how much whites and other non-blacks can really "get" the music. And yet there have been first-rate white jazz musicians—someone as understandably sensitive to racism as Miles Davis included in his band such whites as Bill Evans, and composed some of his most enduring pieces with the very white, very Anglo Gil Evans. Furthermore, jazz is played and loved around the world. It took the adoration of the French to convince white Americans just how artful is this music born on our soil; and the Japanese are famously enthusiastic about jazz. The fact of the matter is no cultures are watertight or hermetically-sealed compartments, and jazz is a music marked by its "boundless capacity to absorb outside influences," as the cultural critic Martha Bayles has written. Jazz historian Ted Gioia aptly calls it "the most glorious of mongrels," and Dexter Gordon said, "Jazz is a great octopus; it'll do anything; it'll use anything."[3] Jazz sprang from the meeting of African and European musics. Its roots are sunk in slave spirituals and the blues and ragtime, but its branches wrap around the march, Tin Pan Alley, Broadway musicals, and later even Stravinsky and Ravel. The truth is that African-Americans are the fathers and mothers not just of jazz, but of all popular music of the twentieth century: the blues, minstrel songs, gospel, country, rock and roll, reggae, soul, rap—none would exist without the African-American musical genius. The debt whites and other nonblacks owe is not to leave black music alone—it already suffuses our churches and concert halls and CD collections—but to acknowledge that truth, and to celebrate it as a wonderful gift.

The third disclaimer relates to the debt nonblacks owe African-Americans, and to the persistent and pernicious racism that has kept us from acknowledging how much we all owe to black culture, not least to black musicmaking. The third disclaimer is that jazz is not, as has so often been supposed, an anti-Christian music. And yes, that supposition is marked by the distortions and obfuscations of racism. Because of this, and because my remarks come particularly from the angle of a theological commentator, this third disclaimer deserves a bit more of our time than the other two.

Way Down Yonder in New Orleans

Christian uneasiness about jazz goes back to the music's birth, but is not merely an historical artifact. As recently as last year, the conservative Christian *World* magazine, running a laudatory article on recent jazz, found it necessary first to struggle with what it called the "evil connotations" of jazz.[4] When I studied at Wheaton College in the late 1970s, the then-president of the college would not allow the music to be played at school functions. We can always rely on a fundamentalist to state candidly what other conservative Christians would rather leave unsaid or bury in tactfulness, and so I turn to David Cloud of the Fundamental Baptist Information Service to place the objection straightforwardly. Mr. Cloud rejects jazz because, he says, it "was born in the unwholesome and sensual environment of sleazy bars, honkytonks, juke joints and whorehouses. The very name 'jazz' refers to immorality."[5]

Now it is true that jazz has had and still has some association with disreputable environs. Nor is there any use denying that, especially in the 1940s, aspects of the jazz ethos embraced blatant drug use and even addiction.[6] Black Christians themselves have had concerns about the music on just such counts. The mother of pianist and one-time Louis Armstrong spouse Lil Hardin denounced it as "worthless immoral music, played by worthless immoral loafers expressing their vulgar minds with vulgar music."[7] African-American churches, not just white American churches, have wrestled with the line between sacred and secular musics. For instance, at one point they permitted tambourines but not drums in their sanctuaries, or allowed dancing with the feet apart but never crossing.[8] So it would be unfair and misleading to *simply* dismiss white Christian concerns about jazz as racist.

But Martin Luther, and later Charles Wesley, famously set the melodies of drinking songs to church lyrics, and the classical music long endorsed by white Christians has its own associations with dancing, sensuality, unsavory environments, and immoral behavior. The Christian appreciation of, say, Mozart can hardly extend to his sex life, and those of us old enough to remember Bo Derek and the movie *10* know that the music of seduction can be found in the classical canon. I am afraid an unwillingness to look both harder and more forgivingly on the history of jazz does have its racist elements.[9]

Namely, tendencies to denounce jazz as "vulgar," "primitive," and even "savage" are all too easily traceable to racist assumptions. Much of this is owed to the emphasis in jazz on rhythm and the supposition that rhythm is the most elementary, "natural," and, yes, sensual component of music. I will later have occasion to say more about misconceptions surrounding rhythm. So for now I merely surface these suppositions, and the then not-so-distant linkage that blacks are allegedly more of the earth, more "natural," and less civilized than whites, and so apt to focus on the supposedly less sophisticated, less thoughtful, and so less genuinely artful aspect of music that rhythm is often imagined to be.

More to the point at the moment is the word *jazz* itself, and the actual history of jazz's nascent environments.

As to the etymology of *jazz*, we will of course never definitely know where or how the word first came into currency. David Cloud is right that some think the word came from *jass*, as nothing less than a reference to semen, and you cannot get more bluntly sexual than that. But others, such as Henry Osgood, argue that sexual meanings were not original to the word, and point to such possibilities as the etymological corruption of the name of a turn-of-the-century New Orleans outfit known as Razz's Band.[10] I find especially plausible, remembering the importance of the New Orleans Creole population to the development of early jazz, the resort some make to the French verb *jazer*, to speed up, to pep up, to exhilarate. Certainly jazz is about speed, pep, and exhilaration, and perhaps this is what the earliest users and makers of the music had in mind. In any event, Wittgenstein and biblical scholars alike would want to save us from the root fallacy, the supposition that a word always carries its earliest meaning, so that the actual and continued use of the word *jazz* need not be attached to crude sexuality, even if that were somehow proven to be its origin.

More substantially, attention to the history of jazz will not support its confinement to origins in unsavory or immoral environments. Storyville, the infamous Red Light District of New Orleans so often imagined as the birthplace of jazz, existed a scant twenty years, from its creation by city elders in 1897 until its closing by the U.S. Navy in 1917. Before and after this brief period, jazz demonstrably drew on the music of the African-American church. Buddy Bolden, sometimes credited as the very first jazz musician, was not devout but often went to church expressly for musical inspiration (and did not play in brothels). The fact is that early twentieth-century New Orleans was rife with venues enhanced by live music—fish fries, picnics, dinner boats, parks, train excursions, fundraisers in milk dairy stables, and, with expressly sacred music, the famous jazz funerals. The great early jazz clarinetist Sidney Bechet commonsensically pointed out that brothels wanted only pianists or small ensembles, so as a matter of course excluded "orchestras," or what we might now think of as Dixieland jazz bands. Bechet testified to have known very few jazz musicians who played in brothels, and historian Ted Gioia estimates that, at its peak, Storyville employed no more than a few dozen jazz musicians.[11]

Thus it is time to put to rest, once and for all, the supposed genetic link of jazz and vice. In terms of environment, the music itself is traced more surely and thoroughly to the house of God than to houses of prostitution. The list of jazz musicians who learned music in the church is lengthy, and extends well after Buddy Bolden. You could, without much effort, make of it something as long as an Anglican or Catholic litany of the saints. Fats Waller's father was a Baptist lay preacher. Duke Ellington trombonist Lawrence Brown's father was a minister. Lester Young's parents were strict Baptists. Charlie Parker's mom was devout. Sixteen-year-old Thelonius Monk toured with an evangelistic troupe. Young Ornette Coleman played in a church band, and later said church music and big band records influenced him more than the blues. Albert Ayler performed saxophone duets in church with his father. Earl Hines said the two greatest influences on his music were the Baptist church and Chopin. Art Blakey learned to "keep rhythm" in the church. Even Miles Davis, decidedly not himself a Christian in his maturity, assigned aspects of *Kind of Blue* to "these bad gospels" he heard walking home from church in his boyhood Arkansas.[12] Contemporary jazz musicians known for their Christian confession include Cyrus Chestnut, Kirk Whalum, Monty Alexander, John Patitucci, Kurt Elling, Eric Reed, and Gregory Tardy. I could go on, but will settle for a hearty "Amen" and end my litany here.

Regarding Heresy and Racism

Far, then, from leaving the extraordinary African-American music called jazz with the onus of proving of its pedigree and fitness for Christian ears, I want to shift the onus for demonstrating a genuine Christianity back to us white American worshippers and our heritage. I mentioned at the outset that black liberation theologian James Cone, in regards to unhappy aspects of that heritage, speaks of the "heresy of white Christianity." *Heresy* is a strong word and is, as such, often deployed politically against those whose convictions and practices we want to rout from the field. Since it is so powerful and prone to abusive overuse, careful theological discussion has tended to limit the term "heresy" to deviation from the core doctrines of the Christian faith—roughly, those convictions affirmed in the Nicene and the Chalcedonian Creeds. Heresy in this strictest sense concerns dogma so central and crucial that deviation from it imperils one's very salvation. Hence the tendency of ancient orthodox creeds to include not only positive affirmations but anathemas, casting those who contradict the affirmations outside the circle of faith.

There is much wisdom in hewing to this careful and restricted use of the word. But especially in a modern context, in which convictions or "beliefs" have conceptually been severed from practices or actual behavior, prudence itself may at times behoove us to apply the term more broadly. That is to say that if white, racist Christians have rarely denounced the doctrine of the Trinity or Christ as Savior, they have often embodied and practiced their faith in such a way that others, whom they subjugated in the name of that faith, could not themselves come to affirm orthodox doctrines. The heresy of white Christianity, then, is one of distorting and deviating from truth in such a way that even if it does not destroy your own faith confession, it effectively prevents or destroys the faith confessions of others.

Up through most of the eighteenth century, American slaveholders did not want their charges evangelized and churched. In part, they probably sensed the incompatibility between baptizing and naming as brother or sister him or her you claimed to own and justifiably treat as subhuman. It also seems quite clear that slaveholders sensed slaves would recognize such incongruities, and perhaps use the faith bequeathed them to challenge their slavery. Despite such misgivings, though, slaveholders gradually came to think that Christianity could be used to domesticate and subdue their charges. Thus a nineteenth-century Alabama judge averred that Christianity "not only benefits the slave in his moral relations, but enhances his values as an honest, faithful servant and laborer."[13] This is, I hope you will agree, a gross distortion of Christian truth: a faith rooted in a people freed from slavery, a revolutionary faith that was understood in its earliest days to "turn the world upside down" (Acts 17:6), is twisted and contorted into an instrument of elite and unjust power. The slavery system even more explicitly warped orthodox Christian faith. For instance, slave catechisms were created to inculcate a sense of black inferiority and white superiority. The doctrine of creation and the Ten Commandments were among the teachings bent to such purposes. So a catechism question asked, "What did God make you for?" and demanded of the slave the answer, "To make a crop." Another inquired, "What is the meaning of 'Thou shalt not commit adultery?'" and expected the reply, "To serve our heavenly Father, and our earthly master, obey our overseer, and not steal anything."[14] These are examples of what Cone, and I here following him, calls "the heresy of white Christianity."

And we need not merely conjecture that this heresy turned slaves away from the God of Israel and the church. Daniel Payne, elected bishop of the African Methodist Episcopal Church in 1852, wrote, "[The slaves] hear their masters professing Christianity; they see their masters preaching the gospel; they hear these masters praying in their families, and they know that oppression and slavery are inconsistent with the Christian religion; therefore they scoff at religion itself—mock their masters, and distrust both the justice and goodness of God." Payne also notes as typical the response of a runaway slave, of whom Payne inquired if he were a Christian. "No sir," replied the runaway, "white men treat us so bad in Mississippi that we can't be Christians."[15]

Right up to the current day, Christianity is sometimes employed—whether subtly or blatantly—to bolster the supposed inferiority of African-Americans and superiority of Anglo-Americans, to reinforce an unjust status quo, and to provide religious sanction to the nation-state and its institutions. At least Cone recognizes all this as a heresy of white Christianity, and does not dismiss Christianity as a whole. It is difficult to blame other African-Americans who have taken heretical white Christianity at its word, as embodying genuine Christianity, and turned to other faiths such as Islam. In fact, Dizzy Gillespie spoke of the movement of jazz musicians into Islam and said that some converted "purely for social reasons." "Christianity" was so identified with "white" that anyone declaring himself or herself Muslim was formally regarded not as a "colored person" but as a foreigner. And as foreigners—as "Arabs"—the musicians could be served in white-only restaurants and lodge in white-only hotels.[16]

Thus has racism created the heresy of white Christianity in its most potent essence, and so can no discussion of jazz or any other African-American art neglect it. But I do not want to confine the remainder of my remarks to a direct consideration of racism. For one thing, such an approach would dishonor jazz itself. There can be no adequate narrative of jazz without taking racism into account, but jazz is not just a reaction to racism. African-American culture is vitally creative, not simply reactive, and hearkens back to resources predating enslavement. Put theologically, God did not only provide African-Americans with resources to survive in a hostile situation determined by their oppressors, but led them to draw on wondrous resources developed in and brought out of Africa. It is some of those resources that shaped jazz and can, through jazz, help correct not only racism but also other crippling errors of white heretical Christianity. Jazz, I want to suggest, can help us correct the heresies of disembodiment, privatization, and the skewing of eschatology. An imposing list, I know, but taken one at a time, not, I hope, an overwhelming list.

The Heresy of Disembodiment

Consider first, then, the white Christian heresy of disembodiment. "White" or "Western" Christianity of course rejects gnosticism, the formal heresy so suspicious of the physical body that it denies the Incarnation and imagines human salvation occurring apart from or even in opposition to the body. Yet western philosophy and Christianity has, especially since Descartes, separated mind and soul from the body and often been awkward at best in recognizing the beauty and rightness of the physical body in the Christian life. Consider, for instance, the limited bodily expression practiced in much or most "white" worship. African-Americans have a wonderful expression for worship really alive and robust; they say, "Now we're having church." The epitome of worship is achieved when most of the congregation is standing, handclapping, raising arms, swaying, and even dancing to gospel beats clearly intended to engage the whole worshiper, body as well as mind. By contrast, we non-Pentecostal whites tend toward stillness and quietness when we move into our most intensely worshipful moods. As the joke goes, if a Dutch Reformed worshiper raised her hands others in the congregation would think she was having a heart attack. Now I do not intend to disallow a place for worshipful quietness and stillness, but I suspect other whites share the awkwardness I sometimes sense about bringing my body into worship. I may be profoundly moved and want to involve my whole person, but any bodily gestures come clumsily and self-consciously, and the self-consciousness itself is a sure sign I am mainly worshiping with my head.

Jazz has been condemned by Christians and other "respectable" Americans because it so enthusiastically involves the body. In the 1920s, the medical officer of a Philadelphia girls' school condemned jazz because "its influence is as harmful and degrading to civilized races as it has always been among the savages from whom we borrowed it."[17] *The Ladies Home Journal* denounced jazz in 1921 because its irregular and sometimes pronounced rhythms supposedly "stimulates [listeners] to extreme deeds, to a breaking away from all rules and conventions," just as the earliest jazz stimulated "the half-crazed barbarian to the vilest deeds."[18] Such concerns have of course been stated more recently, if in less overtly racist terms, by Christians wary of rock music.

There can be no doubt that rhythm affects us bodily more immediately than harmony or melody or other components of music. Turn up a stereo, amplify a bass, or bang the drums harder and you can literally feel the beat in your chest. Lively percussion and basslines are more likely to at least set feet tapping than, say, a stately or lilting unadorned melody. But by Christian confession it is not a bad thing to involve the body. The splendor of resurrection very much includes the body as well as the soul. Karl Barth rightly reminded us that fully Christian theology must speak of an "embodied soul" just as readily as it does of an "ensouled body."

Jazz is a music whose enjoyment disallows the mind-body split; it works complicated changes on melody and chords and can intellectually exercise the most highly trained musician, yet at the same time is built on complex African polyrhythms. As musicologist Christopher Small writes, "In practically all African musicmaking there is a rhythmic polyphony, with at least two different rhythms proceeding in counterpoint to each other, held together only by the existence of a common beat; even the downbeats will quite likely not coincide in different parts."[19] Now it is of course this "irregularity" (better, complexity) of rhythm in jazz to which *The Ladies Home Journal* objected.

But even that objection is more thoughtful than many suspicions about music with a rhythmic emphasis. At least it implicitly recognizes that rhythm in and of itself does not necessarily feed into mindless frenzy and lustful abandon. After all, the regular rhythm of a march can regiment and conform individuals to a group, as armies have long realized. And the work song, another musical form at the historical heart of jazz, employs rhythm to regulate and order labor. Both foes and friends of jazz, rock, and other strongly rhythmic musics have often erroneously associated rhythm with the sexual act. So a spokesman for the Red Hot Chili Peppers has boasted that rock, "being so incredibly rhythmic as it is, [is] very deeply correlated to sex and the rhythm of sex."[20] But if regular rhythm were so tightly and necessarily linked to sex, and a rock band wanted only to sexually excite its audience, it could of course dispense with expensive guitars and sound equipment and simply amplify the ticking of a clock. Or how about the Red Hot Metronomes? As for the actual rhythms of jazz, they are so varied and multilayered that if they remind you of sexual intercourse, I can only say my hat's off to you.[21]

What rhythm actually is, to a degree other components of music are not, is, as I have said, immediate. Or, to clarify, we might say it is eminently accessible; it is the part of music even the most untrained or musically clumsy can most easily discern and follow. But that is not to say rhythm is mindless. As Simon Frith observes, "musical rhythm is as much a mental as a physical matter; deciding *when* to play a note is as much a matter of thought as deciding *what* note to play."[22] And, again, the African polyrhythms that animate jazz are sophisticated and challenging. Listen to Elvin Jones at work, for instance. In a performance such as Coltrane's "Africa," Jones constantly varies volume, tone, and tempo. He treats his trap-set like a complicated orchestra, employing snares, toms, bass drum, cymbals, the highhat, and rimshots like separate instruments—some called on sparingly, others worked throughout, all in their proper places within the whole.[23] Jones's extremely artful and thoroughly crafted performances remind us that excellent drumming is not merely natural or spontaneous, but comes only with much intentional training and practice.

And this is what ethnomusicologists have found when they have actually visited Africa and studied African drummers. Few villagers can play the drums in more than a rudimentary fashion, and even many of those who devote themselves to the art rarely progress beyond the lesser drums and rhythms. The most accomplished drummers, besides possessing unusual musical gifts, practice long and hard, and can vary pitch, vibrato, and timing as skillfully as singers. The musicologist A. M. Jones found that trained African musicians could hear time intervals as small as one twenty-fifth of a second, and remarked, "When we Europeans imagine we are beating strict time, the African will merely smile at the 'roughness' of our beating."[24]

It is also worthwhile noting that African polyrhythms, in their original settings, were used to order and punctuate all of life's activities and were not, as Europeans have so long imagined, fixated on sex. African music was and is used in religious, celebratory, work, and other settings. The mindlessness and abandonment associated with African music in fact owes more to white misperceptions than to actual African and African-American practices of musicmaking. Early white rock stars, in their effort to get across white misunderstandings of black musicality and physicality, exaggerated and theatricalized their performance styles well beyond those of black musicians contemporaneous to them. Think Jerry Lee Lewis, laying into the piano with his fists, feet, and even butt, as if it were a trampoline on fire. Chuck Berry, Little Richard, and Ray Charles began their careers performing in a comparatively sedate and restrained fashion (not to mention the dignified, earlier stage presences of Nat King Cole and the Mills Brothers). Only as they began to appeal to white audiences did they find it necessary to caricature black styles *as their white audiences understood them,* accelerating their singing speed, shrieking and crying out, and sometimes attacking their instruments maniacally.[25]

Such caricature has a long history, extending at least back to minstrelsy. Whites have long found black music fascinating and compelling, but have also been threatened by its artistry and sophistication, enough so that a psychological distance and safety was sought by blackfaced white performers who borrowed (or stole) the music and simultaneously presented its originators as ridiculously comical. After Emancipation blacks themselves worked in minstrel shows and, for white audiences, had to "black up" their performances to conform with stereotypes white ministrel players had been exploiting for decades. The psychological safety this provided Anglo-Americans is evidenced from the testimony of bluesman and jazz artist W. C. Handy. Handy worked in black minstrelsy troupes in the early years of the twentieth century and noted that when the players visited southern towns, they could best avoid harassment offstage "only when dressed in their minstrel costume; those who had the temerity to appear, smartly dressed, as themselves could expect trouble."[26]

In sum, once we try to disentangle racism from our perceptions and interpretations of rhythm, we can appreciate jazz as a musical integration of mind and body. Fine jazz, like fine classical or other musics, "is sometimes erotic, but it is never obscene, because there is always a larger whole—whether spiritual ecstasy, physical exuberance, or emotional catharsis—to which the erotic qualities are joined."[27] White Christians, at least many of us, can use help reclaiming our bodies spiritually, theologically, and worshipfully. Human beings are created and redeemed physically, not merely mentally. And there is a place—a necessary place—for the proper Christian appropriation of the erotic, as an appreciation of physical and material beauty and the right ordering of bodily desires. Jazz, a bodily as well as intellectually involving music, can help us practice resurrection and redemption of the whole person.

Privatizing the Faith

The second heresy of white Christianity jazz can correct is the privatization of faith: the compartmentalization of religion that confines it to the "personal" or nonpublic aspects of our lives. As I indicated, music was pervasive in the everyday and celebratory life of Africa. Just as Africans did not, in European fashion, separate mind from body, so they have not been marked by the European separation of the sacred and the secular. The European or Western or, again loosely speaking, "white" development of Christianity has entailed the separation of religion from politics and economics, and the privatization and individualization of faith. This is reflected in Western music and the modern approach to it.

Consider for a moment our typical experience of classical music. We usually hear live—and certainly orchestral—classical music in a concert hall especially built for the purpose of performing and auditing "high" art. Thus is classical music ideally set apart from everyday life and removed to a separate culture and realm of the fine arts. Indeed, in my home city of Chicago, Symphony Center is set within a six- or eight-block radius of the city's major museums. Alongside the displays of natural history and fine art paintings and sculpture, classical music is itself presented as a kind of museum artifact, presumably representing the highest achievements of Western musical art alongside the highest achievements of Western sciences and visual arts. This is not, at least as we architecturally and semiotically frame it, music for integration and assumption into our everyday lives.

Indeed, we doff our jeans and other casual or work clothes and dress up to enter the concert hall; the classical musicians are clad in tuxedos. The concert hall is windowless and soundproof, intended to be strictly isolated from surrounding life on the streets and neighborhoods. The seats are in orderly, curved rows; that arrangement and the raked floor focuses all attention on the performers and away from the seatmates surrounding those of us in the audience. The musicians have separate dressing rooms and entrances, preventing any mingling with the audience, and they pointedly ignore the audience during their warmup and performance. It has become a part of the ritual to pick up throat lozenges at the doors of the hall, one more way of emphasizing that the role of the audience is a passive one. Listeners are supposed to sit as still and quietly as possible, and direct all attention to the orchestra. All work the listener has to do is strictly mental or intellectual, and solitary or private.[28]

You see of course that I am set to contrast the performance of jazz with that of classical music. But I do not want to demean the undoubted beauties of classical music, for jazz is great on its own merits and does not need to be built up by tearing another music down. Furthermore, the music performed in our concert halls has not always been so segregated from the rest of life and made purely a mental activity on the part of listeners. The concert hall built expressly for that purpose is a development as late as the nineteenth century, and Bach's cantatas, for instance, were originally written for active worship, not as museum pieces for religiously indifferent connoisseurs.

It is exactly our modern, Western, "civilized" framing of classical music that contrasts it with jazz (and explains why some of us do not consider jazz done a favor with its belated welcome into the concert hall). Jazz can be and is played in concert halls, but its ideal setting is a smaller and more intimate one. Furthermore, jazz emphatically resists being made an art object (and so something akin to a sonic museum exhibit). The emphasis in jazz is on the performance of the moment, on music as an activity rather than an objectification. The modern classical musician is bound to the score, and indeed the composer's work, as a kind of ideal object, is made sacrosanct.[29] Perhaps the best short definition of jazz, on the other hand, is that of Louis Armstrong, who said jazz is "music that's never played the same way once."[30] Jazz is improvisational. The nature of jazz as a dynamic activity, unfolding appropriately to the occasion at hand, goes back to the use of African music as an agent of communal bonding. Music drew the community together for celebration or worship or mourning or some other purpose, and was played as befitted the occasion. Dancing, handclapping, and constant verbal or other interaction with the musicians was expected of listeners—in fact, they were never only listeners, but essential participants in the activity of musicmaking. The call and response form of African-American preaching and singing is of the same vein, and deeply marks jazz. That is true in terms of the jazz musician's active improvisational interplay with other musicians, but also in terms of his or her engagement with the audience.

This is most evident when jazz is played for dancing. Perhaps a majority of jazz, up through the era of swing and the big bands, was played for dancing. The interaction between dancer and musicians was direct and vital, so that Lester Young once pined for more jazz played to dancing. He said, "The rhythm of the dancers comes back to you when you're play-ing."[31] But even without the full-fledged bodily commitment of dancing, jazz wants listeners as participants, feeding back verbal and other energy to the musicians as they play. So jazz performances are punctuated by fre-quent applause, with approval of each successfully executed improvisa-tion. As Christopher Small observes, "The improvisers are playing a dan-gerous game, just as they can in any other living relationship, and only the most skillful, quick-thinking and above all 'accomodating to others' . . . can stay the course. This is why listeners see no reason to restrain their applause until the end of the performance, for they are applauding, not one thing, but many skillful and daring acts which are being carried out by musicians as ritual representatives of the whole community."[32] A jazz audience may clap in rhythm, thus becoming additional instruments in the performance. Their engagement and mood helps determine the tone of any given improv-isation, and certainly has much to do with its length or duration.

Consider as an example the Duke Ellington Orchestra's performance of "Diminuendo in Blue and Crescendo in Blue" at the 1956 Newport Jazz Festival.[33] It is a glorious thing, now fully restored and recovered on the Columbia Duke centennial edition issued in 1999. The liner notes help us understand that many things went into this astonishing performance, including the band's anger at waiting hours to go on and having an earlier set prematurely interrupted. The fifteen-minute performance starts ener-getically enough, but really begins to take off about four minutes in, when tenor saxophonist Paul Gonsalves steps up to the microphone. Gonsalves's lead builds the momentum and the band's rhythm takes on a positively oceanic undertow. Then it's chemistry, explosive chemistry. Gonsalves prods the band and it in turn lifts him to more jubilant heights. But also, the liner notes inform us, the listeners become key participants. Some stand up on their chairs and smack their hands. Then a platinum blonde in a black dress can no longer contain herself and, even though she is seated in one of boxes (where she is supposed to behave more as if she were at a classical concert), she's got to dance. She's on her feet and exulting to the music with her whole being. This moves Gonsalves, who has already been swinging like there is no tomorrow, to somehow kick the intensity up another gear or two. Scattered dancers appear like sparks flying through the rest of the audience. "Halfway through Paul's solo," producer George Avakian writes, "[the audience] had become an enormous single living organism, reacting in waves like huge ripples to the music played before it." Gonsalves plays for twenty-seven straight choruses before he relin-quishes control to Duke at the piano.

My point is that this extraordinary moment, now legendary and still incredibly exciting to hear, could not have happened without Paul Gon-salves, but also not without an unnamed platinum blonde dancer and the engaged participation of the rest of the audience. So, as Martha Bayles writes, the jazz soloist plays a priestly role. "This role is sometimes equated with that of the romantic genius, but they are different. The genius is exalted as an individual whose inspired utterances may or may not resonate with the group. The African-American musician, by contrast, is elevated chiefly as a conduit for expression of communal emotion and experience. In both religious and secular settings, he is obliged to interact with his audience through practices such as call and response, collective movement, and the skilled evocation of extreme emotional and mental states."[34] Accordingly, jazz is not a music of atomistic individualism, but of communally engaged musicians who can fully become the musical individuals they are for the duration of a particular performance only through dynamic interaction with other musicians and listeners who commit themselves to be part of the activity of making music. Jazz expects listeners not so much to sink into solitary introspection as to participate in a social performance.

By contrast, I simply ask us to consider how much our white Christian worship, and our practice of faith in general, is more akin to the framing of the concert hall experience than of the jazz performance. Too often, it seems to me, our worship is oriented to the isolated individual's private relationship with God and set apart from the world around us. We order and arrange it so that worshipers are mere auditors, focused as passive and inert spectators on the preacher's words or the singer's solo performance. Jazz as a model would have us recognize the importance of everyone's participation in worship and see the constitution of a social body—not one-on-One relationships with God—as vital to Christian spiritual formation and witness.[35]

Eschatology Askew

The final heresy of white Christianity I will discuss is difficult to characterize. It has to do with eschatology, or the doctrine of last and ultimate things, but certainly we cannot say white Christianity has been without any eschatology. Twentieth-century evangelicalism, for instance, was in large part constructed around the eschatology of dispensationalism. And fears and hopes of the apocalypse are intensely popular in white Christian and American culture in general, as the phenomenal sales of the *Left Behind* novels indicate. One recent poll even has it that forty percent of Americans expect the world to end in their lifetimes.[36] There is also a great deal of diversity in terms of eschatological views.

Yet there are certain tendencies in the eschatology of much white Christianity that, I would argue, skew eschatology and push it away from some of its important bases in the biblical and orthodox Christian tradition. What I think much of white Christianity loses, and what jazz and African-American Christianity can vitally help it recover, is the dynamic and ongoing tension of New Testament apocalypticism. That is, white Christianity tends to radically separate heaven and earth, and the present age from the consummated age to come. So heaven is strictly what happens after you die, and the present age can be considered either entirely unredeemable or, from another political angle but on the same theological basis, not really so profoundly in need of revolutionary redemption.

What I am trying to get at is the reflexive conservatism of white Christianity, a temperamental conservatism that skews its eschatology so that the affairs and state of this world are pretty much to be left just as they are or once were in an earlier golden age. This contributes to a practice and confession of faith that has little place for attempts at social, cultural, and political improvement of the world we inhabit. Accordingly, many blacks cannot relate to the yearning so many white Christians have for a restoration of the America of the 1950s, and this gap is reflected in the notably different voting habits of the black and white churches since the Reagan 1980s. On the other hand, many white Christians who have sensed the need for social and political involvement by Christians have been so marked by the skewed eschatology that utterly partitions heaven from earth, this age from the age to come, that their efforts to integrate faith and politics have collapsed in a rush to one pole or the other. Some, like the secularized sons and daughters of the social gospel, abandon the church and make national politics their new faith. Others, like disgruntled refugees of the religious right such as Ed Dobson and Cal Thomas, give up on politics and emphasize with renewed vigor that faith really has nothing to do with polity.

African-American Christianity has, since its inception, been a rather different creature. Slave Christians devoutly believed in heaven and in a new, just world to come. They did not secularize heaven, and they very much expected a new world to be ushered in by the King Jesus they knew through the biblical narratives. Yet they also saw God at work in their present circumstances, and believed that heaven sometimes broke into even the ugliness and desperation of an earthly life branded and scarred by slave trade. The slave spirituals, then, are grossly misread when they are seen as pietistic and world-denying, as passive hopes for pie in the sky by and by. How so?

The slaves inhabited a world in which open political revolt was unrealistic and unpromising, so their songs featured what some have called "double voicing."[37] "Heaven" in the spirituals then did designate a home beyond death, but it could also refer to Africa, Canada, or the free U.S. North. Canaan, as in "Swing Low, Sweet Chariot," signaled rescue from this world's woes through death, but was also used by the Underground Railroad to refer to transport into the free North. The "band of angels" then were spir-

itual beings, but could also be conductors on the Underground Railroad.
"Steal Away" meant turning to Jesus and could at the same time signal
sneaking into the woods for a secret slave meeting. "Follow the Drinking
Gourd" promised genuine spiritual refreshment and could simultaneously
mean heeding the nighttime orientation of the Big Dipper constellation,
toward the North and liberation. Satan was a transcendent reality, but could
be personified and embodied by slaveholders, slavecatchers, and slave-
traders, as is reflected so clearly in these lines from one spiritual:

> Ole Satan like that hunting dog,
> He hunt them Christians home to God.
> Ole Satan thought he had me fast;
> Broke his chain and I'm free at last.[38]

The power of the spirituals right down to our day is embodied in the
remarkable rendition of "Mary, Don't You Weep" on Aretha Franklin's
album *Amazing Grace*.[39] James Cleveland's opening piano chords in the song
are propulsive, though they call not so much for a smooth march-step as
a stutter-step, anticipating the entire congregation's determined if not unim-
peded advance into a better world. The choir quickly joins in with hum-
ming punctuations of the downbeats and the song gains communal
momentum. After a few bars, Aretha the singer assumes the preacher's
pulpit, picking up the choir's encouragement, "Mary, don't you weep."
Choir and then congregation lend vocal and handclapping support. The
corporate worshiping body is swept into the Gospel of John, standing alongside Mary and Martha days after the death of their brother Lazarus. But
not only does a twentieth-century black church now stand tombside in
first-century Galilee, Aretha suddenly remembers and recalls her congregation to a scene many centuries before Jesus' day, on the freedom side of
the Red Sea, where the Israelites watched "all them men" in Pharaoh's
army drown. "Now if I could," Aretha preach-sings, "I surely would/Stand
right up on that rock/Where Moses stood." She tells Mary and her congregation simultaneously, "I know you know that story/Pharaoh's Army
drowned in the Red Sea."

So the living saints at Cornerstone Institutional Baptist Church in Los
Angeles are brought into communion with the saints dead but not gone,
at the Red Sea thousands of years ago and in front of Lazarus's tomb in
first-century Palestine. In this spiritual as in so many, God brings life and
defines true life Christologically. Aretha now, and in a way I find spine-
tingling every time I listen to it, assumes the voice of Mary addressing Jesus
arrived at the tomb: "My my, my my, my my, my my, my sweeeeet Lord/If
you had been here/My brother would've never died." Then she takes on
the voice of Jesus, calling Lazarus back from the dead, and after that resumes

her place beside Mary and Martha and the Cornerstone Baptists: "He got up walkin'!/ Like a natural man."

Such a performance, like the performances of the spirituals down through the decades before it, is a stirring enactment of biblical eschatology. Jesus already has come and inagurated the kingdom of God on earth. Death itself has been struck a deathblow and Pharaoh's armies of oppression have drowned in the Red Sea. Already. But yet—death remains with us, and surely injustice, and disease and hunger; they are not fully and finally vanquished. What the saints know in the light of Jesus' life, death, and resurrection is that the forces of sin and death and the devil can be defeated, because they have already been beaten, and every time life overcomes death, every time and however fitfully the grip of injustice is broken, there is the kingdom of God on earth. African-American Christian spirituality dwells in the tension between the already and the not yet, the new day dawned but not yet risen to high noon, and so can at once acknowledge suffering and still celebrate, can admit the power of despair and still hope.

When African-Americans sing "Were You There," they *are* there at the foot of the cross, able to empathize all too well with Jesus' scourging and torturous death; when they sing "My Lord delivered Daniel/Why can't He deliver me?" they can at once complain to God with the Psalmist—"How long, O Lord!"—and fully expect that their complaints and pleas are heard and will be honored by the God of Israel met in Jesus Christ. Like Paul, through baptism they pass with the Israelites through the Red Sea and under the cloud in the wilderness and eat the manna in the desert (1 Cor. 10:1–5). Like the writer of Revelation (Rev. 13) they can see the spawn of hell in the present-day government and principalities and powers that pound and beat them down. For African-American Christians, the Bible tells historical stories, certainly, but those historical stories absorb and transform their own stories, private and social, personal and public, individual and corporate. The African-American biblical hermeneutic is decidedly what theologian James McClendon calls a "baptist hermeneutic," with "its awareness of the *present* Christian community" (in Los Angeles in 1972 with Aretha Franklin, in Philadelphia and Chicago and Detroit this Sunday morning) which is also and simultaneously "the primitive [biblical] community" and on top of that a foreshadowing and instance "of the eschatological community" yet to be fully consummated. "In other words," McClendon says, "the church now is the primitive church and the church on the day of judgment is the church now; the obedience and liberty of the followers of Jesus of Nazareth is *our* liberty, *our* obedience."[40]

I am suggesting that white Christianity too often has lost this vibrant eschatological dynamic of past, present, and future interlaid or interwoven in the gospel, and when it has done so has too much seen the biblical past as strictly historical (dead and gone) and the biblical future as strictly future (pie in the sky by and by). And I want to add that jazz, as an African-American music, is very much marked by an eschatological respect of the past, present, and future dynamically connected and marked, each by the others. Jazz of course does not only deal with explicitly sacred music, but its form, if not its substance, is irrevocably eschatological. Jazz musicians are acutely conscious of and respectful to the jazz tradition, even as innovators are accused of taking their music in a fatal departure from the tradition.[41] (Beboppers, for example, though they are now firmly ensconced in the jazz canon, were in their earliest days denounced as apostate.) At the same time, as I have said, jazz is a music concentrated on music as performance and activity rather than as object and static artifact, and as such it has constantly changed and reached ahead into the future. We have seen jazz move from ragtime to Dixieland to swing to bebop to hardbop to jazz fusion to free jazz to acid jazz to who knows exactly what next.

As I said much earlier, jazz is a supremely adaptable and flexible music. It is the music of a people who have long had to live within a society more determinatively defined by others, and know how to make do with limits and material that were not self-chosen. Yet they have never forgotten that you can be creative and transformative even as others set the rules and lay down the conditions of the game. African-American Christians, unlike white Christians, have never presumed they lived in an authentically "Christian nation." For them, as cultural critic Craig Werner puts it, things never changing meant black folk would always remain on the other side of the tracks and at the back of the bus. So jazz is not always sweet and sedate; it can be angry and bring beauty out of that anger, as in Charles Mingus's "Haitian Fight Song." It can mourn heartbreakingly, as in Coltrane's "Alabama," and howl for liberation too long denied, as in Archie Shepp's free jazz. Jazz is not afraid of dissonance because it can transform "noise into music" and thereby "challenges us to *hear* the music in the noise" of an often harsh and even tragic world, and so "to open our ears, our minds, our lives to things we haven't thought about."[42]

Jazz is the eschatological tension that is the human condition set to music, lived as music, able to celebrate and certainly to dance, but also and in the same breath aching and grieving and raging and never satisifed with the tired old world as it is. And in all this it can grant courage and perseverance for present struggles—not for nothing did Martin Luther King call music the "soul" of the civil rights movement.[43] Maybe just a little bit, and in small but important ways, Christians with ears to hear, shorn of white and other heresies, can have jazz make of them prayers to the God "who by the power at work within us is able to accomplish abundantly far more than all we can ask or imagine" (Eph. 3:20).

nineteen

From Holiness to Honky-Tonks

Race and Religion in Country Music

It was Reinhold Niebuhr who suggested that American history is best interpreted through the category of irony. His argument was so suggestive that it was adopted and exploited by a parade of leading historians—from Perry Miller to C. Vann Woodward to Henry May, right on down to Martin Marty in our own day. And if this shotgun matrimony of incongruities, the passionate love-hate affairs of American virtues cohabitating with the vices they deplore most, captures something fundamentally true about the (formerly slaveholding) Land of the Free, then nowhere is it easier to be found than in the quintessentially American art form of country music.

Designating country music an art form straight-away lands us, like Dorothy deposited in Oz by a tornadic dream, deep in the territory of irony. Three-chord song structures, keening steel guitars, rednecks singing out their noses—you dare to call this art?

This essay is dedicated to my late father-in-law, Jess Baldwin, and his dance band, the Sundowners.

Even Nashville, as synonymous with country music as any place on earth, has doubted that it might be so. Blessed with several strong universities (preeminently Vanderbilt and Fisk), Nashville has long styled itself "the Athens of the South." In 1943 the governor of Tennessee denounced Roy Acuff and his Grand Ole Opry for making the state the hillbilly capital of the United States. Little matter. Acuff was then so astronomically popular and so prototypically American that the Japanese, in their banzai charge on Okinawa, cried out, "To hell with Roosevelt; to hell with Babe Ruth; to hell with Roy Acuff!" The fiddler impresario responded to the governor's anathema by twice running for the office.

There is much to be said about the aesthetic status of country music, but mainly I want to concentrate on ironies inherent within the art itself. It is, in fact, no small part of the art of country music that it teems with ironies both delicious and vexing. Three recent books especially equip us to appreciate ironies pervading two key themes that run, root to stem, through country music: race and religion.

On the matter of race, Mississippi-born pastoral theologian Tex Sample (in *White Soul: Country Music, the Church, and Working Americans* [Abingdon, 1996]) provides us with a blunt but inarguable summary: "Without black music, country music would simply not be country." Sample cites a scholar who says country's "sound, structure, and text: all are indebted to African-Americans and their gifts. Country's harmonic origins lie in the blues. Its dramatic employment of stringed instruments (flatpicking and sharp, fluid fingerpicking) traces back to black musical culture."

In fact, black mentors stand behind nearly all the truly great country artists. Jimmie Rodgers, long hailed as the Father of Country Music, in his earliest years listened to black railroad crews who worked in unison by chanting under the lead of a caller setting the cadences. (In his *In the Country: People and Places in American Music* [Pantheon, 1997], Nicholas Dawidoff reports a former worker who remembers "sexy calls" were most effective: "Some callers would talk about the lingerie that a woman wore. Now that caused the crew to really shift that track.") As a young adult, Rodgers spent many of his recreational hours in black neighborhoods, frequenting billiard halls and blues-playing juke joints. In his heyday, Rodgers's music was so transparently African-American that some worried about him as "a white man gone black." At least in terms of his repertoire, there is no evidence Rodgers ever tried to disguise the connection. He is most famous for a series of twelve "blue yodels," and his "Blue Yodel No. 9," recorded in 1930, features no less than Louis Armstrong on trumpet.

Contemporaneous with Rodgers, and equally important to the history of country music, was the Carter Family. The "family" consisted of an eccentric, preoccupied Virginian named A. P. Carter, his wife Sara, and their guitarist-niece Maybelle. The Carters recorded dozens of timeless songs

("Keep on the Sunny Side" would be among the most familiar, but my own favorite is the haunting "Hello Stranger"). Most of these were gathered by A. P., who often disappeared on month-long song-hunting forages throughout the Appalachians. As Dawidoff notes, "A. P. had an excellent ear for affecting music, but a poor memory for melody." To compensate, he took to traveling with black blues singer Lesley Riddle. Riddle not only helped Carter take down songs: he taught A. P. many of his own and coached Maybelle in the strikingly plaintive guitar style that subsequently molded generations of pickers.

Such recounting could go on at length. Hank Williams learned guitar from a black man. Bob Wills's Western Swing—a wondrously odd music that initially struck my pretentiously hip teenaged ears as ridiculous but eventually won me over with its sheer, infectious fun—melded fiddle music and Dixieland jazz, as well as Wills's deep love of the blues of Bessie Smith. (One of our very finest living musician-songwriters, Merle Haggard, was mentored by Wills and prefers to call his own work "country jazz.") Bill Monroe pioneered bluegrass out of an amalgam of fiddle shuffles, gospel hymns, and jazz (whence bluegrass's yen for improvisation), and perfected his mandolin technique with the tutelage of an African-American guitarist whose syncopated licks, Dawidoff says, helped "make old-time string-band music into something livelier and more complex, shaping his notes into sophisticated rhythm structures that experts will be hashing over for generations." Young Johnny Cash, bored with a job selling appliances door-to-door in black Memphis, met a retired street sweeper and banjo picker named Gus Cannon. Most days, rather than hawking vacuum cleaners, Cash brought along his guitar and jammed on Cannon's porch.

But—and here is the irony—despite this monumental legacy, African-Americans and African-American concerns are glaringly scarce in country music. Tex Sample cites one careful study confirming that, "Of the thousands of songs on the country music hit charts since World War II, probably no more than twenty mention race in any connection." Only two black artists have achieved visibility. Deford Bailey performed on the Grand Ole Opry during the twenties. Decades later, Charley Pride recorded a string of hits. Yet his first three singles were released without any accompanying publicity photos, and when Pride walked on a Detroit stage for his first concert he was greeted by stunned silence that was broken only after he joked about his "natural tan."

The racism marring country's ethos—and racism, I am afraid, is what it must be called—can be explicit. Charlie Louvin, one-half of the brotherly duet whose vocal harmonies are spine-chillingly beautiful, can still offhandedly refer to scrub pine trees as "nigger pine." Charlie's late brother Ira alienated Elvis Presley, with whom the Louvins were touring in 1955, by screaming at him that he was a "f—in' white nigger." Mostly, though, country music's racism is a racism of forgetfulness and neglect. It reflects, I suppose, the wider racism of the white, working-class, southern culture from which it sprang, tortured and almost hopelessly complicated by the familiarity and proximity of a people and a culture to which it owes so much but, in its own economic and psychological insecurity, also fears and feels it must denigrate.

This is, of course, finally no excuse. Reinhold Niebuhr seized on irony to interpret American history exactly because it preserves an important capacity for self-criticism. So those of us who love to promote the art need to forcefully remind ourselves that behind the lily-white face of country music courses black blood and pulses glorious black soul.

So race and country music. But what of religion? Most country singers learn how to sing in church. George Jones picked up his first guitar chords in a Pentecostal Sunday school and for a while traveled with an evangelist as a child singer. Young Emmylou Harris sang duets with her father in church. Of the present-day stars in Lesley Sussman's *"Yes, Lord, I'm Comin' Home!"* (Doubleday, 1997), fourteen had strong Baptist upbringings, four Pentecostal, and four Methodist or Nazarene.

Yet, as they mature and decide to pursue careers in music, country artists' venues inevitably and, at best, ironically include not just sanctuaries but honky-tonks. Sussman says "playing gigs in South Oklahoma beer joints" made Toby Keith "feel as if he was betraying [the] spiritual values" of his Christian upbringing. Mark Collie tells Sussman, "You're faced with all your church learning and then you're going out and making a living playing in roadhouses and bars. It's very strange. I would be singing in the roadhouses on Saturday night and then playing the revivals on Sunday afternoon. Many a Sunday I felt like the preacher was speaking directly at me."

So country artists ricochet between the carnal passions of Saturday night and the spiritual ecstasy of Sunday morning. A few notables have tamed this charged dialectic and managed stable personal lives: Dawidoff remarks that Kitty Wells, the first successful female solo performer in country music, "was a devoted wife and mother who didn't drink or smoke, took a Bible with her on the road, and carried herself, the popular Tennessee governor Frank Clement observed, in 'the finest tradition of Southern womanhood.'" Wells and her (only) husband have been married six decades. But many other artists have struggled, on sometimes nearly mythical scales of self-destruction, to balance the Bible in one hand and the bottle in the other.

Hank Williams wrote classics like "I Saw the Light" that still ring out at southern gospel sings, but perished from hard living and heartbreak at age twenty-nine. Carter Stanley (of the Stanley Brothers) made gospel songs the keystone of his career but drank himself to death by age forty-one. George Jones amazes his friends and fans, who have literally given him up for dead more than once, that he is still alive in his sixties.

Yet the uneclipsed standard-bearer in this grim litany of tortured souls is perhaps Alabaman Ira Louvin, who finally, and one can't help but think mercifully, died in a car wreck in 1965. Raised with brother Charlie in Pentecostal fervor, Ira was to his last years telling a local preacher he would perform one more concert, then take to the road as an evangelist. He penned exceedingly preachy songs like "Broadminded," which inveighed against social dancing and drinking: "That word broadminded is spelled s-i-n/I read in my Bible, 'They shall not enter in.'" Trussed on a rack with the church stretching from one end and the honky-tonk from the other, Ira would perform in a bar, revile himself for it, then drink himself into a stupor. In unremitting turmoil, he was given to violence and repeatedly stomped mandolins to pieces. He attempted to strangle his third wife with a telephone cord. She got loose and emptied a .22 pistol into Ira. He survived, and a newspaper quoted her afterward as saying, "If the son of a bitch don't die, I'll shoot him again."

Ira had a high forehead with a widow's peak, an aquiline nose, crazed eyes, and a maniacal open-mouth smile. The cover of the Louvin Brothers' *Satan is Real* album features the siblings in a mock hell, with flaming rocks and a cardboard devil looming behind them. Baby-faced Charlie has his arms extended with palms open, gesturing from the right side across the scene as if to say, "Ain't this a silly picture." Ira, though, appears positively possessed and faces the camera with arms out and fingers curled, beckoning the viewer into the torment. He is scarier, by far, than anything else in the picture.

True, all kinds of great music marinated in misery. The travails of classical composers such as Mozart and Beethoven are well known. Many jazz geniuses have passed short, stormy lives, such as Bix Beiderbecke, who died at twenty-eight, and Charlie Parker, who never made his thirty-fifth birthday. But perhaps no music so consistently and starkly juxtaposes the sacred and the profane as country.

The progressive country songwriter Butch Hancock wryly provides Dawidoff some clue to this irony: "In Lubbock [Texas] we grew up with two main things. God loves you and he's gonna send you to hell, and that sex is bad and dirty and nasty and awful and you should save it for the one you love. You wonder why we're all crazy."

More seriously, Tex Sample challenges the church to put aside its tendencies to sanitize life and mount superficial moralistic façades that obscure unpleasant realities from view. Indeed, it disappoints to hear many of Sussman's subjects insist that they became truly Christian only after they stopped singing about suffering. Susie Luchsinger (Reba McEntire's sister) says, "I'd never been really happy singing country music. So much of it was about turmoil and fear." The talented songwriter Paul Overstreet, according to Sussman, now "leaves it to others to write lyrics about cheating hearts, Sunday morning hangovers and breaking up." Red Steagall unwittingly reveals how far such attitudes are from genuine Christianity, remarking, "I just wish that everybody could have a positive attitude whether they believe in God or not."

A good deal of excellent country music need not offend even the most avid reader of Norman Vincent Peale or the most naive champion of family values. Country songs are forever remembering Mama and harking back to home and the old ways. At their best, these songs reinforce foundational virtues and poignantly invoke healing tears.

But not all country music is informed by the power of positive thinking. I wonder if Sussman's subjects, God bless them, have stopped reading the Psalms or Jeremiah or the Passion accounts in their Bibles. If the Christian tradition is any guide, it is not always wrong or "unhealthy" to grieve or cry out in anger or admit one's sinfulness. I would like to think that, before they grew up and began dragging their guitars and broken hearts into barrooms, country singers gleaned something of these verities in their little rural churches. Isn't it possible, even likely, that George Jones—who Frank Sinatra once called "the second best male singer in America"—first learned something about the artful acknowledgment of suffering at the foot of the cross?

In any event, he learned it somewhere. Dawidoff is at his considerable best in describing Jones's visceral vocal powers on his performance of "A Good Year for the Roses." The song is the lament of the survivor of a shattered marriage morosely surveying his home for signs of his departed wife. As Dawidoff writes, "The vocal effect is like a human bagpipe—the slow release of a deep, mournful sound. He gives you the picture of a man who senses he is about to be unhappier than he has ever been, and will be for a long time. Someone who understood no English could hear Jones sing this song and would know instantly what it is about."

And if that isn't art, art doesn't matter.

Endnotes

1. How Firm a Foundation

1. Richard R. Topping, "The Anti-foundationalist Challenge to Evangelical Apologetics," *Evangelical Quarterly* 63, no. 1 (1991): 45–60 (quote from p. 45). Helpful overviews of foundationalism can be found in Jonathan Dancy, *Introduction to Contemporary Epistemology* (Oxford: Blackwell, 1985), and John E. Thiel, *Nonfoundationalism* (Minneapolis: Fortress, 1994).

2. Jeffrey Stout, *The Flight from Authority* (Notre Dame, Ind.: University of Notre Dame Press, 1981), p. 46. A more detailed account of the historical situation and its results is offered in the first two chapters of Stephen Toulmin, *Cosmopolis* (Chicago: University of Chicago Press, 1990), pp. 1–87.

3. Lorraine Daston, "Baconian Facts, Academic Civility and the Prehistory of Objectivity," in *Rethinking Objectivity*, ed. Allan Megill (Durham, N.C.: Duke University Press, 1994), pp. 52–53.

4. Stephen Toulmin, *The Uses of Argument* (Cambridge: Cambridge University Press, 1958), pp. 127, 249. Descartes is quite explicit about mathematics' appeal and influence on his work. In the first chapter of his *Discourse on Method*, he comments, "Above all I enjoyed mathematics, because of the certainty and self-evidence of its reasonings," and "I was astonished that on such firm and solid foundations nothing more exalted had been built." In the second chapter he explains that since "only the mathematicians have been able to arrive at proofs, that is to say, certain and evident reasons, I had no doubt that it was by the same things which they had examined that I should begin." And in chapter five he writes, "I have always remained firm in my resolution . . . not to accept anything as being true which did not seem to me more clear and certain than had previously the demonstrations of the geometers" (*Discourse on Method*, trans. F. E. Sutcliffe [London: Penguin, 1986], pp. 31, 41–42, 61).

5. Stanley Hauerwas has pointed out to me that *individual* was a term first used in mathematics, to denote a "free-standing entity."

6. George M. Marsden, *Fundamentalism and American Culture* (New York: Oxford University Press, 1980), p. 111. For more on the influence of Scottish Common Sense Realism, see pp. 14–16, 109–18, and Marsden's "The Collapse of American Evangelical Academia," in *Faith and Rationality*, ed. Alvin Plantinga and Nicholas Wolterstorff (Notre Dame, Ind.: University of Notre Dame Press, 1983), pp. 219–64.

7. Marsden, *Fundamentalism*, p. 111.

8. Ibid., pp. 111, 112.

9. One of the central points of this chapter is that words and their truth mean nothing apart from the communal contexts in which they are used. In that spirit, I hope it is clear that I am aware that the word *foundationalism* hardly has a single, univocal meaning. Thus there are some important Christian thinkers, perhaps most notably Alvin Plantinga and William Alston, who call themselves foundationalists but are certainly not foundationalists of the sort worried over through these pages.

10. Toulmin, *Uses of Argument*, p. 183.

11. Ibid., p. 218.

12. I take this example from David S. Cunningham, who clearly fared better in algebra than I did. See his *Faithful Persuasion: In Aid of a Rhetoric of Christian Theology* (Notre Dame, Ind.: University of Notre Dame Press, 1991), pp. 152, 154.

13. Ronald Nash, *Faith and Reason* (Grand Rapids, Mich.: Zondervan, 1988), pp. 23, 26, 28, 30.

14. I know Ron Nash to possess a sense of humor. Accordingly, the smoking metaphor is an attempt to clarify a tendency among some evangelicals—maybe "funly," as a friend of mine often says. It is not intended to mock or disrespect Professor Nash.

15. Nash, *Faith*, pp. 38–39.

16. Ibid., p. 55.

17. Quoted in ibid., p. 57.

18. In a book powerfully pertinent to the contention of this essay as a whole, David Cunningham notes, "Most of our arguments take place precisely because we have no general agreement about the rules of the game; and the absence of such universally accepted conventions makes persuasion essential." See his *Faithful Persuasion*, p. 154.

19. Nash, *Faith*, p. 63.

20. Ibid., pp. 65–66.

21. Kenneth S. Kantzer, "Unity and Diversity in Evangelical Faith," in *The Evangelicals*, ed. David F. Wells and John D. Woodbridge (Grand Rapids, Mich.: Baker Book House, 1977), p. 80.

22. See Stanley Murphy, *Reasoning and Rhetoric in Religion* (Valley Forge, Penn.: Trinity Press International, 1994); McClendon and Smith, *Convictions*, pp. 106–7.

23. Stanley Hauerwas, "No Enemy, No Christianity: Preaching between 'Worlds,'" unpublished paper, p. 17; later published in an edited form, "Preaching as Though We Had Enemies," *First Things*, May 1995, pp. 45–49.

24. I have borrowed William Placher's phrase from his *Unapologetic Theology: A Christian Voice in a Pluralistic Conversation* (Louisville, Ky.: Westminster/John Knox, 1989). He explains that in recent decades "the search for universal starting points and standards for rationality" has come under crippling critical fire. Dialogue need no longer "await universally acceptable starting points" before beginning. "We could admit that of course we all stand within traditions and can never achieve an 'objective' point of view." Given these conditions, and since Christianity "cannot criticize our culture very effectively if it has already accepted many of the assumptions of that culture," it may be that the time has come for a more particular, explicit, and "unapologetic" theology (p. 12).

25. "Yet," he continues, "this does not reduce the choice between different frameworks to whim or chance. . . . The norms of reasonableness are too rich and subtle to be adequately

specified in any general theory of reason or knowledge. These norms, to repeat a point often made in this book, are like the rules of depth grammar, which linguists search for and may at times approximate but never grasp." See *The Nature of Doctrine: Religion and Theology in a Postliberal Age* (Philadelphia: Westminster Press, 1984), p. 130. Cogent arguments that Lindbeck's account of truth is compatible with the mainstream of Christian tradition have been made by one of his former students, Bruce D. Marshall, in "Aquinas as Postliberal Theologian," *The Thomist* 53 (1984): 353–401 (to which Lindbeck responds [pp. 403–6] affirmatively that "Marshall has explained the view of truth which I had in mind better than I explained it myself" [p. 406]), and "Absorbing the World: Christianity and the Universe of Truths," in *Theology and Dialogue: Essays in Conversation with George Lindbeck*, ed. Bruce D. Marshall (Notre Dame, Ind.: University of Notre Dame Press, 1990), pp. 69–102.

26. Kantzer, "Unity and Diversity," p. 71. Contrast this with Nancey Murphy's candid admission that though she considers Christianity historically and ontologically true, "no system fulfills all of these criteria [of epistemological persuasion] perfectly. We always have some inconsistencies and a great deal of incoherence in our networks of belief." She also observes, "No one working with a holist account of knowledge is likely to argue for absolutism" (*Reasoning and Rhetoric in Religion*, pp. 257, 263).

27. In terms compatible with the criticisms I offer here of Nash, Kantzer, Piper, and Grudem, Richard R. Topping critiques the foundationalist apologetics of evangelicals Carl F. H. Henry and Stuart Hackett. See his "Anti-foundationalist Challenge to Evangelical Apologetics."

28. John Piper and Wayne Grudem, "An Overview of General Concerns: Questions and Answers," in *Recovering Biblical Manhood and Womanhood*, ed. John Piper and Wayne Grudem (Wheaton, Ill.: Crossway, 1991), pp. 84–85.

29. See Toulmin, *Uses of Argument*, p. 235. Relativism as the inversion of foundationalism often draws remark. See, for example, Nancey Murphy, "Textual Relativism, Philosophy of Language and the Baptist Vision," in *Theology without Foundations*, ed. Stanley Hauerwas, Nancey Murphy, and Mark Nation (Nashville: Abingdon, 1994), pp. 268–69; and Ian S. Markham, *Plurality and Christian Ethics* (Cambridge: Cambridge University Press, 1994), pp. 142–43.

30. For a lucid discussion of these holistic epistemological rules, see Murphy, *Reasoning and Rhetoric in Religion*, particularly pp. 256–57.

31. See Alasdair MacIntyre, *Whose Justice? Which Rationality?* (Notre Dame, Ind.: University of Notre Dame Press, 1988), pp. 349–88.

32. Likewise, of course, we may be changed and our faith enriched in the same relationship. Or, though we hardly expect it, we cannot deny the possibility that our faith may be shattered in the relationship. I paraphrase here, in my own Christian and theological terms, the summary of persuasion on nonobjectivist grounds presented by Barbara Herrnstein Smith in "The Unquiet Judge: Activism without Objectivism in Laws and Politics," in *Rethinking Objectivity*, ed. Allan Megill (Durham, N.C.: Duke University Press, 1994), p. 301.

33. In this regard I am friendly to Cunningham's description of theology. Seen rhetorically, he writes, theology recognizes that its task "is to persuade others to thought and action. Such persuasion will be unable to operate in a value free, individualistic mode; it must take account of the moral presuppositions of both speaker and audience, as well as the 'material concerns, resources, and strategies in the present situation'" (*Faithful Persuasion*, p. 36).

34. George Parkin Grant, *English-Speaking Justice* (Notre Dame, Ind.: University of Notre Dame Press, 1985), p. 102.

35. For critical surveys of liberalism, see Ronald Beiner, *What's the Matter with Liberalism?* (Berkeley: University of California Press, 1992); H. Jefferson Powell, *The Moral Tradition of American Constitutionalism* (Durham, N.C.: Duke University Press, 1993); and Robert Booth

Fowler, *Unconventional Partners: Religion and Liberal Culture in the United States* (Grand Rapids, Mich.: Eerdmans, 1989).

36. MacIntyre, *Whose Justice?*, p. 335 (emphasis added).

37. This is not to say there are no nonfoundationalist liberals. Nonfoundationalist liberalism differs from its foundationalist ancestor in that it does not, at least not as easily, appeal to universal and acultural norms. But it persists in idealizing individual freedom and eschewing any substantive common good. For nonfoundationalist defenses of liberalism, see Richard Rorty, *Contingency, Irony and Solidarity* (Cambridge: Cambridge University Press, 1989), and "The Priority of Democracy to Philosophy," in *Prospects for a Common Morality*, ed. Gene Outka and John P. Reeder Jr. (Princeton, N.J.: Princeton University Press, 1993), as well as Jeffrey Stout, *Ethics after Babel: The Language of Morals and Their Discontents* (Boston: Beacon, 1988), pp. 220–92.

38. Stanley Fish, *There's No Such Thing as Free Speech and It's a Good Thing, Too* (New York: Oxford University Press, 1994), p. 16. I agree with Fish that liberalism is "basically a brief against belief and conviction," that it "is an incoherent notion born out of the correct insight that we will never [noneschatologically] see an end to these squabbles and that therefore we must do something, and the doing something is somehow to find a way to rise above the world of conviction, belief, passion. I simply don't think that's possible" (pp. 296, 298).

39. For fine guidance on reading the Bible nonviolently and nonhegemonically, see J. Richard Middleton and Brian J. Walsh, *Truth Is Stranger Than It Used to Be: Biblical Faith in a Postmodern Age* (Downers Grove, Ill.: InterVarsity Press, 1995).

40. John Howard Yoder, *The Royal Priesthood*, ed. Michael Cartwright (Grand Rapids, Mich.: Eerdmans, 1994), pp. 112–13.

41. These last two sentences paraphrase Hauerwas, "No Enemy, No Christianity," pp. 3, 4.

42. Yoder, *Royal Priesthood*, p. 373.

43. I am grateful for the draft readings and criticism of this essay by Kelly James Clark, Stanley Hauerwas, Philip Kenneson, Nancey Murphy, Tim Peebles, James Sire, and Brian Walsh. Whatever its remaining faults, it has been much improved through their generosity and intelligence.

6. Tacit Holiness

1. John F. Alexander, *The Secular Squeeze* (Downers Grove, Ill.: InterVarsity Press, 1993), p. 31.

2. Stanley Hauerwas, "The Sanctified Body: Why Perfection Does Not Require a 'Self,'" in *Embodied Holiness: Toward a Corporate Theology of Spiritual Growth*, ed. Samuel M. Powell and Michael E. Lodahl (Downers Grove, Ill.: InterVarsity Press, 1999), pp. 19–38. Henceforth all references to this essay will include parenthetical page numbers in the main body of my text.

3. Michael Polanyi, *Personal Knowledge* (Chicago: University of Chicago Press, 1962), p. 50.

4. Stanley Fish, "Dennis Martinez and the Uses of Theory," in *Doing What Comes Naturally* (Durham, N.C.: Duke University Press, 1989), pp. 372–98.

5. Colin E. Gunton, *Enlightenment and Alienation* (Grand Rapids, Mich.: Eerdmans, 1985), p. 38.

6. Ibid., pp. 38–39.

7. Thomas à Kempis, quoted in Alexander, *Secular Squeeze*, p. 31.

8. Wayne Booth, "Individualism and the Mystery of the Social Self," in *Freedom and Interpretation*, ed. Barbara Johnson (New York: BasicBooks, 1993), p. 81.

9. Ibid., pp. 87–88.

10. Philip Slater, *The Earth Walk*, quoted without further attribution in Lawrence Stone, *The Past and the Present Revisited* (London: Routledge and Kegan Paul, 1987), p. 325.

11. Booth, "Individualism," pp. 78, 79.

12. For a classic statement, see H. Wheeler Robinson, "Hebrew Psychology," in *The People and the Book,* ed. A. S. Peake (London: Oxford University Press, 1925), pp. 353–82. Robinson remarks that such doctrines as original sin are incomprehensible without a notion such as corporate personality. I would add that our thoroughgoing individualism also threatens to render incoherent the doctrines of atonement, of the church, and even, most fundamentally, the Trinity.

13. Bruce J. Malina, *The New Testament World: Insights from Cultural Anthropology* (Atlanta: John Knox Press, 1981), pp. 54, 55 (emphases in original).

14. Charles Talbert, *Reading Corinthians: A Literary and Theological Commentary on 1 and 2 Corinthians* (New York: Crossroad, 1987), p. 31. Also J. Paul Sampley: "Paul thinks of believers' relationship with Christ in terms of solidarity with, participation in, or belonging to Christ. . . . Those who have faith are one together in Christ. This solidarity with Christ is Paul's primary identification of believers."

He adds, "Just as surely as one does not snub the workings of the Spirit, one does not disregard the community in one's life of faith."

And: "Paul's great interest in the health and growth of the individual's faith is always set within his concern for the well-being of the community, and his commitment to community is always located within his conviction that God's renewal of the entire cosmos is under way" (J. Paul Sampley, *Walking between the Times: Paul's Moral Reasoning* [Minneapolis: Fortress, 1991], pp. 12, 43, 118).

15. Dale Martin, *The Corinthian Body* (New Haven, Conn.: Yale University Press, 1985), pp. 4–5.

16. For unpacking of what I mean by such a designation, see the remarks on mass-techno-liberal-capitalism in chapter 12 of Rodney Clapp, *A Peculiar People: The Church as Culture in a Post-Christian Society* (Downers Grove, Ill.: InterVarsity Press, 1996).

17. Robert Inchausti, *The Ignorant Perfection of Ordinary People* (Albany, N.Y.: State University Press of New York, 1991), p. 141. Inchausti's excellent book examines such "religious plebeian" leaders as Gandhi, Solzhenitsyn, Elie Wiesel, Mother Teresa, Martin Luther King, and Lech Walesa who have, out of their religious traditions, recognized the reality of the inimical mass modern system, and called for antidotes that include an "elevated sense of the self as socially and historically constituted and therefore inherently politically engaged and morally responsible" (p. 141).

18. Martin, *Corinthian Body,* pp. 131–32.

19. Tertullian, *De Resurrectione Carnis* 8.6–12, as cited in Mary Timothy Prokes, FSE, *Toward a Theology of the Body* (Grand Rapids, Mich.: Eerdmans, 1996), p. 137.

20. Louis-Marie Chauvet, *Symbol and Sacrament,* trans. Patrick Madigan, S.J., and Madeleine Beaumont (Collegeville, Minn.: Liturgical Press, 1995), p. 376.

10. At the Intersection of Eucharist and Capital

1. Robert W. Jenson, *Systematic Theology: The Works of God,* vol. 2 (Oxford: Oxford University Press, 1999), p. 305.

2. David Toole, *Waiting for Godot in Sarajevo* (Boulder, Colo.: Westview Press, 1998), p. 35. Louis Dumont makes the same point concisely, if more abstractly: "Everyone knows that religion was formerly a matter of the group and has become a matter of the individual . . . [Once Medieval Christianity gave way and Christianity] became an individual affair, it lost its all-embracing capacity and became one among other apparently equal considerations, of which the political was the first born. Each individual may, of course, and perhaps will, recognize religion (or philosophy), as the same all-embracing consideration it used to be *socially.* Yet on the level of social consensus or ideology, the same person will switch to a different configuration of values in which autonomous values (religious, political, etc.) are seemingly juxta-

posed, much as individuals are juxtaposed in society." Cited in Talal Asad, *Genealogies of Religion* (Baltimore: The Johns Hopkins University Press, 1993), p. 28.

3. See Kenneth R. Craycraft, Jr., *The Myth of American Religious Freedom* (Dallas, Tex.: Spence Publishing Co., 1999), p. 141. Although the example of Kennedy is now three decades old (and serves my present purpose because it is both candid and concise), the privatization/neutralization of the church is still very much with us. Given more space, it would be worthwhile to examine in detail Mario Cuomo's famous 1984 speech at the University of Notre Dame, "Religious Belief and Public Morality: A Catholic Governor's Perspective" (found on pp. 32–51 of Cuomo, *More Than Words: The Speeches of Mario Cuomo* [New York: St. Martin's Press, 1993]). Cuomo's central fear in the speech is that a powerful religious body—such as the Roman Catholic Church—might tell its members how to vote, or at least who *not* to vote for (as in the contentious example of abortion). But without telling his listeners (or himself?), he elides a question about the proper authority of the church over its members into a discussion against the church legislatively imposing its will onto the entire populace—not just Catholics, but Protestants, Jews, Hindus, secularists, and all other American citizens. So, though he quite correctly eschews governmental coercion of the national body politic, Cuomo effectively eviscerates any real or actual authority the church might have over its members' "public" or political conduct. Cuomo wants Catholics to give, e.g., the words of the bishops "respectful attention and careful consideration," but he is clear that the same Catholics should not heed in public practice those same words on issues of nuclear war, economics, or contraceptives and abortions. In the end, then, he allows for Catholic public "authority" little more than the polite deference afforded a senile uncle.

4. For an expanded account of retrenchment and sentimental capitulation, see Rodney Clapp, *A Peculiar People: The Church as Culture in a Post-Christian Society* (Downers Grove, Ill.: InterVarsity Press, 1996), pp. 16–57.

5. Jenson, *Systematic Theology,* p. 305.

6. See David C. Korten, *The Post-Corporate World* (San Francisco: Berrett-Koehler Publishers; and West Hartford, Conn.: Kumarian Press, 1999), pp. 33, 42; and Korten, "The Failures of Bretton Woods," in ed. Jerry Mander and Edward Goldsmith, *The Case Against the Global Economy* (San Francisco: Sierra Club Books, 1996), p. 26.

7. See Rodney Clapp, *Families at Crossroads* (Downers Grove, Ill.: InterVarsity Press, 1993), pp. 48–66.

8. See Andrew Kimbrell, "Biocolonization," in ed. Mander and Goldsmith, *Case Against the Global Economy,* pp. 131–145.

9. Ted Halstead and Clifford Cobb, "The Need for New Measurements of Progress," in ed. Mander and Goldsmith, *Case Against the Global Economy,* p. 201.

10. Quoted in David A. Crocker, "Consumption and Well-Being," *Philosophy & Public Policy* 15, no. 4 (Fall 1995): 13. It is of course one of the premier oddities of so-called conservatism in the United States that it routinely supports and promotes consumer capitalism, rarely if ever admitting capitalism's highly antitraditional and nonconservative nature. As Lebow's statement suggests, the vanguard of consumer capitalism recognized that engrained, genuinely conservative habits stood in its way. Even more explicit, in this regard, were the late-1940s comments made by industrial designer J. Gordon Lippincott: "Our willingness to part with something before it is completely worn out is . . . truly an American habit. . . . The prime job that national advertising, research, and the industrial designer are doing in common is . . . convincing the consumer that he needs a new product before his old one is worn out." Cited in Mark Dery, *The Pyrotechnic Insanitarium: American Culture on the Brink* (New York: Grove Press, 1999), pp. 119–120.

11. Cited in Craycraft, *The American Myth,* p. 20.

12. An excellent concise account of the liturgical and patristic renewal is Paul McPartlan, *Sacrament of Salvation* (Edinburgh: T&T Clark, 1995).

13. Michael B. Aune, "'Into the World, Into Each Human Heart': Ritual Behavior in Relation to the *Missio Dei*," in *Inside Out: Worship in the Age of Mission*, ed. Thomas Schauttauer (Minneapolis: Fortress Press, 2000), pp. 155–156.

14. Ibid.

15. Quoted in ibid., p. 156.

16. Asad, *Genealogies of Religion*, p. 33.

17. Ibid.

18. Ibid., p. 136.

19. Ibid., p. 39.

20. George Lindbeck, *The Nature of Doctrine* (Philadelphia: The Westminster Press, 1984), throughout, but see pp. 31–32 for a definition.

21. Charles Talbert, *Reading Corinthians* (New York: Crossroad, 1987), p. 31.

22. The classic proposal and delineation of postliberal theology remains Lindbeck, cited above in note 20. A fine overview of postliberal theology is William C. Placher's *Unapologetic Theology* (Louisville, Ky.: Westminster/John Knox Press, 1989). For interesting exchanges between prominent postliberals and postconservative evangelicals, see *The Nature of Confession*, Timothy R. Phillips and Dennis L. Okholm eds. (Downers Grove, Ill.: InterVarsity Press, 1996). For a penetrating examination and description of postconservative evangelicals, see Gary Dorrien, *The Remaking of Evangelical Theology* (Louisville, Ky.: Westminster/John Knox Press, 1998).

23. The founding text of radical orthodoxy is John Milbank, *Theology and Social Theory* (Oxford: Blackwell, 1990). Catherine Pickstock has published *After Writing* (Oxford: Blackwell, 1998).

24. Baxter's work thus far is a number of intriguing journal essays. Cavanaugh has written *Torture and Eucharist* (Oxford: Blackwell, 1998). For a striking example that these thinkers are already being read to direct effect on church affairs, see the Library of Congress address "Catholic Christianity and the Millennium: Frontiers of the Mind in the 21st Century," by the archbishop of the Chicago diocese of the Catholic Church, Francis Cardinal George. Cardinal George here draws on Baxter, Milbank, Pickstock, and the postliberal William Placher.

25. John Milbank, *The Word Made Strange* (Oxford: Blackwell, 1997), p. 250.

26. Aidan Kavanagh, *On Liturgical Theology* (New York: Pueblo Publishing Co., 1984), p. 176.

27. Alexander Schmemann, *For the Life of the World* (Crestwood, N.Y.: Saint Vladimir's Seminary Press, 1973), p. 25.

28. Ibid., p. 27.

29. Ibid., p. 44.

30. Jenson, *Systematic Theology*, p. 304.

31. A remarkable book working toward the recovery of Christian discipline from a Protestant perspective is Philip D. Kenneson, *Life on the Vine* (Downers Grove, Ill.: InterVarsity Press, 1999).

32. Glenn McDonald, "Imagining a New Church," *The Christian Century*, 8–15 September 1999, p. 852.

33. A statement made by pastor and televangelist D. James Kennedy, in "Flex the Muscle," *Leadership*, Spring 1993, pp. 24–26.

34. Schmemann, *For the Life of the World*, p. 29.

35. Robert Wuthnow, *God and Mammon in America* (New York: Free Press, 1994), pp. 138–141.

36. In a disturbing but richly suggestive book, Mitchell Stephens notes that one of the strengths unique to the medium of video is its ability, with fast-cut editing, to jump immediately from one place to another (say, New York to Tokyo) and even one time to another (the early twentieth to the late twentieth century, e.g.). The written word can also do so, but

in a much less dexterous, less compressed, and ultimately less impressive fashion. It occurs to me that the eucharistic celebration, in the powerfully condensed manner of embodied imagery, concisely executes its own "jump-cuts" from the time of Christ's life and death to the anticipated time of the eschatological consummation. To cite a few words that signal these enacted "jump-cuts" from the temporality of past to present to future, at the anamnesis the celebrant and people declare, "Christ *has* died, Christ *is* risen, Christ *will* come again." On video's strengths, see Mitchell Stephens, *The Rise of the Image and the Fall of the Word* (New York: Oxford University Press, 1998).

37. David Ford, *Self and Salvation* (Cambridge: Cambridge University Press, 1999), pp. 137, 145.

12. From Family Values to Family Virtues

1. Alasdair MacIntyre, *A Short History of Ethics* (New York: Collier Books, 1966).

2. MacIntyre, *After Virtue*, 2d ed. (Notre Dame: University of Notre Dame Press, 1984), p. 222. MacIntyre offers another, and complementary, definition in *Whose Justice? Which Rationality?* (Notre Dame: University of Notre Dame Press, 1988), p. 12: "A tradition is an argument extended over time in which certain fundamental agreements are defined and redefined in terms of two kinds of conflict: those with critics and enemies external to the tradition who reject all or at least key parts of those fundamental agreements, and those internal, interpretative debates through which the meaning and rationale of the fundamental agreements come to be expressed and by whose progress a tradition is constituted."

A generally compelling application of MacIntyre's understanding of tradition to theological methodology is Trevor Hart's *Faith Thinking: The Dynamics of Christian Theology* (Downers Grove, Ill.: InterVarsity Press, 1995). Hart makes the important critical point that not all Christian engagement with its own or other traditions need or should be belligerent, so that a tradition might be better thought of as a "dialogue" than an "argument" (p. 228).

3. Cited in Lance Morrow, "But Seriously, Folks . . . ," *Time*, 1 June 1992, p. 29.

4. See Frances Kartunnen, *Between Worlds: Interpreters, Guides, and Survivors* (New Brunswick, N.J.: Rutgers University Press, 1994), p. 139.

5. Steven Mintz and Susan Kellogg, *Domestic Revolutions: A Social History of American Family Life* (New York: Free Press, 1988), pp. 1–23, particularly 15.

6. For documentation and further discussion, see Rodney Clapp, *Families at the Crossroads: Beyond Traditional and Modern Options* (Downers Grove, Ill.: InterVarsity Press, 1993), pp. 30–34.

7. See, e.g., Judges 17:12. For information and understanding of the Israelite household, see especially Hans Walter Wolff, *Anthropology of the Old Testament* (Philadelphia: Fortress, 1974), and Norman K. Gottwald, *The Tribes of Yahweh* (Maryknoll, N.Y.: Orbis Books, 1979).

8. See Paul Veyne, ed., *A History of Private Life*, vol. 1, *From Pagan Rome to Byzantium*, trans. Arthur Goldhammer (Cambridge, Mass.: Belknap, 1989), pp. 2–205; David L. Balch, *Let Wives Be Submissive: The Domestic Code in 1 Peter* (Chico, Calif.: Scholars, 1981); and O. Larry Yarbrough, *Not Like the Gentiles: Marriage Rules in the Letters of Paul* (Atlanta: Scholars, 1985).

9. These traditionalists support what sociologists call "patriarchy of the last instance," a view of men and women that is largely egalitarian but that insists that in the event of an irresolvable disagreement between husband and wife, the husband's decision is final. Albeit certainly objectionable, this is a form of patriarchy considerably diluted and moderated from earlier, robust patriarchy, which forthrightly understood and treated women as the property of men. See Judith Stacey, *Brave New Families* (New York: Basic Books, 1990), pp. 133–46.

10. Historian John Gillis rightly notes, "Ironically, we are . . . in the habit of updating the traditional community and family periodically so that the location of the golden age is constantly changing. For the Victorians, the traditional family, imagined to be rooted and extended, was located sometime before industrialization and urbanization, but for those who came of age during the First World War, tradition was associated with the Victorians themselves; today

we think of the 1950s and early 1960s as the location of the family and community life we imagine we have lost." See Gillis, *A World of Their Own Making: Myth, Ritual, and the Quest for Family Values* (New York: Basic Books, 1996), pp. 4–5.

11. N. T. Wright, *The New Testament and the People of God* (Minneapolis: Fortress, 1992), pp. 449–50. For an extended biblical and theological argument of this theme, see Rodney Clapp, *Families at the Crossroads,* pp. 67–88.

12. *After Virtue,* p. 263.

13. See *After Virtue,* pp. 23–35. For an extended discussion applying this MacIntyrean insight to the subject of Christian friendship, see Rodney Clapp, *A Peculiar People: The Church as Culture in a Post-Christian Society* (Downers Grove, Ill.: InterVarsity Press, 1996), pp. 204–11.

14. Victor Lebow, cited in Alan During, "How Much Is Enough?" *The Utne Reader,* July/August 1991, p. 73.

15. Quoted in Steve Daley, "Quayle's rehash of 'family values' falls way short on specifics," *Chicago Tribune,* 11 September 1994, DuPage edition, sec. 4, p. 4.

16. *Vital Speeches of the Day,* 15 September 1992, pp. 711–12. Quayle closed the speech with a promise that the Republican ticket would "build an America more secure in the values of faith, family and freedom," apparently with no sense of how these three "values" might conflict. I say more about such tensions below. Here I note that it is disastrously shortsighted not to recognize that rising divorce rates and child abandonment have something to do with the liberal, democratic, and individualistic apotheosis of freedom. This freedom is negative, only a freedom *from* community, tradition, and other strictures. As such it actively corrodes the virtues of fidelity and commitment, and it breeds no sense of constructive freedom, freedom *for* the service of some community's or tradition's purpose.

17. Robert Nisbet, *The Quest for Community: A Study in the Ethics of Order and Freedom* (New York: Oxford University Press, 1953), p. 61.

18. *Whose Justice?,* p. 335 (emphasis added).

19. *Liberalism and the Limits of Justice* (Cambridge: Cambridge University Press, 1982), p. 22.

20. *After Virtue,* p. 26. See his entire criticism of emotivism, pp. 11–35.

21. Ibid., p. 23.

22. Brigitte and Peter Berger, writing in defense of the bourgeois family, list six primary characteristics of that form of family, including romantic love as the major motive for marriage. See *The War over the Family* (Garden City, N.Y.: Doubleday, 1983), pp. 101–2.

23. Eamon Duffy, *The Stripping of the Altars* (New Haven: Yale University Press, 1992), p. 11.

24. Michelle Z. Rosaldo, "Toward an Anthropology of Self and Feeling," in *Culture Theory,* ed. Richard A. Shweder and Robert A. Levine (Cambridge: Cambridge University Press, 1984), p. 143.

25. Rougemont's classic account is found in his *Love in the Western World,* rev. and augmented ed., trans. Hazel E. Barnes (Princeton: Princeton University Press, 1983); first published in French, 1939.

26. See James Wm. McClendon, Jr., *Ethics: Systematic Theology, Volume I* (Nashville: Abingdon Press, 1986), pp. 133–55.

27. "Missing Wheaton couple did it all for love," by George Papajohn and James Warren, *Chicago Tribune,* 28 July 1988.

28. *Ethics,* p. 150.

29. As quoted in Martin E. Marty, "Who says all you need is love?" *Context,* 1 July 1988, pp. 5–6.

30. Diogenes Allen, *Love: Christian Romance, Marriage, Friendship* (Cambridge, Mass.: Crowley Press, 1987), p. 79.

13. The Theology of Consumption and the Consumption of Theology

1. Richard Tedlow, *New and Improved* (Boston: Harvard Business School Press), p. 3.

2. Leslie Savan, *The Sponsored Life* (Philadelphia: Temple University Press, 1994), p. 1.

3. To be published by Princeton University Press as *Financing the American Dream: A Cultural History of Consumer Credit,* 1999.

4. Quoted in William J. Walsh, S.J., and John P. Langan, "Patristic Social Consciousness—The Church and the Poor," in *The Faith That Does Justice,* ed. John C. Haughey (Nahwah, N.J.: Paulist, 1977), pp. 114–15.

5. Robert Wuthnow, *God and Mammon in America* (New York: Free Press, 1994), p. 18.

6. Max Weber, *The Protestant Ethic and the Spirit of Capitalism,* trans. Talcott Parsons (New York: Scribner's, 1958), pp. 59–60.

7. Ibid., p. 60.

8. Quoted in Robert Wuthnow, ed., *Rethinking Materialism* (Grand Rapids, Mich.: Eerdmans, 1995), p. 15.

9. Weber, *Protestant Ethic,* pp. 80–81.

10. Ibid., pp. 103–4.

11. Ibid., pp. 106–7.

12. See ibid., pp. 113–15.

13. On this last point, see ibid., pp. 157–58. For much of the formulation of this paragraph I am indebted to correspondence from Tim Peebles, 22 February 1996.

14. Weber, *Protestant Ethic,* p. 53.

15. Jackson Lears, *Fables of Abundance* (New York: BasicBooks, 1994), p. 46.

16. Quoted in Weber, *Protestant Ethic,* p. 175.

17. Weber, *Protestant Ethic,* pp. 130, 133, 140, 151.

18. Colin Campbell, *The Romantic Ethic and the Spirit of Modern Consumption* (Oxford: Basil Blackwell, 1987), p. 128.

19. Ibid., pp. 129–30.

20. Quoted in ibid., p. 130.

21. Ibid., p. 131.

22. Ibid., pp. 132–33.

23. Ibid., p. 134.

24. Hoxie Neale Fairchild, quoted in ibid., p. 136.

25. Ibid., p. 137.

26. Lears, *Fables of Abundance,* p. 47.

27. Ibid., p. 57.

28. Quoted in ibid., p. 143.

29. On Candler, see Tedlow, *New and Improved,* pp. 22–111, 349; on Wanamaker, see Leach, *Land of Desire,* pp. 191–224, and Leigh Eric Schmidt, *Consumer Rites* (Princeton, N.J.: Princeton University Press, 1995), pp. 159–69.

30. R. Laurence Moore, *Selling God* (New York: Oxford University Press, 1994), p. 38.

31. See Richard Ohmann, *Selling Culture* (London: Verso, 1996), p. 9.

32. Ibid., p. 49.

33. Ibid., pp. 79, 86.

34. Quoted in ibid., p. 78.

35. See Susan Strasser, *Satisfaction Guaranteed* (New York: Pantheon, 1989), pp. 97–105, 133.

36. For both citations, see Ohmann, *Selling Culture,* p. 109.

37. See Leach, *Land of Desire,* p. 10.

38. Cited in Rick Prelinger, *Ephemeral Films: 1931–1960* (New York: Voyager, 1994), CD-ROM. I am indebted to good friend and computer connoisseur Verne Becker for calling this fascinating resource—replete with actual film and television commercials—to my attention.

39. Colin Campbell, "The Sociology of Consumption," in *Acknowledging Consumption,* ed. Daniel Miller (London: Routledge, 1995), p. 118.

40. Cited in Earl Shorris, *A Nation of Salesmen* (New York: Avon Books, 1996), p. 105.

41. Quoted in Lears, *Fables of Abundance,* p. 212.

42. Quoted in ibid., p. 323.

43. Quoted in ibid., pp. 311–12.

44. Campbell, "Sociology of Consumption," p. 118.

45. Quoted in Lears, *Fables of Abundance,* p. 32.

46. Campbell, "Sociology of Consumption," p. 118.

47. Miroslav Volf, "In the Cage of Vanities," in *Rethinking Materialism,* ed. Wuthnow, p. 172.

48. Robert Nelson, *Reaching for Heaven on Earth* (Lanham, Md.: Rowan & Littlefield, 1991), pp. xx, xxi, xxii, 2, 8, 10, 17.

49. Leach, *Land of Desire,* p. xiii.

50. Victor Lebow, quoted in David A. Crocker, "Consumption and Well-Being," in *Philosophy & Public Policy* 15, no. 4 (Fall 1995): 13.

51. Daniel Miller, "Consumption as the Vanguard of History," in *Acknowledging Consumption,* ed. Daniel Miller (London: Routledge, 1995), pp. 17–18.

52. See Steven Waldman, "The Tyranny of Choice," *The New Republic,* 27 January 1992, pp. 22–25.

53. Alan Ehrenhalt, *The Lost City: Discovering the Forgotten Virtues of Community in the Chicago of the 1950s* (New York: BasicBooks, 1995), p. 99.

54. Ibid., p. 272.

55. David Popenoe, "The Roots of Declining Social Virtue," in *Seeds of Virtue,* ed. Mary Ann Glendon and David Blankenhorn (Lanham, Md.: Madison Books, 1995), pp. 87–88.

56. Wuthnow, *God and Mammon in America,* pp. 138–41.

57. Ibid., p. 266 (emphasis added).

58. Gordon Lafer, "Universalism and Particularism in Jewish Law: Making Sense of Political Loyalties," in *Jewish Identity,* ed. David Theo Goldberg and Michael Krausz (Philadelphia: Temple University Press, 1993), p. 196.

59. George Lindbeck, "The Church," in *Keeping the Faith,* ed. Geoffrey Wainwright (Philadelphia: Fortress, 1988), p. 193.

60. Along such lines theologian D. Stephen Long warns, "We must free ourselves from the rationality of the [omnivorous] market and recover a theological rationality grounded in the life and practice of the church. If we are not so converted, the church will simply continue to be incorporated into the transnational corporation until the church can no longer give an account of itself in theological terms, or even feel the need to do so" (from D. Stephen Long, "A Global Market—A Catholic Church," *Theology Today* 52, no. 3 [October 1995]: 365).

61. Ernest Best notes that "priest" in 1 Peter is corporate: "each is a priest . . . but never a priest in and by himself; it is only as a member of the corporate priesthood within one corporate existence of the church: the conception is not individualistic" (from Ernest Best, *1 Peter,* New Century Bible Commentary [Grand Rapids, Mich.: Eerdmans, 1971], p. 108). See also Peter H. Davids, *1 Peter,* New International Commentary on the New Testament (Grand Rapids, Mich.: Eerdmans, 1971), p. 91.

62. See Robert Booth Fowler, *The Greening of Protestant Thought* (Chapel Hill: University of North Carolina Press, 1995), p. 80.

63. See, for example, Wesley Granberg-Michaelson, *A Worldly Spirituality* (San Francisco: Harper & Row, 1984), pp. 62–63.

64. See Christopher J. H. Wright, "The Theology and Ethics of the Land," in his *Walking in the Ways of the Lord* (Downers Grove, Ill.: InterVarsity Press, 1995), p. 184. The creation texts of Genesis 1 and 2 are, of course, much criticized in some discussions of consumption and environmentalism, particularly for the granting of human dominion over the rest of creation. For a helpful treatment of the texts that addresses such concerns, see Phyllis Trible, *God and the Rhetoric of Sexuality* (Philadelphia: Fortress, 1978), pp. 80–92.

65. See, for example, Psalms 65:12–13; 98:8; 148:1–14; Isaiah 24:4, 7; 55:12; Jeremiah 4:28; 12:4; Ezekiel 31:15.

66. Alexander Schmemann, *For the Life of the World* (Crestwood, N.Y.: St. Vladimir's Press, 1973), p. 14. I differ from Schmemann's wonderful portrayal of priesthood on two important points: he tends to see nonhuman creation existing solely for the sake of humanity and clearly excludes women from the ordained priesthood.

67. C. E. B. Cranfield, *A Critical and Exegetical Commentary on the Epistle to the Romans,* vol. 1 (Edinburgh: T & T Clark, 1975), pp. 413–14. For an excellent and theologically responsible discussion on the praise that nonhuman creation may offer God, see Brian J. Walsh, Marianne B. Karsh, and Nik Ansell, "Trees, Forestry and the Responsiveness of Creation," *Cross Currents,* Summer 1994, pp. 149–62.

68. This important point on stewardship is made by Jonathan Wilson in his "Evangelicals and the Environment," a paper prepared for the Evangelical Ethics Interest Group, Society of Christian Ethics, 1996 annual meeting, pp. 7–8.

69. Irenaeus *Adversus Haereses* 5.33.3–4, in *The Early Christian Fathers,* ed. and trans. Henry Bettenson (New York: Oxford University Press, 1956), p. 100.

18. That Glorious Mongrel

1. James H. Cone, *The Spirituals and the Blues* (Maryknoll, N.Y.: Orbis Press, 1972, 1991), pp. 22-23.

2. Quoted in Ted Gioia, *The History of Jazz* (New York: Oxford University Press, 1997), p. 78. I changed the pronouns in Condon's last sentence from plural to singular.

3. Martha Bayles, *Hole in Our Soul: The Loss of Beauty and Meaning in American Popular Music* (Chicago: University of Chicago Press, 1994), p. 23, and Gordon quoted p. 37. Gioia, *History,* p. 364.

4. George Harris, "Faith and All That Jazz," *World,* 6 March 1999, as accessed at *http://www.worldmag.com/world/issue/03-06-99/cultural_2.asp.*

5. David Cloud, "Jazz," at *http://www.whidbey.net/~dcloud/fbns/jazz.htm.*

6. A compact survey of heroin use by Charlie Parker and then an all-too-long string of jazz artists who thought they could pharmaceutically capture some of Bird's genius is found in Charley Gerard, *Jazz in Black and White: Race, Culture, and Identity in the Jazz Community* (Westport, Conn.: Praeger, 1998), chapter 4, "Race and Jazz Communities."

7. Cloud, "Jazz."

8. Bayles, *Hole in Our Soul,* p. 130.

9. The endorsement of jazz by white Christians (and whites in general) often unwittingly reflects racist (and closely related classist) presuppositions. For instance, David Cloud refers to Biola University's acceptance of jazz in the early 1980s on the basis, as Biola officials argued, that "contemporary jazz has become 'classical.' . . . Jazz, in effect, must be considered 'classical' in the broad sense of the term. It is entirely possible for college students to rehearse and perform jazz purely as another style of concert music." (See Cloud, "Jazz.") But why should jazz now be acceptable to conservative evangelicals merely because it has "ascended" to the status of classical music? Again, as I have indicated, some classical music can be challenged on grounds of immorality and secularity. It is difficult to avoid noticing that the "classical" music presumed uncritically to be acceptable is almost monolithically European and "West-

ern" (i.e., not African and black). "Classical" in such contexts all too easily serves as an unconscious codeword for "white."

10. For the full study, consult Henry O. Osgood, "Jazz, That Peculiar Word," at *http//www.cwrl.utexas.ed/~nickle309k/texts/osgood.*

11. See Gioia, *History*, pp. 31-34, and for Bechet, Robert Gottlieb, ed., *Reading Jazz* (New York: Vintage Books, 1996), pp. 8-16. Discussion of "Jazz Funerals of New Orleans," complete with photos and music samples, can be found at *http://www.wwoz.org/html/story_jazz_funerals_NO.html.*

12. See Gioia, *History*, pp. 99, 129, 168, 206, 214, 341, 353. For Hines, see Lawrence W. Levine, *The Unpredictable Past: Explorations in American Cultural History* (New York: Oxford University Press, 1993), p. 186. For Blakey and Davis, see Gottlieb, *Reading Jazz*, pp. 211, 256. A discography of jazz music *explicitly* reflecting churchly settings would be even longer than my litany of church-rooted artists. But it would have to include John Coltrane's *A Love Supreme* (Impulse! GRD-155). Almost at random, I also mention Charles Mingus's "Wednesday Night Prayer Meeting," found on his *Blues and Roots* (Atlantic 1305-2). Mingus writes in the liner notes, "I heard this as a child when I went to [church] meetings with my mother," and explains the scene he wants to capture in the music: "The congregation gives their testimonial before the Lord, they confess their sins and sing and shout and do a little Holy Rolling. Some preachers cast out demons, they call their dialogue talking in tongues or talking unknown tongue (language the Devil can't understand)."

13. Cone, *The Spirituals and the Blues*, p. 23.

14. Ibid.

15. Ibid., p. 63.

16. See Gerard, *Jazz in Black and White*, p. 76. The typically straight-shooting Billie Holiday addressed Jim Crow laws and customs in a manner that reminds us the results of such practices far exceeded mere "inconvenience." Remarking that as she traveled she often was not allowed to use available public restrooms, Holiday said, "Then finally I just said to hell with it. When I had to go I'd just ask the bus driver to stop and let me off at the side of the road. I'd rather go in the bushes than take a chance in the restaurants and town." Cited in Angela Y. Davis, *Blues Legacies and Black Feminism* (New York: Pantheon Books, 1998), p. 193.

17. Quoted in Simon Frith, *Performing Rites: On the Value of Popular Music* (Cambridge, Mass.: Harvard University Press, 1996), p. 330.

18. Anne Shaw Faulkner, "Does Jazz Put the Sin in Syncopation?" found at *http://www.cwrl.utexas.edu/~nick/e309k/texts/faulkner/faulkner.html.*

19. Christopher Small, *Music of the Common Tongue: Survival and Celebration in African American Music* (Hanover, N.H.: Wesleyan University Press, 1987, 1998), p. 25.

20. Quoted in Frith, *Performing Rites*, p. 123.

21. Quoting Bayles, *Hole in Our Soul*, p. 9.

22. Frith, *Performing Rites*, p. 132.

23. The John Coltrane Quartet, *The Complete Africa/Brass Sessions* (Impulse! IMPD-2–168).

24. See Frith, *Performing Rites*, pp. 135, 142.

25. Ibid., pp. 130–131.

26. Small paraphrasing Handy, in *Common Tongue*, p. 150.

27. Bayles, *Hole in Our Soul*, p. 72.

28. I build here on the thoughts of Christopher Small, *Common Tongue*, pp. 60-64.

29. This again is not true of classical music as it has always been performed. Mozart is said to have been an extraordinary improviser, for instance.

30. Quoted in Craig Werner, *A Change Is Gonna Come: Music, Race and the Soul of America* (New York: Plume, 1998), p. 132.

31. Quoted in Small, *Common Tongue*, p. 305.

32. Ibid., p. 301.

33. Duke Ellington, *Ellington at Newport 1956 (Complete)* (Columbia C2K 64932).

34. Bayles, *Hole in Our Soul,* p. 93.

35. The social body I have in mind is of course nothing less or other than the body of Christ. In this regard, it is significant how much, in 1 Corinthians 10–14, Paul interweaves worship, spiritual formation, the participation (in both constructive and destructive ways) of various individuals in worship, and the hopeful expectation that all this will build one body with many members (12:12)

36. Cited by Elizabeth Castelli in "Reality Check: A Religion Professor Examines *Dogma,*" at *http://www.dogma-movie.com/archives/religionnf.html.*

37. See, e.g., Cone, *Spirituals and the Blues,* p. 15.

38. For this paragraph, see Ibid., pp. 15, 80, 81 and 73, respectively.

39. Aretha Franklin, *Amazing Grace* (Atlantic 2-906-2).

40. James Wm. McClendon, Jr., *Ethics: Systematic Theology Volume 1* (Nashville: Abingdon, 1986), p. 31. (I have departed from some of McClendon's italicization in my first quotation.)

41. Country music, for instance, pervasively postures as traditional, yet you can scour the record bins and listen to country radio and find few signs of Hank Williams or Bob Wills among Nashville's contemporary luminaries—even living and still richly talented embodiments of that tradition, such as Merle Haggard, struggle for record contracts and airplay. Rock music is ironically more respectful of its living ancestral masters (how odd that the graying Rolling Stones get airplay on rock stations, while country stations ignore a George Jones now, if anything, at the peak of his extraordinary vocal powers [listen to *The Cold Hard Truth,* Asylum 62368-2), but it cannot match jazz, where young leaders like Wynton Marsalis still compose in classical jazz styles and it is no surprise to see even an avant garde artist such as Don Byron devote an entire album to the music of Duke Ellington and Raymond Scott (Nonesuch, 79348-2). Among living, vigorouly practiced musics only the blues, a close relative of jazz, comes close to a similar respect for its elders and "the tradition." Classical music, of course, respects the past masters, but to the point that even its most ardent practitioners can accuse it of musical necrophilia and an alarming inability to continue the organic development necessary to a *living* tradition.

42. Werner, *A Change Is Gonna Come,* p. 133.

43. Ibid., p. 134.

Acknowledgments

The essays in this book have been written over a span of nearly a decade. The list of people (friends, editors, editors who are friends, authors I have met only via the printed word, unsuspecting folk who invited me to address a topic live and in person) deserving thanks is accordingly lengthy. To remain as brief as possible, I tip my hat (baseball cap, actually) to Dennis Okholm and Tim Phillips, who first allowed a version of chapter 1 at the Wheaton Theology Conference, which they created and masterminded; to the various editors at *The Reformed Journal,* now *Perspectives,* in which versions of chapters 2, 11, and 12 originally appeared; to the redoubtable John Wilson of *Books & Culture,* who in his office as editor first wreaked on the world the havoc of chapters 3, 17, and 19; to Fred Clark and Kristyn Komarnicki, coconspirators at *Prism* magazine, where chapters 4, 7, and 14 first saw the crimson light of day; to David Neff and Mickey Maudlin of *Christianity Today,* host to the earliest incarnations of chapters 5, 8, 9, 13, and 16; to Samuel Powell and Michael Lodahl, really smart Nazarenes who, despite their wisdom, asked me to contribute to their book *Embodied Holiness* (InterVarsity Press, 1999) and so occasioned what is here chapter 6; to Emmanuel Cutrone, who asked me to address the North American Academy of Liturgy and so occasioned the birth of chapter 10; to Bradley Wilcox, then editor of *Re:Generation Quarterly,* who got chapter 15 for the trouble of asking me what I was up to; to Nancey Murphy, Brad Kallenberg, and Mark Thiessen Nation, editors of *Virtues and Practices in the Christian Tradition* (Trinity Press International, 1997), in which chapter 12 first appeared;

and William Edgar, who asked me to indulge my enthusiasm for jazz to a captive conference audience at Westminster Theological Seminary, thus eliciting a version of chapter 18 and granting me rationalization for even more indulgence of a CD-buying habit possibly (well, probably) somewhat at odds with the insights of chapters 10 and 13 through 15.

Certain other forbearing souls are thanked in the endnotes for critiquing chapters originally carried, as swaddling babes, into the teeth of academic audiences, and therefore in need of more-than-the-usual flank-guarding.

I want here also, and finally, to thank Don Stephenson, Bobbi Jo Heyboer, and Rebecca Cooper, cofounders and colleagues at Brazos Press. Group hug. But now what have we gotten ourselves into?